The Hotel

The Hotel

BACKSTAIRS AT THE WORLD'S MOST EXCLUSIVE HOTEL

JEFFREY ROBINSON

ARCADE PUBLISHING · NEW YORK

FIRST U.S. EDITION

ISBN 1-55970-377-6
Library of Congress Catalog Card Number 97-71066
Library of Congress Cataloging-in-Publication information is available.

Published in the United States by Arcade Publishing, Inc.
Distributed by Little, Brown and Company

10 9 8 7 6 5 4 3 2 1

Designed by API

BP

PRINTED IN THE UNITED STATES OF AMERICA

TO MARGARET AND HOWARD ARVEY
FOREVER FRIENDS

AVANT PROPOS

The name of every guest has been changed for the sake of discretion and the numbers of the rooms in which they stayed have been changed as well, for the same reason.

But nothing else has been altered in any way.

The people are real.

The stories are as they happened.

The Hotel is Claridge's.

DRAMATIS PERSONAE

Major Players in Order of Appearance

François Touzin General Manager
John Wingrove Head Hall Porter
Roy Barron Security
Chris Baxter Security
Robert Buckolt Rooms Division Manager
Rory Purcell Chief Engineer
Carole Ronald Executive Housekeeper
Adam Salter Night Manager
Philippe Krenzer Food and Beverage Manager
Andrew Jarman Banqueting Manager
Christian Horvath Head Cashier
Daniel Azoulai Restaurant Manager
Marjan Lesnik Maître Chef de Cuisine
Andrew Pierron Information Technology Manager
Michael Duncan Assistant Manager

The Hotel

~ 1 ~

$\mathcal{B}$ROOK STREET WAS JUST WAKING up as he walked briskly towards the front entrance.

There was hardly any traffic. Only one taxi was in the rank, its driver sitting in the rear seat, sipping coffee out of a thermos. A red Post Office van was parked on the far side of the street. Much further along the block, all the way down at the corner of Bond Street, there were the flashing yellow lights of a maintenance vehicle, where workmen were doing something to a street lamp.

For most people, Monday was the start of the week. But not for him. There was no such thing.

Above the Hotel's entrance, three flags hung motionless. The Union Jack. The European flag. The Stars and Stripes. The other four flag poles were empty.

"Good morning, Mr Touzin." The uniformed doorman always waited until he was just close enough before tipping his hat and greeting his boss.

The ever-polite Frenchman said in his soft voice, "Good morning, Roman. How are you?"

And as his boss stepped into the revolving door, the doorman gave it a gentle push so it would rotate more easily.

"Thank you."

Inside the art deco entrance, with its starburst chandelier, mock tortoiseshell ceiling and blue, star-patterned carpet, Touzin spotted the back of a starched white and gold-braided uniform.

The man wearing it was standing in the middle of the Front Hall, alone in the large, oddly silent room with its stunning black and white marble floor, its period fireplace, its Georgian chandelier, its cathedral ceiling and its grand staircase leading up to the mezzanine.

Moving cautiously towards the man, careful not to make any noise, Touzin got close enough, then poked his finger like a gun into the small of the man's back and whispered, "Stick 'em up."

The senior Concierge swung around, hesitated, grinned and said, "Good morning, Mr Touzin."

"Good morning, John." Trying to catch him with his back to the front door was a game they played often.

The Concierge laughed. Touzin laughed too. But the Concierge understood.

Around the corner to the left was Reception — a light wood counter facing a blue settee, two separate desks at the side of that, with lamps and telephones, and comfortable chairs to sit in, where guests who had never been here before completed a form.

The moment the two young men behind that counter saw him, they stood up and said, almost in unison, "Good morning, Mr Touzin."

"Good morning, Alastair. Good morning, Michael." He asked, "Anyone in yet?"

Michael answered, "Yes, sir. Two early arrivals."

He said, "Good," and walked past them to the door that led into his own small office, where curtained windows looked out on Brook Street.

It was an unremarkable room, with a mahogany desk to the right, a straight-backed chair against the near wall next to a small cabinet, plus two other straight-backed chairs and a tiny round cof-

2

fee table in front of the desk. Another door, in the far corner, opened into the even smaller office of the Rooms Division Manager.

There were a lamp and a computer terminal on Touzin's desk — he turned them both on — and, next to his two phones, a bottle of Evian water he'd forgotten to put away. In the centre of his desk, neatly stacked, were a dozen small black notebooks, like the kind high school kids use to record their homework assignments.

His watch told him it was not yet 7:30.

He always tried to arrive early — leaving home just after his children got up to go to school, getting to the Hotel before the rest of his senior staff — so that he'd have some quiet time to go through those notebooks.

It was an important part of his day because each department manager recorded in them everything, every day, that he or she thought the General Manager would want to know. And François Touzin was the sort of General Manager who wanted to know everything.

Now in his mid-40s, with short brown hair and a friendly roundish face, he was running one of the most famous and most exclusive hotels in the world. Twenty-five years after going into the business, needing to prove to his father that he could succeed in life, he was the first non-British custodian of one of Britain's most distinguished traditions.

Of average height, fighting hard and just about winning the battle against middle-age spread, he tended to wear dark suits, unlike his five predecessors who had, for the past century, traditionally worn morning suits. He kept his office door open most of the time and made it his business to know every one of his employees by name.

This was his second tour of duty here. His first was seven years before, when he had been brought in as Assistant to the General Manager and given the extra responsibility of running the Food and Beverage Department. He stayed two years, a tenure that left him filled with doubts about the Hotel and, in particular, his future there.

In those days, the Hotel was criticized in the press as being a relic, old-fashioned to the point of being archaic, tradition-bound to the point of being stodgy. That bills were handwritten was a nice touch, perhaps, but not terribly practical. That profitability was not always given sufficient importance added to the Hotel's idiosyncratic character.

In those days, the world was sinking in a financial mire, but the Hotel's champagne was always properly chilled.

He'd seen people come to work here, bringing with them all sorts of innovative ideas — the way he had the first time — but changing things at the Hotel was exactly like turning that fabled ocean liner in the middle of the high seas. It needed a lot of water. It needed a lot of patience. And, perhaps most importantly, it needed the rest of the crew to be turning in the same direction.

In the end, he'd seen people leave drained, while the ocean liner sailed on, true to its fixed course, straight ahead.

The older members of staff, the ones who had been here 20 and 30 and 40 years, reminded him when he was here the first time, you can't change the Hotel, the Hotel will change you.

Now he was back, brought in specifically to change it.

But the Hotel will change you.

Their warning kept ringing in his ears.

After ordering a coffee from Room Service, he reached for the notebook on the top of the stack.

The Night Manager's log: Mr Palmer, holding a confirmed reservation for room 315 finally checked in at 2:30 this morning. His flight had been held up somewhere for nearly nine hours. I noticed smudges on the carpet on the 6th floor just outside the main lift. I took extra pillows to room 239. I brought a hairdryer to room 210. 6:45 — A leak reported in the Accounts Office. The Duty Engineer was informed. He couldn't find the source and has notified the plumbers. A bucket was placed under the offending dampness. Mr Hammond, 421–422, was visited at 1:00 by an unknown lady, who left the Hotel at 2:30, and a second unknown lady, who apparently arrived at 3:00. No one realized that she wasn't a guest, until she departed at 4:15. The chimney sweep arrived at 7:00 asking permission to clean the fireplace in the Front Hall. Permission was denied. It was too late in the morning. Guests would have been disturbed. He was told to return at an earlier time.

Checking off each item with the initials FRT — the R was for Robert, after his father — he highlighted the ones he wanted to mention at the morning meeting, put that book aside and picked up the next one.

The Chief Engineer's log: An air-conditioning technician arrived at 19:45 to look at the unit in the telephone PDX equipment room. He left at 20:45 when the repair was completed.

The Rooms Division Manager's log: 17:30 — Mr Robert Latrobbe, room 525, arrived back at the hotel with his brother who'd just missed his flight home. The brother, Mr David Latrobbe, was registered as a guest and a second bed was placed in Mr R. Latrobbe's room.

The Executive Housekeeper's log: One of the maids reported that Mrs V. Cunningham in 340 had suffered an asthma attack. I proceeded to the guest's room to ensure that she had adequate medication and that she was comfortable. She had been to her doctor earlier in the day. She said all she needed were some extra pillows, which I supplied.

Touzin went through them all, one by one.

Afterwards, he glanced at his overnight faxes, stopping at one in particular, from a travel agent in San Francisco who was complaining about the prices his clients were being asked to pay.

That the price of a room might be too high — or, for that matter, too low — had less to do with supply and demand, Touzin believed, than with a guest's perception of what that room was worth.

The price of a room was correct as long as guests felt they were getting their money's worth. Touzin wanted the travel agent to understand that and made a note to ring him. He hoped that a personal phone call could change the man's perception.

After sipping the last of his coffee, he walked into the Front Hall.

No longer the quiet place it had been less than an hour ago, there were people arriving and people leaving and guests coming down for breakfast.

He loved watching the Hotel wake up.

Men with expensive suits and women with somewhere important to be hurried by him.

He greeted those guests he knew by name and introduced himself to the ones he hadn't yet met.

When an elderly gentleman walked up to say hello, Touzin shook the man's hand. "It's nice to have you back with us."

"But there is no honey."

Touzin didn't understand.

"There is no honey," the old man repeated. "I like to have honey with my porridge but they don't bring it to me."

Touzin couldn't recall the gentleman's name, so he asked, "What room are you staying in and I will see to it that you have honey from now on with your porridge."

The gentleman said, "Four-one-seven," nodded thank you, shook Touzin's hand and walked away.

Across the room, huddled into a corner under the grand staircase, Touzin noticed the Hotel's two security officers. Roy Barron was a tall, firmly built, 40-year-old retired veteran of the City of London Police. Chris Baxter was a sandy-haired former Flying Squad officer who'd spent 25 years with Metropolitan Police. They were speaking to a strapping, dark-haired man in an ill-fitting blue suit, and a short, Oriental man in an off-the-rack, undistinguished grey suit.

Touzin nodded hello.

Barron caught his eye and invited him over, to introduce him. The British man was a police officer, assigned to the Diplomatic Protection Group of the Metropolitan Police. The Oriental gentleman was a security officer assigned to the South Korean Embassy.

"We are very much looking forward to the visit," Touzin told the Korean.

The man bowed.

"You are in very good hands," Touzin said, tapping Barron's shoulder. "Is everything going according to schedule?"

"Yes," the Korean gentleman bowed again.

Touzin smiled, shook their hands again and took his leave.

The Concierge was booking a flight for a guest. A gentleman was asking where he could exchange some money. One of the page boys was taking packages from a lady. The uniformed liftman was greeting another. "Good morning, madam."

At Reception, one of the fellows behind the desk introduced him to a French couple just checking in, then added, "Perhaps you could translate."

Touzin took over — *"Bonjour Madame, bonjour Monsieur"* — welcomed them to the Hotel and helped them to register.

Back in his office, he had just enough time to check the name of the guest in Room 417 — Mr Alfred Patrick — before his secretary came in with the morning post.

He was only half through that when the phone rang — it was an old friend from his days in Australia — and he took that call. The hotel business, much like the Mafia, is populated by bosses all over the world who know each other, and even if they are supposed to be competitors they still keep in touch.

Then Robert Buckolt stepped through the door that connected his office to Touzin's.

The tall, smiling, ever-efficient, morning-suited 39-year-old Rooms Division Manager boasted, "Thanks to the Koreans, our yield is way up this week. Here's the final schedule for the visit. The President arrives tomorrow at 11:30."

Touzin took it from him, checked his diary to make certain he had the time right, then asked, "What about the weekend?"

"It drops off considerably."

"You still have the whole week to find new bookings."

"Yes, sir," Buckolt said, as though he wanted to add, if only it was that simple.

By 9, a dozen senior staff members — most of the men were dressed the way Buckolt was, in black tie and tails — had gathered outside Touzin's office. When he saw they were ready, and when he was ready for them, he invited them in with a mannerly, "Please."

The men stood.

Being a European, Touzin invited the women to sit.

There were only three women on his staff, so the chair allotment worked well. But even if there were more chairs, the men would still stand because Touzin believed that people who stood during a meeting said what they had to say in more succinct terms. People who stood didn't linger with non-essential business, the way they might if they were comfortably seated. But then the ladies didn't linger much either because everyone had other things to do.

Especially Touzin.

The meeting began, as it did every morning, with him saying, "Good morning, how is everyone?" then reciting the day's statistics from a computer print-out.

"Last night's occupancy was 77 per cent with an average room rate of £244.50. The month-to-date occupancy is 68 per cent with an average room rate of £241.75. Last year-to-date's occupancy is 66 per cent with an average room rate of £226.60." He put the page aside. "We have the Koreans in this week, which will put those figures way up. But Mr Buckolt tells me the weekend will be light." He looked at Buckolt. "What do you think we'll end the month with?" But before Buckolt could answer, Touzin stopped him. "No. Wait.

I'll tell you." He took a piece of paper, wrote a figure on it, folded it, put it in an envelope and sealed the envelope. "This is what I think." He looked back at Buckolt. "What do you think?"

From the back of the room, Buckolt said, "We should be just about 70 per cent for the month."

Touzin waved the envelope, as if the real figure was his little secret, then reached for the notebooks. "We'll see." He changed gears. "Duty Manager: 11:45 pm. Heat detectors in main kitchen activated. No reason." He turned to Rory Purcell, the young, hyperactive, Irish-brogued Chief Engineer. "It goes off a lot."

Purcell grinned from his place near the door, "It works."

Touzin wondered, "Should it go off so much? It seems to happen almost every day."

"When the heat builds up it's supposed to go off."

"Would you please check it to see if it's functioning properly."

"I will look at it, again. But it's only when it doesn't go off that it's not functioning properly."

Nodding that Purcell had a point, Touzin moved on. "Mr Unger in 425 complained about Room Service. He says he placed his order at 18:30 and it didn't arrive until 19:15."

"He complained," Buckolt said, "because he thought that was very slow. I checked with the Floor Service waiter and found that the order wasn't logged in until 18:55. I presume the guest was mistaken about what time he placed his order."

"Would you ring Mr Unger please and apologize. Tell him that you've made me aware of his complaint and that it won't happen again."

Buckolt made a note to phone the guest.

"Mr Hunter in 316," Touzin read, "complained of indigestion."

Again Buckolt answered, "I saw Mr Hunter this morning and he's feeling better."

"Did he eat in our restaurant?"

Buckolt assured him, "He did not."

Snapping shut that book — "Good" — Touzin picked up the Housekeeper's log. "The clock in 516–517 doesn't work."

Carole Ronald was a compact woman with short, bleached hair. In her early 50s, she was the senior female on the staff. Accordingly, she claimed the chair against the wall, to the left of Touzin's desk. And because she was who she was, no one else ever dared to sit there. "It does now."

Touzin read, "Mrs Widdicombe in 522 stopped me in the corridor and wondered why no one says hello any more."

Everyone laughed.

"She's a dear old lady." Ronald obviously wanted them to understand that this was serious. "She told me that when she first started coming here, which has got to be at least 40 years ago, if not more, all the staff used to say hello to her and greet her by name. Now, she claims, no one says hello."

"Really?" Touzin seemed surprised. "All right, would everyone please make a point of saying hello to Mrs Widdicombe."

A volley of voices mumbled, "Hello Mrs Widdicombe."

He went to another item from Ronald's log. "Mr Stoltz in 131 reported that the laundry lost his shirt."

Ronald explained, "The valet remembers getting it from him and there's a record that we sent it. Except that the laundry claims they have no record of ever receiving it."

"How much?" Touzin asked.

She answered, "Mr Stoltz says the shirt cost him £250."

Touzin raised his eyebrows. "Is that all? Normally shirts that get lost start at £1250." He closed that book and took the Night Manager's log. "Carpet smudge outside lift on sixth floor."

Ronald jotted that down. "I'll take care of it."

"Also . . ." He spotted an item he hadn't seen earlier and struggled with the Night Manager's handwriting. "Light next to entrance . . ."

"It's the sixth floor," Adam Salter offered. Still in his dinner jacket, still wide awake, this was the end of the 26-year-old Englishman's shift. He'd been on duty since 11 the previous night. "It's right next to the lift entrance."

Ronald added that to her list.

Touzin carried on. "Mrs Glass, Room 345, complained about a taxi driver. According to her, the driver was rude." He looked at Salter. "Do you have the driver's number?"

"The lady didn't get it."

"What about the hall porter? Did he know the driver?"

"No."

"Well . . ." There was little he could do, except make certain that the woman was reassured. He asked Buckolt, "Would you please go to see her, say we're sorry about the incident and that we will take whatever steps we can to make certain it doesn't happen again."

As Buckolt wrote that down, Touzin picked up the Food and Beverage Manager's log. "Mr Watkins in 241 complained that the restaurant didn't open until 7:30. He said he thought that was pretty late for some people and wondered why it wasn't open at, say, seven."

Looking at Philippe Krenzer — a thin, dark-haired, shyly quiet man in his mid-30s and the only other Frenchman on the senior staff — Touzin agreed, "I think he's right. At least Mondays through Fridays. Maybe not on weekends, but during the week I think seven is right. Let's see if we can't arrange that."

"We can," Krenzer said.

Now Touzin wanted to know, "What percentage of guests take breakfast here?"

Krenzer guessed, "Including Floor Service, perhaps about 84 per cent."

He thought about that for a moment. "It's too low. We have to talk about finding ways to get that figure higher. Especially in the restaurant. Maybe opening half an hour earlier would help." Then he remembered, "The gentleman who is staying in Room 417, Mr Patrick, came up to me this morning to say that he can't get honey with his porridge. Would you please make sure it goes into his guest history and see that they bring it to him automatically from now on."

As Krenzer wrote that down, Touzin picked up the next logbook.

It was 15 minutes before he finished with them, and, after putting the last one down, he went around the room to see if anyone had anything else to add.

Ronald noted, "I have two maids off sick so we may be a little slow in getting rooms back into service this morning."

Purcell said that workmen would be in at midnight to paint the main lift ceiling, and promised that they would be out before 6 the next morning.

Touzin made a face. "No later than six."

Purcell assured Touzin, "No guests will be inconvenienced."

Banqueting had nothing. Information Technology had nothing. Security had nothing. But Krenzer wanted Touzin to know, "A guest in the restaurant last night didn't like the potatoes."

"The potatoes? What was wrong with the potatoes?"

"He said they didn't taste right."

"Did you speak to the Chef?"

"Yes. He said it was because they were using a different variety of potato. It is not the usual variety."

"Not the usual variety?" Touzin shook his head. "That's no excuse."

"Of course not," Krenzer agreed.

When there was nothing from Personnel, nothing from the Reception Manager and nothing from the Head Cashier, Touzin said to Buckolt, "Okay, arrivals."

One of the women sitting opposite Touzin's desk stood up so that Buckolt could take her place. Balancing a huge logbook on his knees, then finding the correct page, he reeled off the list of guests due in that day.

"Mr and Mrs Pearson are arriving this morning on the Amex

Platinum Fine Hotels Program for three nights in 231. It's their first stay with us. Dr and Mrs Hennessey are back for two nights, and they've asked for 504, which I've given them. Mr Al-Khalili is in 405–406 for five nights. You'll recall that he was with us about six months ago for five nights. He's become quite a regular. Mr and Mrs Hall are coming in this afternoon from Paris, for one night in 104. Mr and Mrs Ryan are arriving tonight by Concorde from New York, for three nights in 440–441. It's their silver wedding anniversary." He paused to ask, "Shall I put something in the room for them?"

"Yes." Touzin noted the Ryans' name in the small red VIP arrivals book that Buckolt made up for him each day. "Let's do extra flowers and a bottle of champagne. And please see that the Duty Manager greets them this evening. He should be the one who takes them up to their room."

Buckolt proceeded down the list of the 45 arriving guests, detailed the rate they were paying, where they were staying and any notes he'd found on them in the Hotel's extensive computerized guest histories.

"Rooms 107–108–109, Ambassador and Mrs Fredericksburg, three nights." Buckolt glanced at Ronald, "There's storage. Last time they left about six suitcases."

She nodded and made a note.

That done, Touzin asked, "Anything else?"

No one answered.

"Have a good day," he said, and they filed out.

After waiting for everyone to leave, he reached for his phone, dialled a room and when a woman answered he said, "Good morning, this is François Touzin. How are you, Mrs Widdicombe?"

~ 2 ~

*A*s soon as the foreign Office reached the point of finalizing arrangements to receive President Kim Young-sam of the Republic of Korea, the Visit Section — which coordinated the specific
details — contacted a man named Lee at the South Korean Embassy
to ask what sort of accommodation the President and his entourage
might require.

Lee had only a rough idea as to the size of the official party, so
he informed the Visit Section that there would probably be 50–75,
but he pointed out that this was just a rough estimate. The Visit Section suggested that Lee ring the Hotel to see if it could handle the
accommodation.

Introducing himself to the Hotel operator, Lee said that he
would like to speak to someone about the possibility of reserving
several dozen rooms. The operator automatically put him through to
Robert Buckolt.

A hotel and catering college graduate, Buckolt had worked his
way up from the bottom — it is the conventional thing in the hotel
business — paying his dues at Reception, as Back of House Manager and as Night Manager. Now he supervised the Reservation and
Reception staff, in addition to the Front Hall personnel and, to some

extent, the cashiers. From the tiny office he shared with the Reception Manager — sandwiched between Touzin's office and the room where the Reservations clerks took bookings — Buckolt asked how he might help.

Lee explained that, although he couldn't go into any detail at this stage, he was wondering if the Hotel could supply 12 suites, including the Royal Suite, 20 twins and seven singles for three nights, mid-week, three months hence.

"This is," he stressed, "a general enquiry and I would not wish to say who the main guest would be."

"I understand." Buckolt easily recognized the planning stage of a state visit because he'd been through this before. It was always the same — a foreign embassy wanting lots of rooms for three days, refusing to say who the star guest would be, creating an aura of secrecy. Perhaps, he thought, it added some excitement to an embassy official's daily grind. "If you would be kind enough to give me just a moment to check, please."

The Hotel comfortably accommodated between 330 and 340 people with a staff-to-room ratio of better than two to one. He had 190 rooms to sell every night and 420 salaries to pay. So he needed to maximize the Hotel's daily occupancy at the optimum room rate. If embassies and their staff secretaries wanted to play games of cloak and dagger, as long as it led to bookings, that was all right with him.

According to his computer, there were several firm bookings for that week, and several more not yet confirmed. However, he saw that he had enough space, even if at this point it meant that the available rooms were spread over the entire hotel. He knew that a group like this would want rooms on the same floor. But then he also knew that wasn't a problem — at least, not yet — because he still had plenty of time to shuffle guests into other rooms.

"Yes," Buckolt assured the Embassy official, "we can indeed accommodate your request."

Lee asked him to hold those rooms tentatively, and promised that he would be back in touch as soon as possible. At that point, Lee did not ask the price of the rooms, nor did Buckolt quote a price.

The moment he hung up, Buckolt stepped into Touzin's office. "It looks like the Koreans are coming."

Touzin was pleased, all the more so because visits like this were sold at "rack" — full price.

Although Buckolt announced the potential visit at the following morning's staff meeting, nothing more was said about it until Lee phoned back to increase his request for both single and double rooms, threefold.

When Lee and several other Embassy officials came to see the rooms and discuss specific requirements, Buckolt conducted the tour, which included a visit to the Royal Suite.

The grand staircase led up from the Front Hall to the mezzanine, where a small staircase — at the far end of the mezzanine — took them up to the first floor. There, in the corner of the building, double doors led into a pale green lobby.

Off to the left there was a dining room, also in shades of green, with a period English table large enough to seat 12. Straight ahead, another set of double doors opened into the large sitting room, in shades of light yellow, with a large salmon pink, plum red and pale green carpet. A large settee faced a coffee table and, beyond that, a working fireplace. There was a writing desk to the right and a beautiful, light wood grand piano in the corner to the left. Made by Broadwood and Sons in London in the 19th century, that piano once belonged to Richard D'Oyly Carte, the British theatrical producer who became famous for staging the operatic works of Messrs Gilbert and Sullivan.

Overstuffed armchairs were scattered around, with side tables next to them.

From the sitting room, an internal hallway led to the main bedroom. Running the length of the first floor, that inside hallway paralleled the main hallway so that anyone staying in the Royal Suite could interconnect with all of the rooms along the front of the Hotel. It created a totally secure area so that the guest in the Royal Suite never had to use the main hallway, except to enter or to leave the hotel.

Although numbers were assigned to every room in the Hotel and prominently displayed on each front door, the Royal Suite was the exception. It had been decided years ago that, for security reasons, it would be the anonymous odd one out. Yet even if there had been a number engraved on a small brass plaque in the middle of the front doors, that would have been misleading. At its smallest, this was a three-room suite. But it was possible to turn it into six, eight, ten, twelve, twenty interconnected rooms.

The bathroom, set off the main bedroom, had that sturdy, old-fashioned, white enamel look, with shiny gold taps on the basins. The bath was heavy, white cast-iron. At some point, very much as an afterthought, a shower had been fitted on, with a glass door that cut off half the bath from the rest of the room.

The main bedroom was surprisingly unspectacular, featuring an ordinary queen-sized bed. But then the list of people who had slept there was quite spectacular: from Nikita Khrushchev to Jackie Onassis, from the King of Morocco — who brought his own bed because he liked that one better — to Enrico Caruso, from Sophia Loren to Ronald Reagan.

Because the Royal Suite was the most special place in the Hotel — it cost £2000 a night for the minimum three-room configuration — not just anyone could have it. Requests for it had to be put in writing to the General Manager. Anyone just ringing up and asking for it was invariably turned down, such as the man who phoned the Night Manager one morning at around 4:15. Refusing to identify himself, he told Adam Salter that he'd like to book the Royal Suite for the remainder of the night.

Without even checking to find out if it was available, Salter apologized that the suite was not available. "I'm terribly sorry, sir."

"Listen, I'm really in a spot," the man confided. "It's only for the rest of the night."

"Sir, I'm afraid the Hotel is fully booked."

"If you knew who this was for, you'd change your mind. But I can't say, you know, for security reasons."

"I understand, sir, but there isn't anything . . ."

"Let me put it this way . . ." The man dropped his voice to a whisper. "My client is an extremely famous pop star. We're talking instantly recognizable, here. The thing is, he's with a young lady . . . you understand, it's not his wife . . . and anything you could do, you know, in the most discreet way possible, would be greatly appreciated."

Admittedly, his interest was aroused. Yet Salter stood his ground. "I'm afraid it's impossible, sir, perhaps another hotel . . ."

"Ah," the man screamed, "to hell with you," and slammed down the phone.

Salter never found out who the pop star was. But that wasn't the point. This was not one of those "celebrity" hang-outs. Even when requests came in writing for the Royal Suite, they were refused to celebrities who might somehow detract from the quiet and discreet nature of the Hotel. They automatically turned down even household names — from actors to pop stars, from teen heart-throbs to heavy-weight champions — refusing to accommodate anyone whom they felt would create a crowd control situation that could disrupt the day-to-day calm and otherwise inconvenience the regular guests.

One rare exception was Clint Eastwood.

When he arrived for his first visit, some years ago, the Duty Manager was notified by the front desk, as was usual, that a V-VIP had arrived.

The first V stood for "Very."

The Duty Manager rushed out of his office to escort the film star personally to the Royal Suite.

"It is a real pleasure to have you with us, Mr Eastwood," he said. "And I would like you to know that my wife has read all your books."

The Foreign Office Visit Section made a firm reservation for 16 rooms, which included suites for the visiting head of state and the most senior people in his party. Those bills would be paid by the British Government Hospitality Fund, excluding personal extras such as international phone calls and hairdressing.

Independently, the Koreans decided they needed 83 more rooms, and agreed to pay all of those bills, including personal extras.

An advance inspection team from Seoul moved into the hotel for three nights, taking nine twins and three singles. There were 18 people in all, including members of the President's Secret Service detail, Korean Telecom engineers and the President's Protocol Secretary.

Touzin chaired the initial meeting in the living room of the second-floor Piano Suite, an exquisitely decorated two-room apartment that cost £1500 per night. Buckolt, Ronald and Andrew Jarman — the young, hefty, large-jawed Banqueting Manager — were there, together with a few other Hotel staff members, and six Koreans.

Noting that the Koreans had expressed the desire to keep as many people as possible on the same floor, Touzin explained that the Hotel had reserved rooms on the first and second floors. Extra allocations, however, now spilled over to the third floor. And, although no one had realized it at the time, additional rooms would need to be found. By then, the only space Buckolt had left was on the fourth floor. It wasn't ideal, but the Koreans accepted that it was the best the Hotel could do. After all, Touzin still had his regular guests to consider.

Lee then went through a long list of requirements. He wanted a dining area in the hotel set aside exclusively for the President's entourage. The Koreans would not, he insisted, want to dine with the Hotel's guests.

Touzin explained that, normally, he would have assigned the main Ballroom to the Koreans, but, unfortunately, all the banqueting rooms were booked for the first night of their stay. Jarman added that he would arrange an alternative dining area for that first day, and make the Ballroom available to them for the rest of their stay.

That led, naturally, to the question of food. They wanted a mixture of European and Korean dishes, Lee said. Jarman promised that the Chef would send Lee his menu proposals.

A protocol officer insisted that food for the entourage was one thing, food for the President was a different matter. The only meal he would definitely take in the Hotel was breakfast, and the President's breakfast was always cornflakes and a three-minute boiled egg. What's more, it could not be prepared, nor could any food be prepared for the President, without his taster being present. Everything prepared for the President would have to be duplicated for the taster.

Touzin wondered if the same held true for the First Lady.

No, the Korean protocol officer said, this was only for the President.

Touzin wondered if tasters could get life insurance, but decided it might not be prudent to ask.

The protocol officer went on to say that the First Lady would need her own dressing table — she would not share one with her husband — and that she also wanted 20 extra hangers in her wardrobe.

Carole Ronald assured him those items would be put into the suite.

Next, Lee said, there would need to be a special express laundry service, available 24 hours a day.

Touzin agreed to provide valet cover overnight, but only for the

16 official suites. The Hotel's regular laundry service would, in turn, handle all other requests on a same-day basis.

Telephone communications was next on the agenda. A Korean Telecom engineer explained how he would install three phone systems to operate in parallel with the Hotel's. The first consisted of 13 regular, unsecured lines, in conjunction with British Telecom. Then there would be two secure, permanently open hot lines — one of them in the President's suite, another in a command post down the hall — going directly back to Seoul. The third would consist of nine point-to-point lines, linking specific rooms, bypassing the hotel switchboard.

Touzin said that was no problem.

Lee then wanted parking spaces out front for 10 government cars, 20 embassy cars and two large buses.

This was difficult, Touzin allowed, because the Hotel didn't control parking. He advised Lee to take up the matter with the Visit Section, which would then act as intermediaries with the Metropolitan Police. As it was, some 200–300 police officers would be assigned to the visit, including members of the Diplomatic Protection Group and motorcycle outriders to escort the President's car.

Throughout the meeting, Korean Secret Servicemen walked in and out, sat down for a few minutes, looked, listened, then got up and, without saying anything, walked out.

It was as if they had nothing better to do.

Little by little, Lee's requests grew more demanding.

He wanted the President's suite to be at a constant temperature of 25 degrees centigrade. That was 77 degrees Fahrenheit.

Buckolt assured him that would be done.

Lee said he wanted cooking facilities to be available to the President's chef 24 hours a day. So the first-floor pantry was designated and two Floor Service managers were assigned as the President's personal waiters.

He said he also needed to know how the Hotel would arrange for luggage on arrival, and how the Hotel would arrange for luggage on departure.

Considering the fact that there would be 400–450 pieces of luggage, it was a serious concern. So a system was worked out whereby everything would be unloaded into the luggage porters' room at the front of the Hotel, taken by them down their lift to the basement, trollied to the back service lift, sorted there and then delivered to each room.

The President's luggage, together with the First Lady's luggage — which when combined would total 45 pieces — had to be handled separately and delivered direct to a valet and maid stationed in the suite, who would then unpack and hang everything.

On departure, all luggage, except the President's and the First Lady's, would have to be in the main Ballroom no later than 9 pm, so that it could be collected at the Hotel by 5 the next morning. Two cots would have to be set up in the Ballroom so that the Secret Service could physically hand-check each piece, then guard them all overnight.

Lee wanted menus set in advance for the entire group, so the Chef devised a buffet — hot and cold European dishes — to be supplemented by Korean dishes that the Koreans themselves would furnish.

After that, Lee required a list of floor staff, housekeeping staff and valets — those people who would need to go into the suites — so they could be cleared for security and issued with special badges.

He also asked that the Hotel provide his Secret Service with floor plans. And, as soon as the Secret Service had them, they selected five rooms that would be used as command posts.

Finally, he said, a large-screen TV had to be put in the President's suite. He paused, then added, in an almost embarrassed tone, that when they visited the suite they noticed that the television there was a Sony, and a non-Korean TV set would never be acceptable.

From past experience, Buckolt doubted that officials on state visits had a lot of time to sit around watching TV. But this wasn't about the President's access to CNN, it was about providing anything the Embassy thought the President might need. It was about helping Lee show his boss that he'd thought of everything, down to the most minute details.

"As for the set itself," Buckolt winced, "unfortunately, this is the standard size we've got. We don't have anything larger and I'm not certain that we have anything else. But I will gladly check. The problem is, we might not."

Lee promised Buckolt, "If that's the case, then we will take care of it."

The cut-off date for room allocations was set for two weeks prior to arrival. Everyone agreed to that. But, at the very last moment, the Embassy commandeered some of the suites which the Visit Section had reserved, meaning that the Foreign Office's 16 official guests were now spread out over two floors. It took Buckolt an extra week to sort it all out. That didn't please the UK hosts, and also created a slightly more complicated security problem for the British police. But that's the way the Koreans wanted it.

A private switchboard was installed for the President in 144 and a second command post in 121–122. Room 124 was set aside for storage — the Hotel's furniture had to come out to make space for the Koreans' computer equipment — and room 129 became yet another command post.

British Telecom showed up to put in extra lines. Then Korean Telecom hooked up their three systems, and also installed a satellite repeater dish on the roof.

Touzin decided that, for a visit like this, the Royal Suite should be freshly painted — there are obviously some people, presidents and royalty, almost certainly including the Queen of England, who must go through life thinking the planet smells of fresh paint — so to get it done on time the Chief Engineer threw bodies at the job. Six painters spent five days there — more time than it ordinarily would have taken, but Purcell ordered speciality finishes to the walls.

The official guest list arrived only four days before the President did.

At the final Heads of Department meeting before the visit — where Touzin assembled 30 people in the Mirror Room, next door to the main Ballroom — Buckolt went over all his background notes. He concluded by warning that the Hotel could have a real problem with this visit.

Touzin was justifiably concerned. "Why?"

"I've just seen the guest list," he said. "It is very important that, when we check the Koreans in, we get their exact initials. The last thing we want is someone to ring the Hotel and have our operators going crazy because everyone seems to be named either Lee or Park."

~ 3 ~

$\mathscr{M}$ARK TWAIN ONCE PROFESSED THAT all saints can do miracles, but few of them can keep a hotel. Not that François Touzin was much of a saint as a French colonial teenager growing up on a tropical island in the Indian Ocean. Then again, he never intended to go into the hotel business.

He was born in Madagascar in 1952, where his father was a doctor in the French Army, a hard-working, dignified man who retired as a Colonel, built a medical school there and served for a time as the President's personal physician. Although Robert Touzin passed away in 1981, his name is still revered in Madagascar.

For François, life couldn't have been more idyllic — the family had a chef, a valet, maids and a chauffeur — except that school got in the way of his affection for the beach and young ladies. Concerned that he should have a solid academic foundation, his father took the drastic step of shipping him off to Poitiers in France, forcing his son to knuckle down in order to get his *baccalauréat*.

It was a rude awakening. From one day to the next, there was no more high living, no more servants, no more ladies, no more beach and very little sunshine.

Once Touzin had his degree — thinking he could now get back

to more interesting pursuits — his dad challenged him to make something of himself. Anxious to live up to his father's expectations, he got accepted at Glion, arguably the most prestigious of the Swiss hotel and catering schools. It wasn't that Touzin dreamed of being in the hotel business, but the hotel business carried a cachet he knew his father would understand.

While there, he fell in love with a young Swedish student, Mia Leffler, and eventually married her.

Following graduation, Touzin took a job as a cook in a kitchen — much to his father's confusion — where he developed a good working knowledge of food and also became quite adept as a butcher. Following that, he waited on tables in a little bistro, at least until he got it into his head that he wanted to learn English, which was when he and Mia came to London. It was 1976 and times were hard. The only job he could find was as a receiving clerk, running the loading bay at the Inter-Continental Hotel.

His father was hardly convinced that this was what graduates of Glion were supposed to do. Touzin tried to make his dad understand that in the hotel business, to get to the top, you must start at the bottom. And Dr Touzin was willing to agree that being a clerk on a loading bay was definitely the bottom.

From there he hotel-hopped, much the way soldiers move from post to post. At the Hyde Park he was Chief Steward, Back of House Manager — he had to make sure the silver was polished and the kitchen was thoroughly cleaned every night — and Coffee Shop Manager. At the Portman he was Materials Manager, then Purchasing Manager. At the Britannia he was Assistant Food and Beverage Manager. And at the Mayfair he ran Food and Beverage.

In the mid-1980s, he and Mia — with the first of their three children in tow — went in search of more exotic adventure and offed to Sydney, Australia, where he was Food and Beverage Manager at the Inter-Continental on Macquarie Street. Then, in the summer of

1988, a head hunter lured him back to London for his first tour at the Hotel.

His original impression of the place was that he'd been caught in a time warp. The Hotel was universally recognized as one of the finest in the world — one of perhaps a dozen in a class by themselves — but the rarefied atmosphere in which it functioned was not the only unreal quality about it. The place was a resplendently grand anachronism patronized by a few privileged clients. It had everything to do with catering to them. Service, he recognized, was indeed the foundation on which profit was built. But bottom line mattered. Here, service seemed to be everything. Profit was one of those things that gentlemen didn't discuss in front of the ladies.

Right from the start, Touzin voiced his concerns to the General Manager. With practised English understatement, his boss tried to allay his fears — "This is a very special place" — and played to Touzin's ego by highlighting his potential. Still, the next 18 months proved to be the most frustrating of Touzin's career.

The Hotel seemed to be all about the status quo, and the status quo seemed to be all about the towering personality of the company's president. An old-school English gentleman, he was the sort of man who didn't walk into a room, he entered it. And when he did — regally — it didn't matter who you were or what you were doing, his presence dominated. And his sartorial elegance was the stuff of legend.

Internationally acknowledged as a truly great hotelier, he had an uncanny knack for understanding the potential of a property. What's more, the old man's philosophy was beguilingly simple. He used to tell Touzin, it is terribly important that the King of Greece be made to feel comfortable because, if he likes your hotel, he will tell people about it. He used to remind Touzin, when the Hotel is full and the guests are happy and the flowers are right and the food is good, you will make money.

But Touzin continued to find himself filled with doubts. He worried that he was being swallowed up by a system he couldn't change. Up to this point, he'd moved one step up the ladder every couple of years. One afternoon, in a weaker moment, he confided in the General Manager, "I'm never going to make it here." The man assured him, "You will succeed me." Touzin, however, saw his boss hanging on forever and decided it was time to look for a property to manage the way he believed a hotel should be managed. He put out feelers. He and Mia hoped they might move to New York.

What he didn't know was how impressed the company president was with him. In Touzin, the old man recognized a protégé with patience enough to pay attention to the most minute details, and with all of the polish of a perfect host. And when, almost out of the blue, the old man offered him the General Manager's job at one of the most fashionable hotels in Paris, Touzin knew he couldn't refuse.

Just off the Champs Elysées, the Lancaster was an incomparable jewel in the Group's crown. A splendidly chic 58-room, five-star hotel with a tremendously impressive guest list and where the staff outnumbered the clients, it was a perfect property for Touzin. Although his only instructions were, "make sure you reduce the losses," Touzin understood right away that here was a place where he could build a solid foundation on service in order to create profit.

He was doing just that when the old man died.

And with that death, the company's main investors decided that a major restructuring of management was necessary.

Coinciding with that, the Hotel's General Manager — a former winner of the prestigious "Hotelier of the Year" award — announced his retirement. So it was decided that Touzin should be brought back from Paris to manage the Hotel. Although emotionally attached to Paris and the Lancaster, and even though it would mean uprooting his family once again, the idea of returning to London was extremely appealing. All the more so because he would be returning to manage what he honestly believed to be the best hotel in the world.

But formidable hurdles stood in Touzin's way.

Touzin's inherited second-in-command was a charming, immaculately dressed man with mannered airs and graces, who epitomized the old regime. The "face" at the front of the house — he knew everyone and everyone knew him — he'd started as a receptionist, worked his way steadily up the ladder and had envisioned that one day he would become General Manager. When he failed to get that job the first time — losing out to Touzin's immediate predecessor — his frustrations simmered just below the surface. Now defeated a second time, the man's irritation was all too evident.

There were several reasons why, Touzin felt, he needed to keep the man happy. First and foremost, it was right for the Hotel. At the same time, the man's continued presence — in full view of the lobby — would serve as a reminder to the rest of the staff that the new regime wasn't changing everything overnight.

But it wasn't to be. The man's immense sense of disappointment coloured their relationship. It grew increasingly clear to Touzin that there wasn't enough room at the Hotel for both of them. The man refused to become Touzin's "greeter." And Touzin wasn't going to permit him to run the place. Their discussions seemed to reach an impasse, until the man — with characteristic style — made the ultimate sacrifice for the sake of the Hotel. After twenty-seven years of service, he announced his early retirement and bowed out gracefully.

The way was now clear for Touzin to hire a new Assistant General Manager. Through a friend in the business, Touzin received the CV of a young guy who had worked at several upmarket hotels. Most recently, the fellow had opened some of the hotels at Euro Disney. Touzin interviewed him and felt he was right for the Hotel. So he announced to the staff that he was bringing in a new, younger "face." When the staff heard that he was a refugee from Euro Disney, some people wondered out loud if the guy had large ears and webbed feet.

♣

At exactly 5 am, the guard at the back door — known as "The Timekeeper" — unlocked the basement entrance to the Hotel and began to accept the day's deliveries.

Three different bakery shipments came in. There were French breads, baked loaves and then pastries. Those were followed by cartons of milk for the kitchen, tins of cream for the kitchen, and some bottles too, for various offices. Then flowers arrived — so many boxes that the driver had to make seven trips from the van to unload them all. After that, there was fruit. After fruit there were vegetables — separate deliveries from three different wholesalers, including one company that brought a lorry from Paris — and then dozens of items for the dry stores, such as tins of oil, chutneys, ketchup, syrups and flour.

Every member of the staff — with the exception of Touzin — entered the Hotel through that back door. They all had to punch time cards, clocking in and out. And they all had to get past the Timekeeper, who stood in his tiny shack of an office with glass walls on two sides so that he could see if someone was attempting to sneak past him.

There were two chairs and a metal basin in his cabin, and a large box where he harboured keys to doors and offices throughout the Hotel. There was a phone on the table, and a security monitor there too, with four split screens, covering the basement, hallways, stairs and back alley. With one switch he could change those views, to check all of the Hotel's 26 surveillance cameras. Nearby there was a VCR that recorded 12 hours' worth of what those cameras saw.

Three Timekeepers worked shifts — Basil the Nigerian, Mohammad the Egyptian and Mustapha, whose real name was Abdul.

They sat there all day, every day — balanced on a shaky old swivel chair with a badly worn cushion — suspiciously eyeing everyone who passed, saying hello to some, nodding to others, knowing all the faces and most of the names of the people who walked by.

If the Timekeeper didn't know someone, he glared with suspicion and challenged the intruder, like a perimeter sentry — friend or foe.

There was a logbook, where contractors signed in and out, and colour-coded passes — yellow for Wednesday, green for Friday, pink for Saturday — so that Security could tell at a glance which contractors were supposed to be in the Hotel and which ones shouldn't be there. Near that was a kettle, and in one corner a TV set, for company at night.

Because there was a pub down the road at the rear of the Hotel, drunks occasionally wandered in. But they never got too far because nobody got past Basil the Nigerian, or Mohammad the Egyptian, or Mustapha whose real name was Abdul — with the exception of two, decidedly sober, cops from West End Central, who walked the beat and every so often stopped by to say hello and have a cup of tea.

Nor did anyone leave without the Timekeeper seeing.

When a young woman started to walk out carrying a quilt, the Timekeeper demanded to see the pass from her department head saying it was all right to have this. She said she'd come in with it. He said she needed a pass. She pointed out that the Hotel didn't have quilts. He said that, without a receipt, it stayed in the Hotel. She said she didn't have a receipt. He held her there for 15 minutes, until he located the Duty Manager and the Duty Manager wrote out a receipt.

Nothing got past the Timekeeper.

Even rubbish that went into the compactor — before it was taken out, he inspected that too.

At 6:50, a truck pulled up to collect food bins. All unused food was taken away for animal feed. Another truck pulled up behind that one and waited with its lights blinking. Five minutes later, the rubbish collectors arrived. They wheeled ten huge bins up to their truck and unloaded them. Then more bread arrived — this time loaves specially baked for afternoon tea sandwiches. Ten minutes later, the Timekeeper wondered about the truck with its lights blinking. He got up from his chair and walked outside to ask the driver what he wanted. The driver said he was waiting for the Purchasing Department to open. The Timekeeper mumbled, okay, and came back inside.

Then came meat deliveries — two different butchers and three different poultry wholesalers — and after that there were deliveries from five different fishmongers, one of whom dealt exclusively in smoked salmon.

That was followed by supplies of cheese and eggs.

The night shift left, handed in their keys, punched their time cards and waved goodbye.

The day shift came in, punched their time cards, took their keys, hurried by and waved hello.

And all the time he looked at every one of them.

Under the previous administration, the Hotel maintained a special royal rate — available to members of Europe's titled families — of £25 a night, inclusive of Value Added Tax.

Not surprisingly, royalty came to the Hotel. And, at least in theory, Touzin was willing to concede that the philosophy behind the price had been right. Successful hotels are run by successfully mixing public relations with business. But in practice, Touzin argued, the price for the exercise was too high for the little business it brought.

When the company president died, the then General Manager doubled the royal rate to £50.

When Touzin moved in, he increased it again.

It cost the Hotel just over £110 per day to maintain a room, whether or not it was rented. To bring the business into profit, Touzin theorized he needed to work off a 30 per cent margin. His break-even point hovered around 52 per cent occupancy. And while some hoteliers believed that it was better to get something for a room rather than let it go vacant for the night — much like the airlines that reckoned that, once the plane took off, the empty seat represented lost revenue — the problem with the royal rate was that royals never stayed in small singles. For their token payment, they'd been pampered enough to come to expect suites.

Touzin's dilemma was that he could get real money for those rooms.

To juggle the Hotel's long-standing relationship with Europe's royals and the realities of modern business — he didn't want to lose their patronage — Touzin sent a personal letter to each of the Hotel's long-standing royal guests, explaining that, unfortunately, he would have to change the royal rate. He told them that, for obvious economic reasons, he had to set it at a commercially viable rate. But he also said that he sincerely hoped they would understand why he was forced to do this, and closed by reminding them that they would always be welcome at the Hotel.

A few of those royals took the time to answer his letter with a personal note of their own, saying that they appreciated the Hotel's past kindness and were grateful Touzin would still consider them special guests.

Almost all of them have since returned.

Some people in the hotel business claim they sell sex. Others believe that what they do is furnish the stage for sex. In reality, they sell sleep.

Logically, then — as Touzin adhered to the theory — the better the hotel, the better the sleep. If clients go away having slept well — which they won't if they haven't been properly taken care of while they're awake — then they'll come back.

For Touzin, it was indisputable that survival at the top end of the market — as opposed to the niche held by those bed factory chains that simply look for volume — hung on repeat business. First he had to work to win a client. Then he had to work to keep that client. If he couldn't manage both, he'd go broke.

Approaching its centennial, the Hotel had arrivals ledgers — gigantic, hard-covered volumes — dating back to the turn of the century. It also had hand-written histories on many guests going back to 1920. They were amusing, but not very useful. Occasionally, someone would ring to say, my parents honeymooned at the Hotel in 1921 and I'd like to have the same room. A secretary would sort through the records to find out which room the couple had. But most of the time those journals were left in storerooms to gather dust.

However, since 1985 the details of every guest who has stayed at the Hotel are on the computer. Besides listing names, addresses, phone numbers and the rooms they liked — or the rooms they didn't like — the guest histories detail all those little quirks that make some clients more demanding than others.

One client wanted a king-size bed but no bedspread. Another insisted that there never be a radio in his room. One liked an eiderdown folded over the settee, the sheets left untucked at the side of the bed and extra Kleenex. Another wanted two hard pillows at the top of the bed, three hard pillows at the foot of the bed on top of the blankets and one regular pillow at the foot of the bed underneath the mattress.

There were guests who hated carnations but loved orchids, and guests who wanted blue tissues in the bathroom, never pink or white. One client always expected to find an exercise bicycle in his room. Another guest needed a barber's chair in his. One couple insisted they must have no fewer than 300 silk hangers, 100 trouser hangers and 100 wooden hangers in their suite. Another wanted every picture taken off the wall at the entrance to theirs.

A guest history stated that a gentleman wanted extra shower curtains, so the Hotel made sure that when he walked into his room there were extra shower curtains. Another guest history noted that a lady always wanted every blanket removed from the room, so the Hotel made certain that when she arrived there were no blankets anywhere to be found.

Someone wanted the desk in his usual room moved to where the dressing table was. Someone else, who stayed in the same room, wanted it put back the other way. Some people only ever slept on a north–south axis. Others only ever slept east–west. One guest history even included a small diagram of how the gentleman liked his room, with a note attached that he needed six pillows — two hard, two medium and two soft.

One woman wanted a hot water bottle left in her room every night promptly at 10, along with extra postcards. Another woman wanted bath mats placed on each side of her bed, with six laundry bags in the room and luggage racks that had to be made of chrome, never aluminium.

There was a gentleman who demanded that his room not be cleaned with Ajax. And someone else who demanded that a maid be available to Dettol his room after he arrived, so that he could see she cleaned everywhere, including the ear piece of the telephone.

Some guests required Tita to be their maid — and wouldn't settle for anyone else — while others wouldn't accept anyone besides Enzo to serve their breakfast.

When Mrs Hayakawa arrived for a three-day stay in 420, a Japanese tea set was already waiting in her room. When Mr Gersten arrived with his lady friend for a weekend in 505, no one addressed his lady friend as Mrs Gersten. When Mr Abbot arrived for one night in 315, a fax machine was already set up in his room. When Mr Oliphant arrived for two days, he went into room 119, because he had a heart condition and felt safer on a lower floor. When Mr May, an exercise fanatic, arrived for two weeks in 204, his rowing machine was already assembled.

Those guest histories, painstakingly updated and constantly referred to, became the nucleus of Touzin's approach to knowing who his clients were, and how to keep those clients coming back.

At the same time, there was also a black list, a ledger affectionately known as NTBT — Not To Be Taken — which indexed some 121 names, various people who had, for all sorts of reasons, outstayed their welcome.

There was a woman who repeatedly caused scenes when she was informed that torn jeans or shorts were not considered suitable dress for the public areas of the Hotel. There was a known art forger. There was a woman who once physically attacked the Night Manager because he wouldn't permit her to take a young man up to her single room at 4:30 in the morning. There was a couple who bounced several cheques. There were men wanted by the police and a couple who caused so much commotion by constantly arguing on each of their previous stays that someone in senior management decided the other guests did not need this kind of disturbance.

When any of those people tried to book, they were politely and promptly informed that no rooms were available.

Touzin often ate lunch in the staff canteen in the basement, around the corner from the main kitchen, even though as General Manager he was entitled to eat in the restaurant every day if he wanted to, or to ring for Room Service.

At first, the maids and the valets and some of the Back of House staff — who always ate their meals in the canteen — stared at him, because senior managers hadn't been regularly seen there. Touzin wanted to show them that the old days were over. But it took a while before they got used to him. And then not everyone liked it. Especially some of the maids.

Until Touzin assumed command, there were several dozen employees living in the Hotel. A series of tiny rooms had been set aside for them on the top floor. It had been that way since the beginning. And even if, emotionally, he was inclined to keep it that way — both for their sake and for domestic stability — it was no longer viable. Intellectually, he couldn't justify it.

Of course, the Hotel found them other accommodation. Of course, the Hotel helped to relocate them. In many cases, next door. But there was no way the Hotel could entirely cushion the trauma that came with that change. Some maids now had to spend time and money commuting to work. It was no longer convenient for them to eat all of their meals in the staff canteen. Some maids quit. Others voiced their discontent but stayed on, putting the blame for their low morale squarely on him. Nor did it help much when, after Personnel failed to find enough well-qualified maids to replace the ones who'd left, Carole Ronald had to announce that every maid would now be responsible for eleven rooms, instead of nine.

As far as they were concerned, Touzin was the bad guy in this piece.

Adding to their criticism of him, changes were made in the way they did certain things, such as how they cleaned the marble floors in the bathrooms. Touzin wanted Housekeeping to set even higher standards. The maids complained that they were already working to the highest standards. But Touzin was looking for one notch beyond excellence.

Again, Touzin appeared to them to be the villain.

Ten years before, the Hotel had 560 employees. When Touzin arrived they were down to 420. He was now as close to the bone as he could cut. Further staff reductions could put service at risk and he refused to do that. The answer, he decided, was space. It was a question of real estate. It was all about yield management. He wanted each square metre to return a certain amount of revenue per day.

In the old days, managers spoke about occupancy and the average room rate. Then again, in the old days, hotels always kept a spare room somewhere, just in case a regular guest showed up. No more. The men in grey suits realized they couldn't bank the average room rate. They began viewing a hotel as an entity and calculated the daily yield. They added up the room revenue for that day, then divided that figure by the total number of rooms.

One way to increase yield was to increase the number of rooms for rent, so Touzin formulated a massive refurbishment plan. The maids' rooms would be replaced by seven luxurious guest apartments, office facilities for guests, a fitness centre, additional banqueting rooms and modern conference facilities. The two penthouses on the roof, both built in 1960, would be restored as two ultra-sumptuous apartments. The terrace, which ran along the south side of the seventh floor, would be covered to become enclosed conservatories serving those apartments.

While this was happening, Rory Purcell saw his opportunity to redecorate and redo the air-conditioning in the entire Hotel. He wanted to put new bathrooms, a new telephone system and a new call system into every room. He wanted to work on some of the common areas of the Hotel, to redo the roof, to install a new lift from the sixth to seventh floors, to add a pair of new Room Service lifts and to renovate a good part of the basement. He also dreamed up an integrated environmental control system for all the bedrooms to show how the room performed over the previous 24 hours — when the heat came on, when the air-conditioning came on, what the constant temperature was. To that he added a new security system, with "intelligent" keys, where access to rooms could be programmed by time.

Touzin took a proposal to the company which, after several lengthy and very detailed meetings, agreed to fund it. He knew they would because along with the restructuring of the company — now in full swing — came well defined priorities. One of those priorities was to create more product. Another was to respect the past and understand the future. The refurbishment plans readily combined the two. This was not just about modernization, it was also about restoration. At the same time, this was about having vision enough to equip the Hotel for the 21st century.

If only, Touzin thought, he could get the maids to understand that by moving them out he was actually protecting their jobs.

~ 4 ~

HE SECOND IN A LINE of five red lights lit up on the back wall panel of the third-floor pantry — a small, fully equipped kitchen with yellow tiled floors and stainless steel worktops — where the Room Service waiter was hurrying to put cups, saucers, napkins, spoons, forks, knives, perfectly rolled butter balls, small pots of jam, cream jugs and sugar bowls on breakfast trolleys before the rush began.

It was much the same scene in the pantries on all the other floors.

At the same time a bell went off, just in case the third-floor waiter hadn't seen the light.

He stopped what he was doing, checked the light to see which part of the floor the call had come from — each floor was divided into five areas — then hurried out of the pantry. Because each room had three tiny lights above the door — red for the waiter, white for the maid, green for the valet — all he had to do was go to the indicated section of the corridor and spot a red light.

To avoid walking in when someone wasn't expecting him to appear — waiters and maids had all learned from experience how embarrassing it was to stumble in on an amorous couple or discover someone just stepping out of the bath — the waiter knocked on the door at room 325 twice, loudly, listening for the client to say, come in.

Not hearing anyone, he knocked again.

He hesitated another few moments, and was just about to open the door ever so slightly with his pass key and announce very loudly, "Waiter," when a gentleman in one of the Hotel's white terry towelling bathrobes got to the door first. "Good morning."

"Yes sir, good morning," the waiter said.

"Two Continental breakfasts, please. Both with coffee and warm milk. Oh, and margarine, no butter."

The waiter nodded, "Certainly sir," reset the call button to turn off the little red light and promised to return shortly.

On his way back down the corridor, he noticed two more call lights that had just come on — rooms 335 and 319 — and stopped there to take both orders.

As soon as he got into the pantry, he logged all three orders into the computer — for billing and inventory purposes — and kept a record for himself, just in case one of his clients asked the next day for "The same breakfast I had yesterday."

Cooked meals came up from the kitchen on one of three dumbwaiters. That might be anything from the usual kippers and eggs — with two eggs, with four eggs, with egg whites only or with egg substitute for those clients who counted cholesterol — to the less obvious cream of vegetable soup and spaghetti Bolognese. Basic breakfasts such as the Continental — juice, coffee or tea, a basket of breads and rolls — were prepared by the waiter in the pantry.

Each pantry was stocked with four kinds of tea — China, Earl Grey, Assam and Darjeeling. Assam was automatically served in the morning and Darjeeling was automatically served in the evening, unless the client specified another variety. And there were four flavours of herbal infusion — mint, chamomile, linden and mango. Coffee was filtered — it was the Hotel's special blend — and served with hot milk, unless a client asked for cold. There was also decaff, Espresso, Turkish and Arabic coffee, and hot chocolate too. Bread was white, brown or wholemeal. There were Danish pastries, muffins, croissants, rolls and brioches. There was a large selection of jams and jellies — apricot, raspberry, black cherry, strawberry, marmalade and honey. There were yogurt and cereals — Raisin Bran, Rice Krispies, oatmeal and porridge — and there were bagels. It's an American thing, but then the bulk of the Hotel's clients are American. It is only the occasional European who orders a bagel. One in particular scooped out all the dough and ate only the crust. Europeans, it seems, still have a lot to learn about bagels.

Most hotels centralize their Room Service — preparing everything in the same kitchen and sending it upstairs with whichever waiter happens to be available. Not here. This is the old-fashioned way. Every floor waiter starts with a two-month formal training course. And then it takes another six months on the job before he can be considered up to standard. But then, waiters working here stay on the same floor for years, and over the years they get to know their guests.

There was a supervisor for each shift — the Italian Enzo who began there in 1958 and the German Kurt who started two years later — roaming from pantry to pantry to make certain that everything was running smoothly. The last thing anyone wanted to hear from a guest was that service took too long or that their food was not hot.

Kurt had just stepped into the third-floor pantry as the first two breakfasts were being wheeled out of the door. "What's next?"

Over his shoulder the waiter pointed, "There's 335 and 319."

Someone wanted porridge so Kurt started preparing it. While that was cooking, he noticed that the coffee was running out, so he made a fresh pot. By the time the waiter came back, two more call buttons were lit. The waiter phoned down to the kitchen for a portion of fresh fruit, logged in two more Continentals, took the breakfast with the porridge to 319 and fetched the next orders. Now Kurt phoned down to the kitchen for sausages and tossed two slices of bread into the toaster. Seeing a trolley ready to go, he put a small pot of cream on it.

When the waiter came back, he instantly spotted Kurt's mistake. Without saying anything, he took the cream off the trolley and replaced it with a small pot of skimmed milk. Then he wheeled out the order.

Later, he would go around to the various rooms to collect the trolleys, throwing away everything that hadn't been eaten. Bread, butter, jam, cream — everything that came back — was binned. Unlike some other hotels, nothing was ever recycled into someone else's breakfast.

Later still, when breakfast was finished, he would wash the pantry, scrubbing and polishing everything, disinfecting the stainless steel worktops, cleaning the coffee maker and scrubbing the floor. The procedure would be repeated after the lunch service and again, for the third time, after the dinner service.

It is a labour-intensive business. But guests feel that there is also something wonderfully decadent about being able to push a button at the side of their bed and have a man in a dinner jacket arrive to serve them. How else could anyone explain why one glass of juice, two cups of coffee and a couple of pieces of toast cost £15?

Carole Ronald lived in flat shoes.

An extraordinarily patient woman, she believed that people born under the star sign Taurus, as she had been, make the best housekeepers. She also believed that if she got to spend an hour a day at her desk, sorting through the mountain of paperwork that piled up for her, that was a lot.

The moment Touzin's morning meeting was finished, she raced up to the sixth floor, pushed through a set of double doors, and went halfway down a small hallway into an office cluttered with old couches, old chairs, a filing cabinet, a fridge, and boxes filled with cleaning powder. Her assistant, her floor housekeepers and the Public Area Housekeeper were all waiting for her there.

Two maids were off sick, two had just quit because they were angry at Touzin, and one floor housekeeper was on holiday.

It was a crisis day.

On a memo board at the side of the room were the names of demanding guests, to remind the housekeepers, and the maids too, which guests needed special care. On the desk in front of her there were four boxes of index cards — compilations of the guests' special requests — detailing precisely what it was that made them difficult. Next to those was a large red book where she'd logged the really strange requests, the ones the Hotel staff referred to as "seriously demanding." The gentleman who was so finicky about his health, he insisted all door handles be wrapped in Kleenex, so that he never had to touch a door handle that had been touched by someone else. Or the client who refused to allow anyone to service his room until 11 pm. No one ever figured out why. But no one ever asked him, either, because as long as that was what he wanted, that was the service he got.

Each of Ronald's housekeepers carried a layout of their specific floor with all the rooms colour coded. Black meant occupied. Red meant departing today. Yellow meant vacant. The letters "OOO" stood for "out of order," meaning that the room was being decorated, or that some sort of maintenance was going on.

"Please check the carpets and floorboards in 404," she began. "Please take a look at the carpets in 109–110 because there was a spillage. Also the corridors. Please tell your maids to keep an eye out for dust around the radiators."

Then she went through all of the day's arrivals. "246, no smoking, one night. 539 one night. 240 two nights. 304 one night. 321 three nights, a regular but no specials. 101–102 six nights. 342 two nights. 233 one night, arriving at seven this evening. 540 four nights arriving at ten pm. And we need great care here. She's a regular with no specials, but be careful. 440–441, three nights, crossed." That meant twin beds had to be put together to make a large double.

Now she warned, "107–108–109. There are specials on this one. Also, there's storage so please check to see what's there."

Each floor housekeeper was responsible for making sure that the rooms on her floor were ready for guests when they arrived and properly maintained while they were in residence. The floor house-keepers also had to make certain that, when a room was vacated, it was cleaned and prepared for the next client as soon as possible. Any room out of service had to be logged into the computer so the front desk knew which rooms were unavailable. When rooms were ready, that too had to be logged into the computer so that the front desk could take guests up to them.

Ronald had started in the business 20 years before, after a long stay in America. She came home, didn't know what she wanted to do and wound up as a floor housekeeper in a medium-sized commercial hotel. Within a few years she'd worked her way up to unit head housekeeper in a 900-bedroom operation. Making a go of a place like that was an invaluable experience, which ultimately stood her in good stead because she was headhunted out of there to be Executive Housekeeper at the Inn on the Park. Six years later, the Hotel offered her what might be considered the best housekeeping job in the hotel business. But no one warned her when she came here that along with the title came a bleeper that would go off almost non-stop.

Mrs Saint-Martin in 537 needed a hairdryer.

There were no bathrobes in 408.

Extra towels had to go into 311.

The new carpets were in for 305–306 but no one could find the carpet fitter.

No one warned her when she came here that a day with two maids off sick, two who'd just quit because they were angry at Touzin, one floor housekeeper on holiday and a hotel full of demanding guests was merely business as usual.

It was also business as usual for John Wingrove.

The senior Concierge, with his half glasses falling off the end of his nose, picked up the ringing phone and heard Mr Saperstein in 437 ask if someone could fly to Antibes, in the south of France, at his expense, to pick up his watch.

A magician and a diplomat, Wingrove hardly flinched.

He came to the Hotel in 1955, at the age of 15, the most junior of nine pages, to spend three years sitting on a bench wearing white gloves and carrying messages on a silver salver. Since then, he'd worked as a lift operator, cloak room attendant and telephone operator. He'd worked in the enquiry office, handing out room keys and giving people their messages, as postman, packer, junior hall porter, assistant hall porter — for 20 years — and was now the head hall porter. It meant that, over the years, he'd heard just about every possible request. Besides the obvious — tickets for Wimbledon, the theatre, the Chelsea Flower Show, Ascot, Henley, Cup Finals and boxing matches — a man once asked him to go to his room and sing Happy Birthday to his wife. Another rang from the States and asked him to deliver a bouquet of flowers to Maria Callas who was singing at Covent Garden. The actor Edward G. Robinson asked him to buy two French poodles for him. And a client once rang from Greece to ask Wingrove if he could send someone to a gun auction at Gleneagles. On behalf of that client, Wingrove spent £45,000 on three hunting rifles, then arranged for the permits, export licences and the shipment to Greece.

When he wasn't running errands, he was offering advice — on

anything and everything, from sightseeing and shopping to airlines, car hire and restaurants. And restaurants were usually the most delicate. If a client asked about a restaurant that Wingrove knew was either a rip-off joint or simply bad, he would say so. But he had to be careful not to put someone off a restaurant or otherwise be seen to be pushing someone towards a restaurant — if the client had a bad meal he would resent the Concierge for sending him there — unless he was asked. So if someone wanted a reservation, he would make it. If someone also wanted advice, he would give it. But he never volunteered.

The other "never" was when it came to girls.

The reputation of the Hotel was such that his answer was always, "I'm sorry, sir, that's not something I can help you with. We can't arrange that." It wasn't done and most guests knew that was the case, so most guests didn't bother asking. It saved everyone a lot of embarrassment.

But, to a concierge like Wingrove, fetching a watch in France was child's play. "Give me a few minutes, sir," he told Mr Saperstein, "and I'll see what I can do. I'll ring you right back." Hanging up he turned to the other Front Hall porters. "Anyone want to fly to the Riviera for the day to pick up Mr Saperstein's watch?"

None of the four assistant hall porters was terribly keen but one of the young pages said he'd love to go, so Wingrove got on the phone, booked a seat on the noon flight to Nice and one on the last flight back, then rang Mr Saperstein to say he had someone ready to go.

Saperstein gave Wingrove all the details, and the Concierge passed them on to the page. He got some cash for the boy's expenses, sent him home for his passport, and then to the airport for the flight to France. The page was back in the Hotel that evening brandishing the watch as if it was first prize in a contest.

Wingrove was still on duty and more than curious to see what sort of a watch someone would go to all that trouble for. A gold Vacheron, perhaps. A Rolex Oyster. A Piaget.

It turned out to be a totally unspectacular, ordinary wrist watch.

And later, when Wingrove worked out what it had cost Mr Saperstein to retrieve it, he thought to himself, the watch didn't cost as much.

A gentleman arrived to check in, announced that his name was Bjornstad, and added, "I've got a meeting right now and don't have time to go to the room."

"No problem, sir," Michael said, noticing on his computer screen that 431 wasn't ready yet anyway. He handed the gentleman his preprinted registration form — so that the guest could check it for accuracy — took his credit card and put it through the machine.

Touzin had instituted a disciplined credit control policy. He reasoned that someone staying in a room at £250 per night for three nights could spend nearly as much again on Room Service, the restaurant, telephone calls, theatre tickets, whatever. So, instead of asking the credit card company to clear an amount equal to the price of the room, the Hotel multiplied the room rate by the number of days, and then doubled it to cover those extras. £250 times three times two came to £1500.

Recognising that while in the Hotel someone might go out and charge even more to their card, putting it over their credit limit — which meant that when it came time to pay the Hotel, the credit card company would refuse the charge — Touzin dictated that on certain occasions Reception use a discretionary multiple. In other words, instead of asking the credit card company to clear a charge of £1500 they might ask for say, £7500. That way, credit was safely held aside to ensure that the Hotel would be paid without ever embarrassing a guest.

"Your bags will be in the room when you return, sir. I'll cut your key-card for you then, or give it to you now, whatever you'd like."

"Hold it here. Fine," he said, scribbling his name on the credit card slip. "See you later."

"Yes sir, and welcome back."

No sooner had he left — Michael breathed a little sigh of relief and pointed to the screen to show Alastair that 431 should have been ready and wasn't — than Mr and Mrs McGrath arrived, exhausted by their overnight flight from Los Angeles. They were booked into 320, and that room wasn't ready yet either.

It was their first stay at the Hotel so, while Alastair helped them fill in the registration form, Michael tried to find another room for them.

That's when Housekeeping returned 431.

Checking Mr Bjornstad's guest history to see if he had a room preference — he didn't — Michael decided he could make life easier for the McGraths by putting them in that room. So he told Alastair, "Four–three–one for Mr and Mrs McGrath."

A slightly bemused Alastair showed them upstairs.

While he was gone, Michael took a call from Mr Welton in 240, saying he wanted to stay for another day. That meant he'd now have to find another room for Mrs Guerrero, who had been due to go into that room.

That's when the Hotel's office at Heathrow Airport rang to say that no one could find Mrs Guerrero, who was supposed to have been on a flight from Chicago.

And just as Michael was about to say, "She isn't here yet," he glanced up and found a woman standing in front of him, looking tired and somewhat bewildered. He said into the phone, "Just a moment," and took a chance with, "Good morning, Mrs Guerrero."

"Good morning," the woman said.

"Did you have a good flight?" He put her registration card on the counter.

"Yes, thank you."

"Mrs Guerrero, I'm terribly sorry that you weren't met at the airport. I believe a car had been arranged . . ."

"It's all right," she said, signing the form. "I took a taxi . . ."

"If you would let us know how much your fare was, we will reimburse you . . ."

"Thank you," she said.

He whispered into the phone, "No problem, we've got her," hung up and tried to find a room for her.

By the time she'd filled in her registration card and he'd taken an imprint of her credit card, Alastair was back. So Michael told him, "Mrs Guerrero is in 427," and Alastair took her upstairs.

At that point, one of the cashiers came up to Michael to report, "There are no charges coming in for 132."

"No?" He punched some buttons on his computer. "Mr Oberman?"

"That's right."

He made a face and dialled Housekeeping.

Because people usually spend money while they are in residence — they eat breakfast, or they call Room Service for a late-night snack, or they use the mini bar or they make phone calls — when the cashier didn't see any charges coming in over the course of a few days, he began to worry. One possibility was that the client had skipped without paying his bill. Another, even worse, was that he might be dead.

When the first-floor housekeeper answered the phone, Michael asked, "Mr Oberman in 132."

"What about him?"

"Is he there?"

"He was this morning."

"Breathing?"

"Yes. Why?"

"Thanks," he said and told the cashier, "He's still with us."

A few moments later, Monsieur and Madame Guilmet arrived from Paris for one night — booked into room 327 — and it was

Alastair again who showed them up. But the minute they saw the room, they decided it was too art deco for their taste and said, flatly, they didn't like it.

Picking up the phone, Alastair rang Reception. "What else have we got?"

"With the Koreans holding everything . . ." Michael hurried through the list on his computer until he noticed something. "It's one night, right? I just got 320 released. Do you want to give that a go?"

Alastair wasn't sure they'd want that either — it was only slightly less art deco — but as it was nearby, he figured it was worth a try. So he cheerfully invited the Guilmets to look at 320 and, when they got there, they decided it was perfect.

Back downstairs, Alastair made a face. "Now what do we do with Mr Bjornstad?"

Michael assured him, "He'll love art deco."

Across the hall, at the cashier's desk, Mr and Mrs Cameron were checking out.

"What's this?" the gentleman wanted to know, pointing to his bill. "These charges aren't mine."

The young clerk explained, "It was Floor Service this morning, sir."

"What Floor Service?"

"Did you have breakfast in your room, sir?"

He hesitated a moment. "Coffee was all," he said.

"Just a moment, sir. Excuse me." The clerk left the couple there while he went into the back office to ask Christian Horvath, the Head Cashier, to come out.

Horvath, a smiling, fair-haired young English fellow, promptly appeared and greeted the guests by name. "Good morning, Mr and Mrs Cameron. I understand there's a problem."

"This extra charge," Cameron said.

Horvath glanced at the bill. "It appears to be two Continental breakfasts this morning, sir."

"Well, I had one but my wife only had coffee. She didn't touch the bread."

"No problem, sir." He took the bill and made an adjustment in the client's favour for £5.

"Thank you," Cameron said, shook Horvath's hand and gave the clerk his credit card.

Horvath returned to his office, forever amazed that someone could spend several hundred pounds a night for a room, then worry because his wife didn't eat the bread. It was even more bizarre, he thought, the week before when a client complained about £4.50 on his phone bill — "I never made this call" — when the total bill came to £3100. But then, he already knew the answer. It wasn't the money, it was the principle of the thing. Some people always needed to think they came out ahead.

The Hotel's computer was hooked up to the phone system so that it recorded the cost of calls and hooked up to Food and Beverage so that it recorded all charges for Room Service, the main restaurant and the Causerie, which was the Hotel's second restaurant. The mini bar, the laundry, charges with the Concierge, theatre tickets, hairdressing, car hire, photocopying and cash advances were all manually posted. Occasionally, Horvath was willing to concede, computer mistakes happened. Seven out of ten of those were because someone put a charge on the wrong room. But the remaining complaints were usually down to client error — asking the Concierge for stamps and saying, I'm in room 243, when they're actually in 234. What's more, guests sometimes forgot what they charged.

The Hotel's clients did not sign bills. This was another thing Touzin wanted to change. He wanted the guest's name to appear on all their bills and that they should sign them too. That, he reckoned, would eliminate most of those complaints.

Jeffrey Robinson

He'd already expunged more serious complaints. The worst of them related to early arrivals. When someone wanted to get into their room before normal check-out time — before the room might normally be expected to be available — the Hotel held the room for them from the night before, and charged them the extra night. It was standard practice in most hotels. But the letter they used to send out caused a lot of confusion. It didn't state clearly enough that there would be that extra charge. Touzin changed that. The new letter said, the room will be held at a rate of ... and then listed the amount. It totally eliminated that problem.

Occasionally, clients paid cash. When the Hotel hosted an international banking meeting, several Russians settled their bills with US dollars. One American in particular, who came to London a couple of times a year to gamble, once handed Horvath $50,000 in cash, to be credited to his account. He took two suites plus two deluxe rooms, extensively used Room Service and also charged a lot of extras. When he handed the money to Horvath, he said, "Here, you count it," as if he couldn't be bothered. But, generally speaking, the Hotel was not considered a cash business. Most clients used credit cards. Still, the daily cash float — the amount of money with which the Hotel started each day — was £31,000. And even then, he sometimes ran out.

A privileged few clients maintained a personal account with the Hotel. They charged what they wanted and were billed monthly for their charges. A couple of guests even maintained credit balances. One of them sent the Hotel a cheque for £25,000 every six months and his credit balance was now £43,200.84. The Hotel did not pay interest on the money, although they got interest on it, but that didn't seem to matter to the gentleman, who openly admitted that he didn't have a clue how much was in his account. He stayed there for six to eight weeks at a time, several times a year, and simply found it convenient to leave his money there.

To get credit, a client had to supply two banking references, both of which were then followed up at the Group Head Office. The average limit was only £3000. And because it was so strict, the Hotel had very few outstanding accounts.

Anyone in the Hotel for more than a week was asked to settle his bill on a weekly basis. And whereas the previous management was fairly relaxed about it — some people were permitted to stay on for weeks at a time — Touzin put his foot down. He didn't want a repeat of the story of the English gentleman whose bill had run well into five figures.

Booked into a large suite for three weeks, the guest ran up his bill with Dom Perignon and Roederer Cristal Brut champagne. He was asked to settle and promised he would, but he never bothered. Then he announced he was leaving and, in a slight panic, two senior managers went to his suite to insist he settle his bill immediately. The guest appeared quite surprised that they should take such a firm approach and handed them a Platinum American Express card. He said — as if they should have asked for it earlier — "Here it is. No problem." The managers became very sheepish and said thank you several times. Then the man asked, "Why don't I just open an account?"

They said they would have an account request form waiting for him when he checked out.

Downstairs, they put the credit card through the system and it cleared immediately. That meant the man was definitely good for that amount of money. When he was ready to leave, an account form was waiting. He filled it out and the application was sent on for a reference check.

Over the course of the next six weeks, while the request was still in the system, the gentleman returned to the Hotel. On the first occasion, he had a lot to drink in the restaurant and caused a scene. On the second, he stumbled drunk into the Hotel at 3 am and demanded a room. The Night Manager was quite concerned, all the more so when the gentleman insisted, "I have an account here."

Checking the gentleman's guest history, it appeared he was well known to the management, so he was given a room. The next morning, when the General Manager saw the Night Manager's report, the Head Cashier was asked about the man's account. He looked to see that the account had, by coincidence, actually only been opened that day. But one day was more than enough for the Head Cashier. He got cold feet and the gentleman's account was closed.

Another client who'd run up a good-sized bill went to see the Head Cashier, said he had no money and offered his watch as payment for the room. The gesture was refused in lieu of suitable arrangements with a member of the fellow's family. He was then placed on the NTBT list.

Then there was the reservation that came in on a company letterhead three months in advance. Two days before the guest's arrival, he asked for credit facilities. He was turned down. First, there wasn't enough time to arrange it. But, secondly, it struck the credit controller as being suspicious. Why reserve that far in advance and not ask that a credit account be set up at that time?

The Hotel had about £1 million outstanding with credit clients per month. But Touzin is so strict about who gets an account that last year the Hotel was stuck for only £2000.

Back at the Concierge's desk, one guest wanted a chauffeured car, another wanted theatre tickets, two wanted dinner reservations, and someone wanted an elephant.

Wingrove asked, just to make sure, "An elephant, sir?"

"Yes," the gentleman explained. "I'd like to take my friends on an elephant ride through Regent's Park. Can you arrange that?"

"I have no idea, sir." But he quickly added, "I'll try."

"Oh, one other thing." The guest apprised him, "It must be an Indian elephant. I don't want any African elephants."

Wingrove acceded, "Of course not, sir."

Waiting for the client to leave — no magician worth his salt would ever let the audience see how he did his tricks — he reached for his little black book. A treasure trove of phone numbers, it listed a career's worth of contacts — out-of-hours florists, shooting schools, invisible menders, professional shoppers in any language, yacht rentals, helicopter and private jet hire, horse-drawn carriages. It also listed a contact at the London Zoo.

Some years before, a client had phoned from the Gulf to ask, "If I were to bring a camel over, where could it be kept?"

It was a serious enquiry, so Wingrove gave it serious consideration. He eventually found someone at the London Zoo who said, if your guest can get his camel through Customs, we'll take care of it for him.

As it happened, the guest couldn't get his camel into the country. But Wingrove duly wrote the Zoo's number in his book. Now he phoned his connection there, told him what he wanted and asked how to rent an Indian elephant.

That turned out to be the easy part.

However, he discovered, in order to ride it in Regent's Park, he'd have to obtain a special permit. To get the permit meant fighting his way through officialdom and a mountain of red tape. Still, he was willing to do it if that was what the client wanted. But when the guest heard how difficult it would be to get the permit, he lost interest.

And for the very first time in Wingrove's 40-plus years at the Hotel, a client actually said to him, "Cancel the elephant."

~ 5 ~

A WORKMAN PREPARING THE ROYAL Suite for the Koreans' visit accidentally put a nail through a floor board in the master bedroom and punctured a pipe. One floor below, in room 57, Mrs Lazarus had just got up and was about to have a bath, when water came pouring through the ceiling. Terrified, she grabbed the phone and told Reception, "There's a flood in my room."

Reception alerted Robert Buckolt, who dropped what he was doing and went racing up the grand staircase to the mezzanine room where he found Mrs Lazarus, in her nightgown and bathrobe, angry almost to the point of rage. She said she had an appointment and couldn't possibly use her room under these conditions.

In his most reassuring tone, Buckolt agreed that the room was unusable.

It did little to calm her down.

With his sincerest apologies, he promised to move her into a new room straight away.

Water continued to gush down from the ceiling.

He took the phone, dialled Reception, asked which available room was the closest to 57, was told 148, and grimaced.

On each floor, next to the main lift, there were two tiny

rooms — known as types 38 and 48 — which were designed to accommodate servants who accompanied guests. Her Lady's maid. His Lordship's valet. The family chauffeur. The only other time those rooms were used was when someone specifically asked for a type 38 or 48, knowing that the Hotel rented them out for about half the price of a normal single, at £80 plus VAT.

Buckolt knew the room wouldn't suit her, but the woman was plainly desperate to get out of this one. So, against his better judgement — she was getting more upset by the minute and he didn't think it would be a good idea to waste any more time by phoning Reception again to look for another room — Buckolt announced, "I have something for you just up one flight of stairs." However, he felt the need to caution, "I'm afraid it is not as large as this room."

She said she didn't care about that. She said that all she wanted to do was wash, dress and get on with her day.

Buckolt now wondered how he was going to get her to that room. He explained that they would have to go up one flight of stairs and offered to wait outside while she changed from her bathrobe into something more suitable.

But the woman was in no mood. "I don't have time. Let's just go."

All right, he said. And, checking that the coast was clear, Buckolt literally rushed her upstairs, down the corridor and into room 148.

The moment she saw the room — small and dark — she exploded with irritation. "What kind of a room is this?"

He knew enough not to offer any excuses. "If you would give me a moment to find something else for you . . ."

"No." She refused. "I don't have the time to keep running around. Kindly have my things sent over here."

He did.

An hour or so later, on her way out through the Front Hall, she spotted Buckolt and reiterated, "I am very annoyed about this."

Buckolt duly noted her displeasure in his log and Touzin brought it up at the next morning's meeting.

"She was extremely unhappy," Buckolt admitted, "to say the least."

Touzin agreed with her. "I would be as well."

Buckolt tried to rationalize, "It was purely a matter of circumstances. She was in a hurry and this was the closest available room."

"You took her down the corridor in her nightgown?"

"Yes. Of course, I made certain there was no one around. She wasn't in the least embarrassed. It was just the choice of room."

Touzin asked, "How would you feel?"

Buckolt granted, "I understand."

Looking around the room, Touzin wanted everyone to understand, "Our guests should leave here thinking they've been treated well, and this woman clearly hasn't been."

The Hotel was filled with flowers. There were large arrangements in the Front Hall and the Foyer, and flowers in the restaurant and the Causerie. And flowers in all the rooms, too.

Three professional florists worked out of two rooms — someone was there seven days a week — at the end of a dingy hallway in the middle of the Hotel, well hidden from the guests, near a staff elevator. One of these rooms was just for storage. It was air-conditioned in summer, left unheated in winter, and filled with flowers. The other room was where flowers were cut and arrangements were made. Vases, pots and wicker baskets, in every conceivable size and shape, lined shelves. Vases, pots and wicker baskets that were too big for the shelves were scattered around the floor.

The Hotel's annual flower bill exceeded £75,000. The florists created and maintained nearly 50 large arrangements a day. In addition, fresh bouquets for the restaurant were made every Monday, checked again every morning and had flowers added to them on Friday so that they were still fresh over the weekend. They put flowers in every room — they used 1000 dozen roses a month — and came up with special arrangements for certain occasions. For one wedding, they did an arrangement ten feet high and six feet wide, composed of 700 flowers. Over Christmas, they put a five foot tree in every suite, and a three foot tree in every bedroom, each fully decorated with lights and bows. One year, to deck out the rest of the Hotel, they made, from scratch, 11 variations on the 'partridge-in-a-pear-tree' theme.

Whenever the Queen Mother dined at the Hotel, they put sweet peas on her table. For Barbara Cartland, only pink flowers would do. And when singer Harry Connick Jr decided to propose marriage to his fiancée, he booked himself into the Royal Suite and asked the florists to fill the suite with 1000 red roses. He proposed, his fiancée accepted, and the florists then dried all the roses, making a pot pourri out of the petals, for his apartment in New York.

Now, for the Koreans, special arrangements had to go into all the suites and four went into the Royal Suite.

There was a huge arrangement for the piano, and another, just as large, for the coffee table in the sitting room. Both featured exotic flowers, such as bird-of-paradise, ginger lilies and anthuriums. The third, a flat arrangement, went against a wall in the hallway. The fourth went into the bedroom.

Roses were cut on an angle, then put in hot water. Lilac stems were bashed before being put into warm water. Foliage stems were bashed too. Every vase was bleached, so that they looked clean and didn't have that stale flower smell. They used irises, carnations and alstroemeria. To that they added gerbera, cornflowers, larkspur, chrysanthemums and roses. They also used lilies, in nearly a dozen different colours.

And because lily pollen badly stains clothes — especially when someone makes the mistake of rubbing off the pollen instead of lifting it off with Sellotape — the florists always pull the stamens out of every lily in the Hotel.

♣

Daniel Azoulai, the Restaurant Manager — a dark-haired man with dark eyes and Mediterranean complexion — arrived by 10:30. The first thing he did every day was check the bulletin board in the narrow hallway around the corner from the kitchen just behind the restaurant to see who was working the lunch shift. Names were written on strips of paper backed by Velcro — so that he could peel them off and replace them in other positions — and sorted into stations. The restaurant was divided into four stations, with a head waiter, *sommelier* and busboy at each. Then there was one waiter for the sweet trolley, a carver and an assistant for the meat trolley, in addition to Azoulai and his assistant who manned the door.

Next to the daily rota was another bulletin board, this one with colour photos of place settings to show the waiters exactly how the tables are supposed to look. There was also a sign that read, "Handling Customer Complaints: Without guests = no business, no hotel, no job."

From there he went into the restaurant to look at the luncheon reservations — each one recorded by hand in a heavy blue ledger on the maître d's podium — sat down at a table and began copying each reservation from the ledger onto the daily sheet.

That's when he first noticed the problem with table 104.

A ringing phone cut into his thoughts.

It sounded twice before he glanced around, saw that no one was there to answer it, then jumped up to grab it. "Restaurant, good morning."

The gentleman on the other end introduced himself as Mr Swenson. "I'd like to come for lunch this afternoon. Around one o'clock. We'll be four. Can you accommodate us?"

Still having tables to sell, Azoulai answered, "Of course I can. No problem, sir."

"Well, that's a good start, for a change."

Azoulai didn't quite understand the man's comments. "Has there been a problem in the past, sir?"

Swenson explained that he'd been to one of Azoulai's main competitors twice in the past month and had two very unsatisfactory experiences. "It began when they got my reservation wrong. Then there was a problem with what one of my guests ordered. First they had it, then they didn't, then they had it again but cooked it wrong. After that there was a problem with the service. I've really had it up to here with them. And I've been a client there for years."

"We will do everything we can for you, sir. And we look forward to seeing you this afternoon." When he hung up, he marked "V-VIP" on the ledger. Stealing a regular guest from the competition was a very satisfying game. "It's a harsh world," he mumbled, and went back to worrying about table 104.

Born in Marseilles in 1951, he'd worked in restaurants most of his life. When he came to the Hotel in 1990, to manage this restaurant, he saw right away that changes were needed. The old-established clients were dying off and he believed that unless the restaurant found new clients it too would fade away. But the older crowd resented change and the management wouldn't even permit him to rearrange the tables.

A large, high-ceilinged, art deco room, there was a little balcony at the rear with more tables. That little balcony was also the way into the Orangerie, a private dining room in the far corner that could comfortably seat a dozen. Table numbers started at 100 and went to 165. Except there were only 46 tables. No one knew why the numbers worked that way, although it was obvious why there was no table 113.

By the time he'd finished with his daily reservation sheet, the waiters had come in and were starting to dress the tables.

"Take 160 and 161," Azoulai called out to them, going down his list, "and make them into a table for four; 131 for six. There's a note in the ledger, do not present bill." The client had already given Azoulai his credit card number because he did not want his guests to see the tab. "One-two-four for five. Extra flowers for table 124. Orangerie — private luncheon for eight."

He assigned tables to clients, trying to spread them out around the room to make the service easier. Of course, if they asked for a specific table, they would get it. Unofficial policy was that new clients were seated at the back of the room and that, over the years, they could slowly work their way forward. The front tables, which some people believed were the best in the house — because it allowed them to be seen — had to be earned. Tables numbered 100–110 were given to the most regular guests. Table 101, for instance — the first table just inside the door — was held every Wednesday lunch for Barbara Cartland, even when she hadn't booked. She'd been dining there for 50 years and would never have considered sitting anywhere else. Nor would Azoulai have ever considered asking her to sit anywhere else.

There was one gentleman who wanted 114 because he liked being in the corner. There was another who was happy with 135 because he didn't mind sitting in the middle. Table 131 was called "the Royal Box" because it was set inside the alcove at the side of the room. It was where, legend had it, kings, prime ministers and presidents were served. In reality, it was available to anyone who asked for it, as long as Azoulai had it free. Table 107 was called "the Greek Cantina" because that's where Aristotle Onassis liked to sit. In the old days there were eight Greeks at his table every day. Many Greeks still insisted on that table, hoping it would bring them the sort of good luck Onassis had. Other Greeks avoided it, fearing it would bring them the sort of bad luck Onassis had.

Experience taught Azoulai to hold back a few tables every day, just in case a regular showed up at the last minute or someone seemed particularly unhappy with the table he'd been assigned. And even if it wasn't often that he needed an extra table, when he did he was glad to have it. But now, two very long-standing clients had both booked for 1 o'clock, and both of them claimed possession of table 104.

Standing next to that table for a moment, he thought about what to do. Normally, he would have given the table to the better client. But he didn't know if Sir Bernard had been eating there longer than Lord and Lady Hawthorne because both of them made a habit of reminding him that they'd been clients of the Hotel for more than 30 years. In the end, he decided the safest thing would be to give the table to whoever showed up first, hoping that he could make suitable excuses to the other and put them at table 105.

As the waiters set up each table for lunch, Azoulai personally checked it. It seems that someone long ago had told him, in life, you can only ever really trust yourself, and he believed that.

He took some flowers off one table and put another arrangement there, inspected all the glasses to see they were clean, noticed a glass missing on table 160 and straightened the napkins on table 135. After going into the kitchen to ask about the soup of the day and any specials, he was ready to summon his staff.

They gathered in a semi-circle at the back of the restaurant.

First, he subjected the busboys to a close inspection, looking at their uniforms and checking their nails. The waiters — all of them either French or Italian and at least his age — were spared the routine. Then, he took up his place on the steps of the little balcony — so that he could see them all and they could all see him — and recited the day's menu, item by item. He explained each dish, giving them enough detail that they could speak knowledgeably about the dish to their clients. Next, he listed the tables, explaining who was sitting where.

"One-sixty is Mr Bergman, Mrs Rowlinson and Mr Lewis. Three cold salmon platters. And be careful, you know how difficult Mrs Rowlinson is." To that he added, "Highlight the salmon and the brisket."

Pointing to the sweet trolley, he said, "Don't wait until it's empty. Keep it filled with fresh sweets. Dessert waiter, because you have nothing to do until the first dessert orders come in, I want you to clear stations. Don't stand around. Oh, and by the way, this goes for anyone of you who answers the phone. Yesterday, three bookings were put onto the wrong page. Please be more careful."

Finally, he explained the problem with table 104. "It's the first time they've ever been here at the same time. It's very delicate so I will handle it. Do not mention it. Do not get into any conversation about it. If one or the other brings it up, just smile. Okay?" No one had any questions. "Let's go."

Within ten minutes, guests began arriving.

Sir Bernard got there at ten to one. A frail man who walked with a cane, he was alone. Perhaps, given a chance, Azoulai could have steered him to another table. But, without stopping at the door, Sir Bernard went straight to table 104 and sat down. Fifteen minutes later, Lord and Lady Hawthorne came in. Both of them were portly and in their 80s. Azoulai met them at the door, and was just about to explain the situation when Lady Hawthorne noticed that someone was sitting at her table.

"I'm terribly sorry," Azoulai started to say.

His Lordship didn't want to know. "But that man is sitting in my place."

"My Lord, I'm terribly sorry . . ."

Lady Hawthorne stormed past Azoulai and went up to the interloper. "This table is ours."

Sir Bernard, in the middle of his entrée, was startled. "I beg your pardon?"

"You are sitting at our table," she said. "I would ask you to kindly move."

"You would ask what?" He wasn't going to have it. "I will not."

She proclaimed, "My husband and I have had this table for 30 years."

He told her, "And I have been sitting at this table for 32 years."
Azoulai was right there. "I'm terribly sorry about this . . ."

It took some doing, but he ultimately managed to quieten them
down, and then to talk Lord and Lady Hawthorne into sitting at
table 105. "It's only this one time." He assured both parties, "This is
entirely our mistake . . . please accept my apologies . . ."

The Hawthornes stared icily throughout their meal at Sir
Bernard for having the gall to sit at their table while Sir Bernard
glared spitefully back at the Hawthornes for having the nerve to suggest that he should give up his table.

There was little else Azoulai could do, except apologize to them
both when they left, then hope — and even pray — that it never
happened again.

Late Monday afternoon, the day before the President's arrival, a large
van pulled up at the Timekeeper's door and unloaded two large crates,
containing identical Korean-made, Samsung 33" television sets.

The Timekeeper automatically paged Buckolt, who seemed
surprised to find two sets there. He spoke with the delivery men,
who didn't know anything more than what they'd been told —
which was to deliver both sets — and then made a fast call to Mr
Lee, who said one set was to go into the Royal Suite while the second would be used as a backup. So Buckolt told the delivery men to
take one upstairs and, while they were doing that, he phoned around
to find an unused room on the third floor to store the other one.

After unpacking the set in the suite, there was a lengthy discussion about where to hide the empty box. It wound up in an unused
room on the fifth floor. That's when Mr Lee proclaimed the TV was
too large for the low table that had been used to hold the smaller
Japanese model.

He said he wanted a bigger table.

So Carole Ronald was paged. She showed up, listened to Lee's concern, wasn't convinced that the table was too low but pointed out, in any case, that it was certainly too shaky to hold such a big set. The last thing anyone wanted, she suggested, was to have the television come crashing down on the President's toes.

Thinking of where she might be able to get a more substantial table — "It must also be higher," Lee insisted — she tried to recall if there was one they might be able to commandeer from a room further down the hall.

A maid was dispatched to check.

Now Lee decided he didn't like the way the set would look in the corner. "It doesn't give our President any room to adjust it. The corner is too small. It will make the television seem too cramped."

Buckolt wondered if it would be better on another side of the room, but the carpet was being shampooed and it was still very wet there. Anyway, Lee said, that wouldn't work because it must be easily visible from the main settee.

"Perhaps," Buckolt suggested, "we could move that writing desk under the window to the left. That would give the television more space in that corner."

"No," Lee said, "the writing desk fits very well in front of the window."

Ronald took Buckolt's side. "There really isn't any other place it can go because that television takes up so much space."

Lee and eight others in the advance party huddled off to the side, discussed it for several minutes and finally compromised. "Yes. We will ask that you move the writing desk. It will have to be okay like that."

The maid returned with a table. It wasn't any sturdier than the first one, but it was slightly higher. Buckolt moved the desk while Ronald put the table in the corner and then the delivery men lifted the TV into place.

Looking at each other, Buckolt and Ronald nodded then both in turn assured Lee it would be fine that way. And Lee agreed. At that point, someone in the Korean party wondered what the room temperature was.

Buckolt acknowledged that they were trying to meet the request to keep the suite at a constant 25 degrees centigrade, but conceded it wasn't easy because there wasn't a thermostat in the room. "Are you sure that the President wants it this warm?"

"We are sure," Lee confirmed. He pointed to a humidifier that Housekeeping had installed the day before. "Is this heater working?"

"That's not a heater," Buckolt said. "We are trying to get the temperature up but when you overheat a room like this, the air gets very dry. This is a humidifier . . ."

"We will be bringing our own humidifier," Lee said. "I would prefer it, for security reasons, if we used our own."

"No problem," Buckolt said. "I will have this one removed."

"But the temperature . . ." Lee refused to give up ". . . will it be kept at a permanent 25 degrees?"

"Of course we will try . . ." Buckolt knew he needed to be careful here because there simply wasn't any way he could accurately regulate it.

"How hot is it now?" Lee asked.

"It's warm," Buckolt agreed. "But without a thermometer . . ."

"Can we get one to find out?"

"Yes. Of course." Buckolt turned to one of the housekeeping staff who had been lingering in the background and told her that he needed something to measure the temperature.

The woman went off to see what she could find.

A few minutes later, Irene, the Hotel's resident nurse stepped into the suite and handed Buckolt an oral thermometer.

~ 6 ~

*T*HE CHEF HAD THE BEST office in the Hotel.

It was in the basement, up a tiny ramp from the pastry kitchen, around the corner from the Hotel's main kitchen — where all the banqueting food was prepared — just next door to the fish and larder stations.

There was a narrow room where his secretary worked and, behind that, there was his. The two were separated by a sliding glass window and a venetian blind, which he always kept closed, unless he needed to speak to someone in her room.

He had a large desk, built in at right angles to surround him in his chair, with phones and a computer screen at his left elbow, and an intercom there too, which connected him to every part of the kitchen. The rest of the room was a small museum to antique cooking utensils. There were copper pots, pans and moulds. There was a large silver-plated duck press, an old-fashioned knife polisher, a raisin stoner, an apple corer and a glass butter churner. There were also about 250 antique corkscrews.

Behind that was his private dining room — with more antique pots and pans and ladles and choppers and scales — where he ate every afternoon with his sous-chefs, held meetings, had tastings and occasionally hosted a lunch for a few selected guests.

Bay windows surrounded his office, looking out towards the hallway and the side to the pastry kitchen, where the walls were decorated with posters depicting all sorts of exotic fish. Even if he couldn't sit at his desk and stare into every corner of the kitchen, no one could enter or leave without walking past his window, and after a while the people who worked there came to believe that he could see them even if he couldn't.

He referred to it as unsupervised supervision.

A thin, agile man with dark hair and a dark moustache, Marjan Lesnik — his friends called him Mario, everyone else called him Chef — patrolled the kitchen in his checked trousers, white jacket and well-worn white leather sabots. An intense, no-nonsense sort of man — he once confessed that his secret wish was to rule the world — he imposed his presence on the Hotel and made no bones about suffering fools badly.

In sharp contrast to the Hotel's guests, many of whom were born with silver spoons in their mouths, Lesnik was born in 1951 with a wooden stirring spoon in his.

His village was Jeruzalem, not far from the Radenska Spa, in a wine-growing region in the north-western part of what used to be Yugoslavia and is today called Slovenia. Bordering on Italy, Hungary and Austria, it was the most industrialized corner in the republic. His mother, grandmother and great grandmother had all cooked in restaurants. But it was rare to find a man cooking in those days in that part of the world — his father wholesaled wine and fruit — and anyway Lesnik's boyhood dream was to go to sea.

Living on a smallholding, his parents grew much of their own food. They kept chickens, ducks, rabbits, turkeys and pigs, which they slaughtered each year, curing and smoking their own meat. By the time he was 15, Lesnik was spending more and more time helping his mother in her kitchen. His father felt he displayed some talent and advised him to go to catering school. But Marjan wanted to see the world.

Accepted at a merchant marine school, he lasted only a month because they said his eyes weren't good enough. Consoling him, his father again suggested cooking school. His argument was, you can always cook on a ship and sail around the world with it, and this way, as the Chef, if the ship sinks, you won't have to go down with it.

After giving that some thought, Lesnik decided it made a lot of sense and headed off to catering college. When he finished there, he worked in several small kitchens around Yugoslavia, cooked in Vienna for two years, and in Bavaria for eight months, until his wanderlust returned. He started looking into the possibility of cooking on a cruise ship, but didn't speak English and that, the cruise lines told him, was essential. So he signed on for a couple of seasons at a resort hotel in Jersey, in the Channel Islands, where he learned to speak English well enough to fall in love with a British girl.

It was the end of 1975. He told her that he wanted to go to sea. She wasn't so sure that was a good idea. Four days into the new year, he received word from the Swedish American Line that a job was waiting for him on a ship bound for the Caribbean. If he wanted it, he had to be in Göteborg by January 8. The British lady balked. He called the cruise line and told them he couldn't possibly make it at such short notice. They gave him another option, to meet the ship in New York in a fortnight's time. He said he'd be there. But she had other ideas. A fortnight later, the two were living in London.

He found work in a large hotel kitchen as a demi-chef — moving from station to station, depending on where he was needed — then larder chef, then cooking in the banqueting kitchen. He left there to cook in a restaurant, until 1977 when a good job opened up at a Group property in Mayfair. Seven years later — now as first sous-chef — he was promoted and awarded the kitchens at the Hotel.

The man he replaced had been at the Hotel for 45 years.

♣

"No joy with the potatoes," announced William, stepping into the Chef's office. The amiable banqueting chef with a permanent slightly hassled expression was Lesnik's number two. "It's just not working."

The Chef pulled himself out of his chair and went with William to a far corner in the kitchen where a stainless steel tray was covered with crisps. He sorted through them, pushing aside the ones that were obviously cooking too dark. A couple seemed all right at first, but the colour quickly changed. Crisps had to be very light and very crunchy. These were anything but.

Nearby, a potato peeling machine stood idle because the potato peeler never used it. He was a large chap named Stanley, except that he was never referred to by his name. Much the way all electricians are Sparks, Stanley was Spuds. He could peel a potato better and faster by hand than any machine and the scars on his giant hands proved he'd been doing it that way for many years.

"This is the last of them," Spuds said to the Chef. "All 15 varieties."

The Hotel used 50 kilos of potatoes every day to make fresh crisps. That was Spuds' job — peeling them, slicing them and cooking them in fresh oil. But because their starch content varied, potatoes never cooked the same way from year to year. The new crop was either too watery or too doughy. The texture was too loose. The crisps discoloured too quickly. Or they didn't retain their crispness. Every year it was trial and error until they found one that made perfect crisps. And every year, until they did, Lesnik had to take the blame.

There were certainly enough potato suppliers around and he knew, inevitably, he would find a solution somewhere. The year before he'd discovered a small supplier of wonderful potatoes in Scotland. They were a very old style of potatoes, grown the same way for several hundred years. He'd loved the texture and the taste and would have been happy to place an order with the man. But the supplier was too small to guarantee regular deliveries and couldn't possibly cope with the sort of volume that the Hotel needed.

In any event, that was last year. There was no telling if the man's designer potatoes would crisp properly this year.

The crisis was now in its fourth week, with no end in sight.

Much of Lesnik's first year at the Hotel was spent trying to change the kitchen's philosophy. He did it as gradually as he could, creating a period of evolution because he understood how the old guard, so well entrenched in the Hotel, would never stand for revolution. But he needed to widen the kitchen's repertoire, to bring in new menus, to modernize the cooking techniques.

Taking his time, he waited them out. Little by little, the average age of the kitchen staff began to come down. As it did, the kitchen began to be transformed. However, hand in hand with that came staff cutbacks. He started with a brigade of 85 and reduced it down to 60. Management felt there was scope for more. He argued that they were hindering his ability to produce the kind of cuisine the Hotel's clients expected. They believed the only damage was to his ego.

Under the old regime, the kitchen prepared two different sauces for meat, regardless of the meat, and just one sauce for fish, regardless of the fish. Lesnik prepared a different sauce for each dish. Then he got rid of tired, out-of-fashion dishes like fish dumplings on a skewer glazed with lobster sauce. He brought in a lighter, more modern cuisine. He refused to offer 12 different soups a day — many of which never got sold — reducing it to a more manageable four. He stopped his cooks from preparing dishes in advance that they could simply reheat when a client ordered them. He forbade them to use frozen ingredients. And he changed the luncheon in the Causerie where the menu had been the same for years, adding to the buffet 36 different daily dishes.

Then he set his sights on the kitchen itself. Few changes had been made in 50 years. A big, unwieldy, poorly planned series of interconnecting rooms, it served all of the Hotel's outlets. But it was no longer capable of providing for all the Hotel's needs. In those days, there were 600 staff working at the Hotel and he had to provide four chefs simply to look after the staff. Lesnik politicked, not merely to have a new kitchen built but for the right to design it. He won on both points and was given £5 million to spend.

He put the kitchen on two floors.

Upstairs, he built a full kitchen to serve the restaurant. Downstairs, he created a maze of yellow-tiled rooms where he cooked for banquets and Room Service, in addition to supplying food for the Causerie. Preparation of certain ingredients needed in the restaurant kitchen — such as soups, stocks and salads — was also done in the basement. So too was all the Hotel's pastry and bread. Further down a corridor, at the far end of the Hotel — beneath the Ballroom — there was a smaller kitchen to serve the staff canteen and, next to that, a large finishing station for banquets.

The way he designed it, with stainless steel worktops, neon lights and the constant hum of an air-conditioning unit, the basement felt like the hold of a ship.

In a funny way, the little boy had finally gone to sea.

The main kitchen had four solid-top stoves, four small ovens and two grills, in addition to 16 bains-marie. Many of the fridges had glass doors because he believed that fridges with glass doors kept themselves clean. No one left a mess when they knew that everyone else could see it.

At the rear, there was a huge roasting oven — they called it "Big Red" — a relic from the Hotel's original kitchen. Nearly a century old, named for its colour and the fact that it was large enough to cook eight baby lambs, it had been restored a few years previously at a cost of £10,000.

Off to the side of that, double locked and connected to an alarm, was the truffle freezer.

Each year, during the season — which ran from late November through February — the Chef bought truffles. Whatever wasn't served fresh during the season would be peeled and cut on a huge white cloth — to catch all the trimmings, because at the price he had to pay for truffles it would have been brazenly wasteful to throw away even the smallest slivers — put in plastic packages and logged into the freezer.

The Hotel used 50–60 kilos of truffles a year and the freezer held a year's supply — about 200 bags. Each packet bore its own docket number, the date it was frozen, the name of the supplier, the country of origin — he bought almost exclusively French — and the cost per kilo, which was around £480.

Only the Chef, William and a couple of others had access to the truffles. Like top secret safes in the Pentagon, each time the freezer was unlocked, an entry had to be made in a log. The docket number of each packet was copied into an accounting book. And whereas the Chef oversaw a stock-take of the entire kitchen once a year, he did a monthly audit of the truffle freezer.

When Philippe Krenzer calculated what was in there — somewhere between £25,000 and £30,000 worth of truffles — he couldn't believe it. The Food and Beverage Manager's immediate reaction was, how could the Chef tie up so much money? If the kitchen needed truffles, he reasoned, the Chef could order them from a supplier.

Not surprisingly, Lesnik saw it differently. He insisted the Hotel had to provide the finest ingredients, and that meant keeping those ingredients on hand. He conceded that to an accountant it might seem as if the Hotel had a lot of money invested in truffles. But, he reminded Krenzer, "I'm buying them at a good price. The truffle season is so short that when we can buy them, we need to buy a year's supply. This way we get them fresh. If we had to buy them out of season, we'd have to buy them tinned and then the price would be twice as much."

Price shouldn't matter, Krenzer retorted, because the kitchen would ultimately pass those costs on to the client. "Anyway, the money tied up in truffles would be better off sitting in the bank."

"Not true." Lesnik had heard this argument before. "And even if you had the money we spend on truffles, you wouldn't put it in the bank. You'd spend it on something else."

Krenzer stood his ground. "You cannot justify an expense like this."

Lesnik wanted him to understand, "If truffles cost the kitchen too much, the client won't pay for them. What am I supposed to say to our clients, I'd love to give you truffles, but I can't afford them and neither can you?"

The discussion got nowhere.

Krenzer walked away.

But Lesnik knew he'd be back.

When he came back, this time it was about a bottle of vinegar.

Lesnik was preparing a menu for a banquet several months down the line and decided to do a special salad that required Balsamic vinegar. There were plenty of varieties available on the market but he wanted a particular one. Made only in Modena, Italy, it was a heavy, thick, pungent 35-year-old vintage — a small bottle of which cost £192.

"No." Krenzer couldn't accept such costs. "I'm not paying for it."

The Chef asserted his artistic independence. "I need it."

Krenzer insisted, "It should go back."

The Chef refused. "This is an important ingredient."

Krenzer pointed out that the kitchen was already several thousand pounds over food-cost budget for the year. "It must be returned."

The Chef put him on notice, "This is the way I cook."

Non-confrontational by nature, Krenzer again walked away.

But the stand-off was evident to everyone.

The following day, a fax came in from the Group press office wanting to know if the Chef would see a journalist who was doing a magazine article on smoked fish.

Lesnik responded politely that he didn't have time, but that he would write something for her, explaining to her readers how to smoke fish at home, and add a few recipes. That was fine with the press office. So he sat down for half an hour with his secretary — a French woman named Marie — and dictated a couple of pages to her, which included one recipe for freshly smoked salmon fillets and another for smoked duck breast. And because Balsamic vinegar was on his mind, he made a point of using it in both recipes.

Marie sent the text off by fax and Lesnik forgot all about it, until two days later when one of the women from the press office stopped by to see him. She said that the recipes he'd sent sounded too much like something written by a chef for other chefs, and that for an audience of housewives it needed some translation. Reluctantly, he agreed to help her put chef-speak into newspaper-speak.

And the first thing she wanted to know was, "What's Balsamic vinegar?"

He had to laugh. "It's a particular vinegar made from Trebbiano grapes and it's expensive."

She looked at him. "Where do you get it?"

"Speciality shops."

"How old is it?"

"I prefer the 35-year-old."

"What does it cost?"

He answered, "A small bottle goes for a couple of hundred pounds."

"Oh!" She stared at him, worried that the journalist who'd asked for these recipes would say that the average housewife couldn't possibly afford to spend that much on vinegar. "Is there anything else you can use that might not cost so much?"

"No." And probably just for Krenzer's benefit, he told her, "You can quote me. This is the way I cook."

There were 195 people coming to a private dinner that night and the main course was halibut. But when he saw the fish he got annoyed that it came in several different sizes. So he cut one to show the cooks how he wanted it.

"Put elongated pieces on one tray," he commanded. "Put square pieces on a second and end pieces on the third." When the fish was ready to be served, he would prepare the plates in such a way that each table would get the same-shaped pieces, so that no one would think someone else was getting a larger piece.

"Leftovers in a fourth tray," he reminded the cooks.

One of the secrets of a successful kitchen is that there should never be any waste. Those leftovers would be used to make hors-d'oeuvres or fish mousse or go into a salad.

Two types of lobster were waiting in a nearby stainless steel sink, with the water constantly running. A shipment had just arrived. One was the very large blue Scottish lobster — it was used only for stocks and sauces and not for its meat because the meat was too tough — and the other was the smaller dark brown Canadian lobster, which was the eating kind. He inspected them both then went to the cold room — a huge walk-in fridge — to check on two trays of grey mullet which had been cut into portions for a private luncheon.

Throwing open the door, he shouted, "William?"

William appeared. "Chef?"

Lesnik pointed to the fish. "They're too small."

William explained, "That's all they sent us."

"Look how irregular they are. No. I don't like this. We'll have to get more. These won't do."

"Okay," Christian said.

Reaching for a fork, Lesnik tasted it. "This is much better. When you get it right it will be a good-looking starter." It was also a good way to use up odd pieces of fish.

Spotting another of his sous-chefs in Marie's office — a burly German fellow named Henry — Lesnik opened the blinds and asked him to come in to look at Christian's dish. "What do you think?"

Henry smelled it, nodded a few times, then took a forkful. "It's good, Chef."

Lesnik told him, "Maybe it's too adventurous for a starter. Should it be a main course?"

"No. It's a starter." Henry was very sure of himself. "Why not put it in place of the risotto?"

Lesnik thought about that. "We could use it to replace the risotto." He handed the plate back to Christian. "I'm not sure about the scallops. Maybe we use too many scallops. I see scallops all the time."

Henry reminded the Chef, "They come in boxes of 200."

"Buy smaller boxes."

"They don't come smaller."

Christian offered, "How about pieces of sole?"

Henry said, "No. Not substantial enough."

"Chef." William stuck his head into the Chef's office. "We can cancel that extra asparagus order. I have enough."

Lesnik nodded.

"Spinach." Henry proposed, then corrected himself. "No. How about fresh-water prawns?"

Taking a blank plate form, Lesnik started to draw the dish. "We risk over-decorating the plate." He continued to draw. "Say you put five little prawns here . . . and then your vegetables with chive sauce . . ." He stopped because out of the corner of his eye he noticed Philippe Krenzer walking into Marie's office.

"They came in small. I checked with the supplier but he didn't have any more."

Lesnik shoved the trays back onto the shelves — "I'll see about that" — and stormed past William.

At his desk, he punched a pre-programmed button on his phone, and waited until the fish supplier answered. He asked for the boss by name and a man came onto the line right away.

"The grey mullet was too small." Lesnik asked, "Why would you send me fish like that?"

"That's all I could get," the man answered. "I don't have any other grey mullet. And I don't even know if I'll have any tomorrow."

"Okay." Lesnik hung up, pushed another pre-programmed button and got another fish supplier on the line. "Grey mullet," was all he said.

"Sorry," the man responded. "Nothing at all."

He tried a third, then a fourth and only got lucky on his fifth call. He told that supplier he needed the fish immediately and, because the Hotel was the sort of account that most suppliers would die for, the man on the other end promised to send a van within the hour. Hanging up, Lesnik pushed the button on the intercom and called out, "William?"

William's voice came back at him, "Yes, Chef?"

"It will be here in an hour."

"Thank you, Chef," William said, and Lesnik snapped off the intercom. Just as he did, the pastry chef walked into his office carrying a plate.

"Attempt number two." Derek was a young, blond, Englishman who'd made the rounds of all the stations in the kitchen, and stopped at pastry because he appreciated the precision that a good *patissier* needs. "And you don't have to say it because I already know."

In the middle of the plate there was a slice of puff pastry with sliced strawberries on top, and a scoop of vanilla ice cream with some raspberry sauce along the side. It was for a banquet of 105 people they were doing in two days.

Lesnik studied it for a moment, knowing what Derek was thinking. "It's better. But you're right, the pastry is still too thin." He drew his thumb around the edge of it. "And I think it should be much bigger. It should fill up the plate. We want to be able to see the layers." He broke off a piece with his fingers. "Also, it should be cooked just a little more. You can see by the colour that it's not quite right." He paused, then added, "The edges could be sharper."

"That's the problem with the round cutter. I think they should be cut with a knife . . ."

"Well then, half-cook the pastry, cut it, and then finish cooking it. That should give you the sharper edges." He picked up the plate and studied it closely. "I also think this needs a lighter sauce to set off the colour of the pastry."

"I used a raspberry sauce just to show you, but I'd probably want to use a strawberry sauce on the night."

"But lighter in colour," the Chef insisted. "And . . ." He thought for a moment. "Maybe something dramatic on top." He reached for a sheet of paper with a huge circle pre-printed in the middle of it — he called them his empty plate forms — and drew the dessert inside the circle. "If you make the pastry bigger, putting three small spoons of ice cream around it like this, and encircle it all with sauce, then put a whole strawberry dipped in chocolate on top . . . how's that?" He finished the drawing and pushed it towards his pastry chef. "What do you think?"

Derek stared at the drawing, nodded, "Okay," mumbled, "Hopefully it's not another plum dumpling," and left. He would keep doing it until they both agreed that it was right.

The plum dumpling reference was part of the kitchen's legend.

The Prime Minister of Slovenia had arranged to host a banquet at the Hotel and Lesnik, with nationalistic pride, had decided that

for dessert he'd reinvent his mother's version of a typical Slovenian plum dumpling.

His mother told him how she cooked it, but he knew he couldn't trust her recipe because she never cooked a dish the same way twice. Like so many women who'd learned family cooking by watching their own mother, she depended entirely on her eyes, her nose and her taste buds. Putting her recipe on paper so that one of his chefs could duplicate the dish was an impossible task. So he gave Derek a close approximation. When he saw the results of the first effort, Lesnik wrote changes into the recipe. Derek did it again. And Lesnik made more changes. The pastry chef kept cooking it and Lesnik kept changing it, refining it each time, until he finally decided it was as close as it was ever going to be. But to get that far, Derek had to make the dish 21 times.

A few minutes after Derek left, Christian — the most junior of Lesnik's sous-chefs, a tall, strong fellow with dark hair — brought in a plate. He worked in the restaurant kitchen and had been looking for a new pasta dish for the à la carte menu. It was tagliatelle, with small pieces of fish, including scallops, and some oriental spices. But even after three attempts it still wasn't coming together.

He wondered, "Maybe it should be ravioli."

"No, tagliatelle is right," Lesnik reassured him. "Ravioli wo be a problem because it would mean we'd have to prepare all the ings. This is faster and lighter." He kept turning the plate. "It l better than the last time. What did you do, toss the pasta in oil basil leaves?"

"Yeah."

"How about sprinkling some tiny tomato juliennes into the just to give it a little colour?" He studied the fish. "What's he grey mullet, red mullet, sole . . ." He thought about it for a s "You need to cook the fish a little more aggressively, to gi golden colour. Maybe you should roast it with the pasta, very

His venetian blinds were still open. So, just like that, he yanked them shut.

When Touzin first arrived at the Hotel, he spent a lot of time thinking about the product he was being asked to sell. He wanted to know everything there was to know about the Hotel, and to see it the way his clients saw it. So he slept in a different room every night, ordered Room Service, ate in the Causerie and ate in the restaurant. One of the things he spotted early on — because paying attention to details was the way he did things — was the bread and butter pudding.

Without saying anything to anyone — he knew he needed to get the staff on his side and rushing in to change things was precisely the wrong way to do that — he ordered it a second time. His conclusion was the same. So he casually asked Daniel Azoulai about the dessert trolley and was told that this was the way they always served it.

Not wanting to make it seem as if he was focusing on something as minor as the bread and butter pudding — after all, there were plenty of other things that, in his opinion, needed to be put right long before a dessert — he mentioned it to the Chef, but then only as an afterthought. "You know, there's something not right with it."

His softly-softly approach had the desired effect because now Lesnik took a closer look.

The pudding came out of the kitchen in a large ceramic dish. The waiter was supposed to spoon some onto a serving plate, then take it back into the kitchen to be kept warm. In the rush to keep things moving, Lesnik discovered that there were times when the waiters served it cold. So he reported back to Touzin, "It's the restaurant. They're not serving it properly. They're not respecting a traditional dish."

Touzin kept the Chef's remarks in mind, ordered it again and conceded that Lesnik had a point. The problem with it was that it looked messy. Lesnik's solution was to change the chafing-dish. He told Derek, instead of making one large portion, make several portions for two. This way, the waiters would have to serve the dessert out of the smaller dish directly at the table and couldn't mess it up.

Because chefs instinctively distrust their restaurant staff — the way they see life, the restaurant is where a perfectly good dish can be ruined by the way it's served — Lesnik asked Touzin to keep an eye on it. So Touzin risked his waistline by ordering the bread and butter pudding for ten straight days. He ate it until he was firmly convinced that the new improved version was now part of the restaurant's routine.

Lesnik liked Touzin. They understood each other.

Which was more than he could say for Krenzer.

Lesnik was the Executive Chef and Krenzer was the new kid on the block, so Krenzer didn't have much choice — he had to tolerate Lesnik. But Lesnik couldn't see why he had to tolerate Krenzer. He'd been around hotel kitchens too long to have much time for Food and Beverage managers. In weaker moments he was willing to concede that someone had to coordinate food and beverage, but administrating was one thing, interfering with the kitchen — which is what he felt Krenzer was trying to do — no, that wasn't on.

It was once very different. Years ago, it was taken for granted that the Food and Beverage Manager had to be an ex-chef. That's what used to happen with chefs. They'd get too old for the daily grind or too weary from the kitchen heat and be promoted to a desk job. They'd trade their apron for a suit, take on the airs of an elder statesman, and rule the roost at feeding time. They knew the kitchen. They understood the chef's problems. They knew costing and purchasing too. But no more. Now chefs died at their stove and Food and Beverage was nothing more than a required step on the management ladder. If someone was a successful Food and Beverage Manager, he got moved on to the next rung. The failures — true to the Peter Principle — stayed right where they were.

One of the best Food and Beverage managers Lesnik ever dealt with was Touzin. Because Touzin had worked in kitchens. He knew food. He could discuss it intelligently.

But then, Lesnik and Touzin shared a secret.

They were both serious collectors of corkscrews. It was a little thing that sort of bound them together.

They could talk.

Lesnik had no secrets with Krenzer.

$$\sim 7 \sim$$

ℛoy Barron's bleeper sounded.

Sitting at a cluttered desk in the tiny Security Office lost at the back of the first floor — a cramped room with TV monitors, just like they always have in security offices, and metal lockers just like they always have in police stations, and fading photos of men in uniform lined up at some police Academy graduation just like they always have in the movies — he glanced at the LCD display on the palm-sized unit that hung off his belt, and checked the phone extension of the person looking for him.

It was the Public Area Housekeeper.

Barron dialled her and when she answered she told him, "We have a problem."

He understood that, otherwise no one ever rang him. "What can I do for you?"

"One of our brass ashtrays, the one at the Ballroom entrance, has taken a walk." Large, heavy and beautifully polished boxes, which sit on the floor at various points in the public areas, they cost around £400 each and would, undeniably, make a handsome souvenir. "It's gone."

"When did you last see it?"

91

She hesitated. "Around half an hour ago."

A man who skilfully hid a healthy dose of cop's cynicism behind an amiable face, Barron already knew the answer. "All right," he said, "I'll get back to you," and took the rear stairs down to the Timekeeper's shack.

Some people genuinely believe that, included in the price of a room, is everything they can steal. They genuinely believe that they are entitled to help themselves, not just to the soap, hand lotion, shampoo, pencils, pens, notepads, shower caps and little plastic shoe horns — which are placed there with every intention that the guests will take them home and are, indeed, included in the price of the room — but also to the bathrobe, towels, bath mat, pillows, taps, trays, the Gideon Bible, the shower-head and whatever else will fit into their suitcase.

It is a very real and very costly problem for all hotels.

Stories abound how someone once got out of a Hilton with a sofa from the front hall, and out of an Inter-Continental with a desk. Admittedly, furniture is more difficult to steal than a shower curtain — although many hotels have reported mattresses stolen — but at the Ritz in Paris a guest once checked out with the TV set from her room.

In lots of hotels, the management do not hide their distrust. There are commercial inns all over the world — including some instantly recognizable chains — where pictures are bolted onto the walls, the television is riveted onto a stand and the radio is fixed into the bed's headboard. By design, the towels are too small for anyone to want to steal, the pillow cases are not monogrammed, the Room Service cutlery is ordinary and they don't give you a bathrobe. There they remove temptation.

Guests probably never realize it, but even at finer hotels, when the Room Service waiter comes to pick up a tray, he knows how many spoons, forks, coffee cups and tea pots are supposed to be on it. Although in most fine hotels, if a knife or monogrammed napkin goes missing, no one ever says anything, for fear of embarrassing a guest. Sometimes, however, a guest gets too greedy and crosses the line of a manager's patience.

At one well-known place in Paris, a Texan decided to help himself to an entire breakfast service. The first morning, he took a cup and saucer. The second morning, he took the same thing again. On the third morning, the coffee pot was not returned. And it went on like that for the rest of the week, with a little more missing each day. The floor waiter mentioned it to the General Manager, who grew increasingly concerned as the gentleman stocked up on the hotel's property.

At the end of the week, the Texan announced that he was checking out. He rang for someone to fetch his bags and went downstairs to pay his bill. As they'd been asked to do, the front desk notified the General Manager. As he'd been instructed to do, the porter held back the gentleman's bags.

Before confronting his guest, the General Manager went to inspect the bags. Sure enough, they were suspiciously heavy. The bags were locked — he wouldn't have opened them even if they weren't — but he had the porter shake them and, after listening carefully, it was evident to both of them that the crockery was there.

Now greeting his guest at the cashier's desk, the General Manager asked discreetly if he could have a word. He told the gentleman, in the nicest way, to please forgive him if there was some mistake or confusion on his part, but a number of items that had been delivered during the week by Room Service had not been returned.

Instantly, the Texan took the defensive. "Are you accusing me of stealing stuff?"

It was the classic reaction of a man who had something to hide. "No, sir. I was simply asking if you might know anything about these items."

"You'd better not be accusing me of stealing . . ."

"Certainly not, sir." Satisfied that the man was lying, the General Manager concluded there was no reason to continue this discussion. "I'm sure there's been an error. And I apologize if I've caused you any embarrassment."

He left the Texan to pay his bill and went back to where the porter was waiting with the bags. "Take them to the top of the service stairs," the General Manager directed, "then toss them down to me."

The porter was confused. "Toss them down to you, sir?"

"That's right."

Doing as he was told, the porter carried the bags up the stairs. And one by one he tossed them down to the General Manager, who made no effort whatsoever to catch them.

"Now," the General Manager told the porter, "please deliver the luggage to the gentleman."

No one knows the Texan's reaction when he got home and found more pieces of crockery than he expected.

At the Hotel, major items had never been taken out of the rooms, probably because the clientele was too wealthy. Not that the rich are necessarily above stealing; it's just that rich folk tend to steal larger sums than poor folk, which may well account for the reason some of them are rich. Perhaps people who are paying £300–£400–£500 a night for a room don't care much about a monogrammed towel — all the more so when the initials are not their own. It is a different story at weekends, when guests come into hotels everywhere on special packages — some of them are the sort of guest who doesn't normally stay at hotels — when acquiring souvenirs seems an integral part of their weekend.

Every room was checked every day by the floor housekeeper. Occupied rooms were checked to see that the maids were cleaning them to standard. Vacant rooms were checked to be sure that no one was actually using them. Rooms where someone was departing were checked as soon as possible after the guest vacated the room, both to make certain that the guest hadn't left anything behind and also to be sure that everything which was supposed to be in the room was still there.

Bathrobes were the biggest single item to go missing. The Hotel's were heavy terry towelling, very bulky, and not necessarily something that was easy to stuff into an otherwise full suitcase. If someone really wanted one, they were on sale at £42 each, which could be considered a lot of money for a clean, but otherwise used, bathrobe, no matter how good a bathrobe it was.

Security is, by definition, preventative. So Barron and Chris Baxter spent a lot of their time telling members of staff what to look for and reminding them to keep their eyes open. They personally briefed every new member of staff on their security obligations, issued them with ID cards which they were required to carry, explained to them what was expected of anyone holding a pass key to the rooms, and reminded them often that they were never to allow someone into a room just because he said, "I'm staying in this room and I forgot my key." Any guest who'd misplaced a key was to be directed to Reception where a new one had to be issued.

A critical element in the overall security strategy was the fact that the keys weren't really keys. They were plastic cards with lots of holes punched in one end, marking a special code that could be identified by the computer. Every time a card was used anywhere in the Hotel, the computer recorded its use. A print-out revealed what time any locked door was opened and which card opened it. From their own register of who held which cards, Barron and Baxter knew who opened the door.

Expensive to install throughout the Hotel, the system paid for itself several times over. As it did when a woman who'd never stayed there before reported that someone had taken jewellery out of her room. The police were summoned to make an official theft report. She told the officers that she'd gone out of the Hotel at around 11 am and hadn't returned until after 5:30, which is when she discovered the theft. But the maid reported that when she went in to clean the room — using her pass key to open the door at around 11:30 — the woman was still there.

The computer print-out showed that the maid went into the room at 11:36 and that the door was not opened again until 3:27, when the woman herself returned to the Hotel — two hours earlier than she'd told the police.

Barron duly reported that to the police. Some weeks later, when the woman's insurance company wrote to him asking for corroboration of their client's story, he furnished them with a copy of that same report. Nothing more was ever heard about the woman or her claim. Nor did she ever return to the Hotel.

Because maids had access to all the rooms, the Hotel purposely never hired dailies. Maids were either hired directly — with references that were checked — or from highly trusted bonded agencies where they'd worked for years. It was paramount that the maids could be trusted to go inside guests' rooms. Not only did they have access to people's belongings, they also knew all the angles. And in Barron's ten years at the Hotel, there was never a single case of theft by a maid. In fact, as far back as anyone could remember, there was only one member of staff involved with theft.

One morning, early, a gentleman named Connally reported cash had been stolen from his room. It had been foolish on his part to leave it there because the Hotel made safe-deposit boxes available. Baxter took his report. The gentleman said he'd hidden £2200 in £50 notes, plus five $100 bills in his suitcase. He was now missing £1000 and $300. He also told Baxter he'd come back into his room the previous night at around 7:30, left before 9 and returned at around 1 am.

It was the fourth theft that year, and in each case only a portion of a guest's money was stolen. A textbook typical "MO" — *modus operandi* as the cops call it — Baxter knew right away it pointed to someone on the staff. Had a thief somehow broken into the room — which had never happened at the Hotel because there was so much security and the staff were constantly on the lookout for anyone who didn't belong — he would have taken everything. When someone took only a portion of the money available, it was because they were hoping the guest wouldn't notice that money was missing.

First, Baxter printed out an access report to the room. It corroborated pretty much what Connally told him. He came in the night before at 7:39. The next time a key was used to open the door, it was the floor waiter at 8:53. The door had then been opened at 21:55 by one of the receptionists, before the guest himself returned at 1:02.

Next, Baxter went to see the waiter, who explained that Connally had asked him for a carrier bag for his running shoes. He said he gave the guest a plastic bag and, sometime later, delivered ice and clean glasses to the room.

Then Baxter went to see the receptionist, who said that a fax had come in for Mr Connally and that he'd carried it upstairs and had put it on the desk in the sitting room.

Armed with that information, Baxter returned to speak with Connally. Yes, the gentleman said, a fax was waiting for him that time. The time at the top of the faxed page confirmed the receptionist's story. But Connally denied ever having asked the waiter for a carrier bag.

Now, by cross-checking the dates of the three previous thefts with personnel records, Baxter discovered that, while the receptionist had not been on duty at the time of the similar incidents, the floor waiter had.

But to make a case stick against someone, Baxter knew he had to catch the thief in the act, or at least find the stolen money on his person. Unfortunately, it was too late for either. The only thing left to do was set up a sting. Baxter and Barron set it up and the General Manager was the only other person on the staff who knew.

A couple who'd been regular guests at the Hotel were invited to stay for a weekend when the floor waiter was on duty. They were put into room 405. The room next door was left vacant.

Baxter took ten £50 notes and five £20 notes to the Head Cashier, where the bills were photocopied and the serial numbers recorded. He then placed the money in a briefcase, along with other papers, and left it, easily visible, in the couple's room.

That evening, according to plan, the couple ordered an early dinner in their room and casually commented to the waiter that they were going to the theatre. When dinner was done, they left.

In the meantime, Baxter and Barron were waiting in the vacant room next door.

Within an hour, the waiter came into 405. He didn't linger very long — hardly even long enough to rifle through the suitcase — then left with the trolley. As soon as he was gone, Baxter and Barron hurried into the room and checked the briefcase.

A hundred pounds was missing.

Briefcase in hand, they went to the pantry and confronted the waiter.

With the marked money in his pocket, there was nothing he could do but confess. He was taken to West End Central Police Station where he was charged. A few months later, when the case came to court, the now former employee pleaded guilty and was sentenced.

While Barron was looking into the case of the stolen brass ashtray, Baxter was attending a coordinators' meeting at West End Central to discuss the Korean visit. Briefing the group, an intelligence officer warned that there might be a demonstration outside the Hotel during the President's stay. Apparently, some animal welfare groups were trying to organize a protest.

Returning to the Hotel, Baxter went straight into Touzin's office. "We may have a crowd control situation. Animal rights activists. They don't like it that Koreans eat dogs."

Touzin grimaced. "I can see why."

Although they had no operational role to play with high-level visits, Barron and Baxter escorted the various protection organizations around the Hotel, facilitated their stay and kept the staff out of the way. However, they didn't necessarily keep the guests out of the way.

Once when Ronald Reagan stayed at the Hotel — he'd already left the White House — Margaret Thatcher came to visit him. The Front Hall was understandably filled with Secret Service men. Four little old ladies had just finished having tea in the Foyer and were getting ready to leave, when one of them asked Baxter, "What's going on?"

He told them, "We're expecting a visit from Mrs Thatcher."

The women wondered if they could stay to see her. He said, sure, and escorted them to a corner where he waited with them until the British Prime Minister arrived. When she did, one of the little old ladies started to applaud. The other three joined her. Mrs Thatcher turned to look at them, cut through the cordon of security men and came over to shake their hands. She chatted with them briefly, then went upstairs to see the former President.

At that point, one of the little old ladies turned to Baxter — not realizing who he was — and said that she was surprised to see how many bodyguards Mrs Thatcher had. Baxter explained that they weren't all for her, that Ronald Reagan was here too. So now, having already met Mrs Thatcher, the four decided to wait, hoping to get a glimpse of Reagan. He came down half an hour later with Mrs Thatcher, and they applauded again. He liked that, broke away from his minders, walked over and shook their hands.

Thanks to Baxter, there are four little old ladies somewhere for whom the Hotel will always be a very special place.

It was a slightly different story when a sitting President showed up. George Bush came to the Hotel and outright security paranoia reigned. A full detachment of Secret Service moved in, armed to the teeth with automatic weapons. It made the British authorities extremely nervous, yet such was the power of the American Presidency that any country refusing a US Secret Service demand to protect the President their way would almost certainly be grounds for the White House to cancel the visit. So this time the Secret Service were everywhere, and so were the Special Branch and the Diplomatic Protection Group. No one was going to get close to the President.

Except that, when Bush walked into the lobby, a little girl broke through the security net and raced up to him with a pen and paper asking for an autograph. He stopped and signed it for her, while all the fellows in dark suits with automatic weapons up their sleeves tried to figure out how anyone — even a child — could get that close.

There was a time, of course, when no visiting foreign dignitaries were permitted to have their own armed guards accompanying them. Because of Britain's strict gun control regulations, visitors needing protection were catered to by Special Branch during the day and the Diplomatic Protection Group at night. But that was a vestige of a gentler time. More and more, visiting foreign dignitaries asked that their own Secret Service be included when it came to their protection. By special agreement, some delegations were permitted to arm their personnel.

The Koreans didn't have the muscle the Americans did. Anyway, the threat assessment for this visit was very low. Police presence became as much a gesture of status as it was anything else. Lots of bodyguards made guests feel important. The problem was that the

Korean Secret Service took their President's security seriously, regardless of the British threat assessment. They used the CIA's training manuals and accepted every word in the literal sense. So when they asked to be authorized to be armed for this visit, the British reluctantly agreed that ten men — but only the ten working close protection — could carry handguns.

There were, in fact, some guns stored in the Hotel.

But it wasn't a service that was frequently discussed.

In the basement, just next door to the secure property storage room where some guests left furs and small valuables, there was a gun room — certified by the police — where hunting rifles and shotguns were securely held. Although the Hotel energetically discouraged guests from leaving guns there, a few clients were accorded that privilege, especially certain Americans who come to England every year to shoot and didn't want to go through the hassle of bringing their guns through Customs each time.

The room was tightly locked — to the strictest police requirements — and access to it was so rigorously controlled that many people working in the Hotel didn't know it even existed.

Barron retrieved the video tape from the Timekeeper's office.

Discreet security cameras, 26 of them, monitored the entrances and exits and all of the public areas of the Hotel. They watched the Front Hall, the grand staircase, the cashier's desk, the street at the front and the mews at the rear. The outdoor cameras even had infrared devices on the lenses so they could see at night.

It was a very effective weapon against crime, which had only sort-of failed on two occasions.

The first time, a guest at the Hotel was having a banquet and decided to bring in his own wine. When the driver from the company delivering the wine pulled into the mews, he noticed that there were other vans and lorries waiting to make deliveries. So he parked 50 yards up the block to wait out of everyone's way. Because those other deliveries were taking too much time, the driver chose to off-load the wine right there. Knowing that he could get a trolley from the Hotel to help him bring the cases inside, he emptied his van, left the cases on the kerb and walked back down the mews. He told the Timekeeper what he wanted and the Timekeeper called for the man who looked after the wine cellar. Together, they went to fetch a trolley. By the time the driver got back to the mews, the van was still there but the wine was gone. The security camera showed that, after the driver walked away, a white transit van pulled up, someone hopped out, loaded all of the wine into the van and drove away. The gentleman who'd ordered the wine was less than pleased, but he understood when he saw the video that this was not a question of the Hotel's negligence. Unfortunately, the camera did not show the transit van's licence plate.

The other time was when someone lifted a valuable antique barometer from the mezzanine wall. It had hung there for years. And one day, it was gone. Someone had unscrewed it off the plaster wall and got it out of the Hotel without anyone seeing anything. Barron and Baxter were able to determine that the theft took place in under 15 minutes. But that's all they were ever able to find out about it. In those days, there were no cameras covering the mezzanine.

There was, however, a camera covering the Ballroom entrance where the brass ashtray had been.

Taking the video tape to his office, Barron slipped it into his VCR and found the camera angle he wanted. The time code at the bottom of the picture read 10:28. And at the side of the shot he could clearly see the ashtray.

People walked up the hallway and other people came down the hallway and until the time code read 10:49 that's all he saw. Then he spotted a man wearing overalls stop in front of the ashtray. The man looked around — to make certain that no one was watching him — reached down, lifted the ashtray and headed out the door.

What he obviously hadn't counted on was that the camera clearly showed the back of his overalls and there, in large letters, was the name of the contracting firm setting up a function in the Ballroom.

Barron stopped the tape and checked his watch.

It was now 11:17.

He dialled the Public Area Housekeeper, got the phone number of the contractor and rang the man in charge.

By noon, the polished brass ashtray was back in the Ballroom entrance.

~ 8 ~

WHEN ANDREW JARMAN AND PHILIPPE Krenzer told the Chef what they intended to do, he vigorously protested. "It's wrong."

The Banqueting Manager wanted to put all his menus in English because the bulk of his clients were English and he felt they should know what they were eating.

The Food and Beverage Manager wanted to put the restaurant's à la carte menu in English, for much the same reason.

"I'm telling you, it's wrong," Lesnik repeated. "French is the language of cuisine." He was well aware of the irony of trying to convince Krenzer, a Frenchman, that French belonged on the menus. "We have traditionally put all our menus in French and English. I can't understand why anyone would want to change that."

Jarman tried to reason with him. "Not all our customers can read French."

"So, let them read the English translation."

Krenzer insisted, "They must be in English."

The Chef's secretary always checked the French on the menus to see that it was perfect. However, occasionally, the English translations that Jarman and Krenzer came up with were less than ideal, such as the way they'd described an asparagus dish served *tiède et froid,* as "cold and hot."

"Correct English," Lesnik reminded them, "is 'hot and cold'. And even that's not technically right, because in French the dish is described, literally, as lukewarm and cold."

But Jarman and Krenzer stood firm. And when the meeting broke up, Lesnik knew they were going to do it their way, no matter what.

The Food and Beverage office was on the mezzanine floor, a narrow room crammed with five desks and a table cluttered with huge appointment diaries. Krenzer and Jarman worked there, together with a Sales Coordinator and two secretaries, all of them only just managing to stay out of each other's way.

Until Touzin brought Krenzer in to oversee the department, the Hotel had been without a Food and Beverage Manager. But Touzin knew from his own experience that he needed someone to supervise the restaurant, Room Service, banqueting and banqueting sales activities.

A graduate of Lausanne's hotel management school — the closest rival to Touzin's Glion — Krenzer was born in Strasbourg in 1963. At the age of 24, when he first started looking for work, there were no hotel jobs to be had anywhere. It was the year the Americans stayed home, discouraged by an all-too-weak dollar and sufficiently scared by Middle Eastern terrorism. The best Krenzer could come up with was taking Room Service orders working at the Inn on the Park.

Two years later, he moved to a large American group, where he got his first operational post, as Restaurant Manager. But he didn't know how to handle employees who were out-of-work actors or cocaine addicts, or both, so within six months he was back in London, this time at the Ritz as Assistant Food and Beverage Manager. Anyway, his girlfriend was there and getting out of the States meant coming back to her. He stayed for 18 months, before going to Hong Kong for two years — where he was Assistant Food and Beverage Manager in a 700-bedroom hotel with seven restaurants — and then Bali for 15 months, where he was Food and Beverage Manager. That's when Touzin brought him back to London.

After eight years in the business, he'd formulated staunch notions about how a hotel should run its food service. Critics were always putting hotel restaurants in the same category as private restaurants, and Krenzer believed that was unfair. Cooking in a big hotel kitchen is not the same as "designer" food. A small private restaurant might serve 30,000–50,000 meals over the course of 250 business days a year. The Hotel served in excess of 200,000 covers a year. To compete on an equal footing with a starred Michelin restaurant would require a prohibitive investment that would push the price of a meal way out of proportion with what the market could bear. Furthermore, whereas a designer restaurant could spend the morning setting up for lunch, at the Hotel, breakfast clients were in the dining room sometimes as late as 11:30 am, giving the staff less than an hour to turn everything around for lunch. The last lunch might not finish until 3:30, which meant they had to start setting up for dinner. Throughout the day, there was also Room Service to contend with, meaning that the kitchen virtually never closed.

Anyway, a hotel restaurant and a designer restaurant serve very different purposes. Someone might go to Le Gavroche or the Waterside Inn once or twice, but people staying in a hotel treat the restaurant there as if it were their own dining room. What's more, in this particular case, the Hotel had guests who'd been eating there regularly, several times a week, for the past 30 years.

And yet he also understood that guests in the Hotel weren't enough to keep the restaurant going all by themselves. He very much agreed with Azoulai that they needed to bring in new clients from the outside, always keeping in mind that they couldn't change so much that they risked losing their old, established clientele.

Krenzer wasn't looking for a fight with the Chef — that wasn't in his nature — but it was obvious to him that some things needed to change.

One of them was the *prix fixe* lunch. Priced at £29 — which many people would consider a lot of money for lunch — the way it worked before Krenzer got to the Hotel was that there were all sorts of extras. Preparation time, the number of cooks assigned to lunch, serving time and food costs were driving the prices too high. The bill for two people never came to just £58. And clients resented that surprise. Regulars complained and many first-timers never came back. Krenzer wanted the *prix fixe* meal to contain a starter, a main course, a dessert and coffee, and to ensure that the price of it would be the bill the client got.

Knowing in advance that 70–80 per cent of the restaurant's guests went for the set-price lunch, he insisted that the kitchen focus more acutely on efficient preparation. That's why he vetoed the Chef's routine of preparing a new menu every day, in favour of a weekly menu.

Lesnik objected. As long as he was willing to go to the trouble of coming up with new dishes every day — after all, a daily menu meant that the Hotel's clients weren't seeing the same food two days in a row — he couldn't figure out why Krenzer should interfere.

Krenzer answered that the cost of putting three or four new dishes on the menu every day far outweighed the benefits of having six new dishes on the menu each week. The kitchen could buy better and prepare better. The cooks and the waiters would also be more familiar with the food they were selling. It had to do with running a more efficient operation.

Lesnik retorted that a daily menu gave him the chance to cook to the market.

Krenzer reminded him that, even with a weekly menu, if there was no trout in the market that day the Chef would know by 11 am and he would still have time to prepare another dish. Because it took only five minutes to run the menu through the computer, they could easily print a new menu without trout on it. And then, there was still a daily special, so that the menu was not exactly the same every day.

Furthermore, he'd calculated that nine out of every ten luncheon guests came from outside the hotel. Eight out of ten dinner guests also came from outside. So, he reasoned, a new menu every day didn't serve the overwhelming majority of their clients. He'd also observed that, for some strange reason, many British clients ordered the same lunch every day. He didn't necessarily find the British ardently adventurous, but that wasn't the point. If someone had a good lunch on Thursday and wanted the same thing on Friday, this way they knew they could have it.

The Chef grumbled that he couldn't run his kitchen on the off-chance that someone wanted the same lunch two days in a row. His arguments fell on deaf ears. Then again, that was the same reception that Krenzer's explanations got when he voiced them in the kitchen.

The old regime hadn't necessarily spent much time worrying about food costs. Krenzer was brought in because the benevolent days were over. Before he arrived, the restaurant closed for Saturday lunch and the Causerie stayed open. He shut the Causerie at weekends and kept the restaurant open every day. Now, instead of three brigades at weekends — breakfast and dinner in the restaurant and lunch in the Causerie — there were two. The first did breakfast and lunch in the restaurant. The second did dinner in the restaurant. The savings on labour costs alone were significant.

Next, Krenzer brought in a full-fledged *sommelier* to build up the restaurant wine list. Because there was more money to be made on wine than on food, he wanted to sell more wine.

The changes he made gradually became visible on the bottom line of the restaurant's balance sheet. To accomplish the same with the kitchen, he needed to do more than simply get rid of the truffles and the Balsamic vinegar.

The buzz words became "menu engineering."

Krenzer was looking for the Chef to work on something like a 34 per cent food cost basis. If the restaurant charged £10 for a dish, £3.40 of it was what it should cost to produce. The rest of the price reflected what it cost to serve, and profit. He'd already got the Causerie down from 45 per cent to 30 per cent. But he was smart enough to stop there, knowing that he was playing with a double-edged sword. If the food cost came down too much, the client wasn't going to get value for money. Nevertheless, the restaurant figure was still too high.

Every percentage point he could save there translated directly into £3500 profit.

In principle, he'd been taught that the Food and Beverage Manager was supposed to make everyone's life easier. In practice, he'd long ago discovered the kitchen staff understood food and the restaurant staff understood service but neither of them understood figures. Adding to his worries, there was the constant battle between this kitchen and this restaurant. It was a vicious cycle — the restaurant wasn't talking to the kitchen so they promoted dishes that they thought the clients wanted. In turn, the kitchen was constantly angry with the restaurant.

Krenzer was stuck in the middle.

Andrew Jarman spent a lot of time on the phone, but that's how business came in.

A gentleman rang to make a tentative reservation for a reception in the Ballroom six months down the line. A woman rang to ask how much it would cost to hold a wedding there. And a regular guest rang to ask about a picnic. Although he wasn't staying at the Hotel, he maintained an account and wanted to know if the kitchen could prepare a dozen breakfast hampers, which his chauffeur would fetch at 8:30 on Sunday morning. Without so much as flinching, Jarman asked the gentleman what he wanted in the hampers.

The Hotel

The son of a British military officer, Jarman was born in Germany in 1966. At the age of 19, he found a job as a busboy in the Hotel restaurant. He went from there to the kitchen of another hotel within the Group, then into Room Service, then into the office that, for the lack of a better title, was called General Services. They dealt with furniture and property, made the Hotel's mattresses and brewed the house coffee. But after two and a half years, he missed the buzz of hotels, so he applied for a Night Manager's job at another place and was turned down because someone there decided he had no personality.

Miffed, he returned to the Hotel to do 18 months as the Assistant Night Auditor, a year as Back of House Manager and a year on Reception. For the next several months, he was an assistant manager without portfolio — a permanent Duty Manager in charge of nothing except lost property. He greeted guests and smiled until his face dropped off. Then, when the Assistant Banqueting Manager suddenly resigned, he moved there.

He had four main function rooms to sell, plus the Orangerie.

From the Ballroom entrance at the east end of the Hotel along Brook Street, a polished marble corridor led back through a marbled Rotunda to a high-ceilinged reception room and, behind that, the main Ballroom. Designed in the 1930s, 40 feet wide and running 80 feet at the rear of the Hotel, it was an elegantly chandeliered room that comfortably sat 210 people.

Three large doors at the side led into the grey, yellow and white Mirror Room, so called because of the large mirrors dominating the room. It was about half the size of the Ballroom. Further along the rear of the Hotel, and only just a bit smaller, was the pink French Salon, with its two marble fireplaces. Then there was the Drawing Room, about the same size, decorated in the 18th-century style, with paintings, mirrors and crystal lampshades.

Clients could have one room, all of them or any combination of them for any type of event, from a candlelit dinner for two to a full-blown party for 1000. Each booking was confirmed by Jarman and inked into one of those huge diaries. Each page in each diary was dated, with spaces allocated for the four main reception rooms, plus the Orangerie. There were two pages set aside per day — one for breakfast and lunch, one for dinner — and, although each diary covered only six months, there were diaries enough sitting on the office table for bookings two years in advance.

The Koreans had reserved the Orangerie during their stay, just in case the President wanted to have a private meal. The Ballroom was theirs on Wednesday and Thursday, so the entourage could eat together. Around that, Jarman had filled the week.

He'd booked a retirement dinner for 160 in the Ballroom for Tuesday night. There was a kosher breakfast for 24 on Wednesday morning in the Mirror Room — because the Hotel didn't have a kosher kitchen, food was brought in from an accredited caterer — and a cocktail party for 100 in the Drawing Room on Wednesday night. He had a private dinner for 45 in the Drawing Room on Thursday, and a dinner for 115 in the Ballroom, once the Koreans were out of there, on Friday night. There was also a private luncheon for eight in the Orangerie on Saturday.

Because Banqueting was one of the most profitable sides of the Hotel's business — the 700 functions they did every year subsidized the restaurants by keeping the kitchen working — Jarman arranged breakfasts, luncheons, dinners, cocktail parties, afternoon teas, fashion shows, conferences, book launches, wine tastings, dinner dances, weddings and Hallowe'en parties. In the past he'd transformed the Ballroom into the sewers of New York for a kid's Ninja Turtle birthday party, and a "theatre night" setting, where every table was a different show. He'd turned it into a speakeasy where guests had to knock to get into the Ballroom, all the alcohol was served in teacups and the waiters were dressed in gangster suits. And he'd filled it with birch trees for a Teddy Bears' picnic where each table had condiments on a 00–gauge model railway and the waiters were dressed like Rupert the Bear. The one happening the Hotel shied away from was strippers.

Now, for the first time, he was going to oversee a Royal State Banquet.

Some months before, he'd taken a call from the Embassy of the State of Kuwait, who asked to reserve the Ballroom for a Thursday night so that the Amir of Kuwait could host a formal dinner in honour of the Queen of England.

The Hotel had a long history of catering for such occasions — only one other hotel in London was trusted enough to handle an event of this importance — but Jarman had never been involved with one. He was very excited about it, until the moment he heard the date. Then his heart sank. And when he checked the large diary, his worst fears were confirmed. He'd already reserved the Ballroom for a buffet dinner.

If it had been any other occasion, he would have regretfully explained that he couldn't take the booking and would have then tried to accommodate his client on an alternative date. But this wasn't just any occasion. This had to be considered the ultimate banquet. So Jarman diplomatically told the Embassy that he would be extremely pleased to pencil in the date, awaiting their confirmation, then rushed downstairs to inform Touzin, "A Royal State Banquet . . . except we're booked."

Mumbling a French expletive, Touzin immediately wanted to know, "Can we move the other booking?"

It wasn't something Jarman liked to do or normally did, because it put the Hotel in a difficult position and almost always annoyed at least one of his clients. But this time he promised, "I'll try."

"Just tell her what the problem is," Touzin advised.

"I wanted you to know first."

"Go ahead and get it moved."

So Jarman phoned the woman who was, unwittingly, standing in the way of the Queen's supper with the Amir. Careful not to upset her — well aware that he risked losing a client — he took the direct approach, apologized that he had to present her with this problem, and asked her to understand that he was caught in the middle of a very embarrassing situation. He told her about the State Banquet and asked her if there was any way she could reschedule her dinner.

She was understandably disappointed.

He was sympathetic.

And, probably because he handled it so well, she agreed in the circumstances to reschedule her event for five days later.

That burden lifted from Jarman's shoulders, he arranged an appointment through the Kuwait Embassy for the Ambassador and his wife to visit the Hotel. They arrived with half a dozen Embassy personnel in tow, and were joined there by a flawlessly groomed, perfectly dressed — regimental tie and all — British Army Lieutenant-Colonel who worked out of the Lord Chamberlain's office as the Queen's aide-de-camp. He'd been assigned by her to help the Kuwaitis plan the evening and carry it off. It was also his job to decide who should be invited and where they should sit.

Touzin and Jarman took them on a tour of the function rooms.

The Ambassador explained that the Amir would be staying at Buckingham Palace, as a guest of the Queen, for three days. He would arrive on Tuesday and, that night, the Queen would host a State Banquet in his honour at the Palace. Wednesday evening, there was a dinner planned in his honour in the City. On Thursday he would leave the Palace for a private residence, and on that evening he would host the Return State Banquet for the Queen and other members of the Royal Family. There would be anywhere from 140 to 170 guests. The Embassy would have a themer — an outside design group who would decorate the Ballroom — but the Hotel would be expected to provide the food.

The meeting lasted 20 minutes.

Jarman now knew the date and the approximate number of guests, so he and the Banqueting maître d' started booking staff. For functions like this, they hired special waiters — freelancers who only worked banquets at the big hotels — and carefully selected the best of them. Going down the lists, there were quite a few Jarman didn't want.

At this point, no one knew if there would be any formal toasts, if anyone would say Grace — Jarman suspected it might be inappropriate at a dinner hosted by a Muslim head of state — or, in fact, what the formalities would be. But all those decisions were left to the Queen.

At this point, no one knew what the menu would be. That would have to be coordinated with Buckingham Palace.

But he knew enough to worry because menus for any major banquet were always a problem.

Each time an order came in from the restaurant, the sous-chef working that kitchen took the pink ticket from the waiter, called out the dishes, then punched the ticket into a computerized clock, which stamped the time on the top of it. Lesnik had installed the clock, reckoning it would be worth every penny he had to spend on it because the waiters were always complaining that their orders were taking too long. Now when they clamoured, "I've been waiting 25 minutes," he could show them the ticket to prove it was only half that.

The gadget cost £600.

And the waiters still complained.

Before long, Christian — who was usually assigned to the restaurant kitchen — got so fed up with the waiters that he took his gripe to Lesnik. Daniel Azoulai was angry enough with Christian that he also complained to the Chef. Lesnik asked to see the pink slip copies of the orders, and after separating them into two distinct stacks — one for *à la carte* and *plat du jour* orders, and one that included off-menu orders — he easily spotted the reason for the stress.

Nearly 40 per cent of the pink slips coming in from the restaurant included dishes that were not on the menu.

The kitchen could always grill a T-bone steak, bake a chicken or do veal cutlets. If someone came into the restaurant with kids, it was easy enough to make cheeseburgers. There were also a bunch of vegetarian dishes they did that weren't on the menu. But when the waiter came in with an order for an Omelette Arnold Bennett — a flat omelette with glazed haddock on top — or grouse stuffed with *foie gras* and black olives, Lesnik felt he needed to know why. It meant that someone in the kitchen had to stop doing whatever they were doing, perhaps go to a book to look up the recipe, get the ingredients and then prepare the dish.

He never said no, unless it was absolutely impossible. A client asking for venison out of season, or a steak and kidney pie, which took several hours to prepare, didn't leave him much choice. But when a woman asked for Charantais melon, and there wasn't any in the kitchen, Lesnik sent someone out to buy one for her. Given 24 hours' notice, he would gladly cook anything for anyone, on condition that the ingredients were available in the market. Yet, he wasn't convinced that clients were asking for off-menu items as often as he was getting them. In fact, he had good reason to suspect that, most of the time, it was the waiters who were pushing off-menu items.

The Hotel's regular clients — especially the long-standing ones — could be very demanding. He knew that they wanted whatever they wanted and couldn't care less if it was on the menu or not. However, he was convinced that the waiters — who worked on commission and therefore took home a percentage of the bill — played up to them. A client would say, I feel like having some veal, and it was the waiter who would suggest Veal Holstein, which is breaded veal with a fried egg, capers and anchovies on top. He was convinced that the waiters were encouraging their clients to have anything they wanted, no matter how outlandish it was, no matter how it disrupted the kitchen.

In theory, Lesnik believed, there were four elements that made a meal. Food was, without any doubt, the most important, and he rated it as high as half the dining experience. What remained, he felt, was an equal helping of atmosphere, service and the client. As the Chef, he controlled the food. There wasn't much he could do about the client, and he had his own ideas about atmosphere — he would have preferred the restaurant to be smaller, more intimate, but there was no way he could change that. His main complaint, however, was about the service.

That he couldn't control the way the waiters were treating his food was the crux of his problem with the restaurant.

In the 1970s and into the 1980s, many chefs who'd made their reputations in hotels left to open their own restaurants where they directed the dining room. It meant that the maître d' worked for the chef.

That's what Lesnik really wanted.

Except he knew it was never going to happen here. He could see very clearly that the Food and Beverage Manager would never concede anything of the sort.

In that respect, he'd read Krenzer perfectly. Personalities, Krenzer had no doubt, were best left to designer restaurants. At some, it was not unheard of to have the chef — who thought of himself as the star attraction — insist that his clients eat at his taste level. Ask there for meat well done, and the chef might refuse to cook it that way. But at the Hotel, when the client ordered lamb with truffle sauce and then wanted mint sauce to go on top of that — a combination which would horrify any Chef — the client had to be given his mint sauce.

Lesnik insisted that wasn't the point.

Azoulai sided with Krenzer.

And the Food and Beverage Manager thought to himself, I am not so much a coordinator as a referee.

Because the Hotel had such a diverse clientele, it was the Chef's job to deliver a wide variety of food that was, for want of a better description, put under the heading of "International Cuisine." When 100 people came into the restaurant, they brought with them 100 different taste levels. No one walked in expecting only French food or only Chinese food, the way they would if they went to a smaller restaurant that featured the cuisine of the chef. They came to the Hotel expecting a menu offering a wide variety of dishes where, at the same time, they knew they could satisfy their own particular tastes.

So Azoulai was willing to agree with Lesnik that the food always had to be the major consideration. But his claim was that the food didn't stand on its own, that it had to work in tandem with everything else. If there was something wrong with the service, the setting, the welcome or how comfortable the client was made to feel, it didn't matter how good the food was. That's why, as far as he was concerned, it was more important to satisfy the client than it was to satisfy the Chef. He argued, you can't run a car from the back seat. In his mind, chefs already had too much power.

Krenzer evidently agreed. It was obvious that he was fast losing his patience with the Chef.

Azoulai had come down on Krenzer's side in the battle of the menu, so to Lesnik it seemed only natural that Krenzer should come down on Azoulai's side in the battle of the kitchen.

It was equally obvious that the Chef had no patience for Krenzer.

~ 9 ~

THE MORNING BEFORE THE PRESIDENT arrived, they test flew the Korean flag.

In the darkest bowels of the Hotel's basement there was a large windowless workshop — where the upholsterer and his apprentice, the carpet fitter, the carpet shampooer, the French polisher and the seamstress worked — and in one corner of that room there were cupboards where the Hotel stored 60 national flags, including four Union Jacks and three Stars and Stripes.

Each flag was roped and toggled, ready to fly.

They used to have more than 60, but a few years ago there'd been a minor flood in the basement and they lost a couple of dozen. Among the casualties were the French and Spanish flags. No one ever mentioned it to Touzin. Whenever they needed one, Joe the upholsterer — who was also the flag expert — could get it at two hours' notice. He had phone numbers for places that rented flags, and if none of them had what he needed — say for one of the smaller nations evolving out of the former Soviet Union or some obscure African country — he knew whom to ask at the various embassies.

Because it wasn't always obvious with some flags which way was up, he checked his well-thumbed coffee-table book on the world's flags, then carried the Korean flag upstairs and, together with the help of a maintenance man and the doorman, hoisted it next to the Union Jack.

Satisfied that he had it right, Joe took it down and stored it again in the basement cupboard, ready to be rehoisted in time for the President's arrival.

With only one day to go, Carole Ronald moved into the Hotel, taking a tiny room on the sixth floor for two nights, to be there just in case. She assigned a valet to be on call for the President overnight, put two valets on duty during the day, then made her final inspection, to see for herself that Housekeeping was ready.

Rooms 102 and 103 were a command post. Beds had been pushed aside and desks set up. Rooms 135 and 137 were bedrooms for the security staff. The Koreans insisted that these rooms, like several others, must have twin beds, well separated.

To be as flexible as possible, many rooms in the Hotel had double beds that could be stripped down and turned into two singles. So, where they'd asked for well separated twins, she checked to see that each bed had been twinned, and that they were far enough apart. There was also a note on her pad about a broken shelf in the bathroom of 137. She crossed it off only when she saw it had been fixed.

She looked in on the four painters redecorating room 123, and satisfied herself that the carpet was being Scotchguarded in 128. On her way down the corridor, a maid stopped her to say that there was a broken toilet seat in 146. She added that to her list, to get it repaired right away.

As she was making her rounds, Korean Security teams swept each of the rooms they were going to use, putting little green and white stickers everywhere — on ceiling panels, cabinet doors, plumbing access traps, electrical access gates and otherwise locked doors — to indicate that they'd inspected everywhere and that the rooms were considered safe.

For two weeks after the Koreans left, Carole Ronald's maids were still finding those little green and white stickers all over the Hotel.

Late that afternoon, two police officers arrived at the Hotel with sniffer dogs — a golden retriever and a cocker spaniel. They were escorted by Buckolt and Barron into the Royal Suite where the dogs ran around, tails wagging, shoving their snouts under the settees and under the bed and behind the heavy curtains. When the officers agreed that there were no explosives, they handed over responsibility for the suite to the Korean Secret Service.

Just after dawn on the first morning of the visit, the police secured the street at the front of the Hotel. Meters were capped. No parking was available to anyone who was not somehow associated with this visit. Unmarked police vehicles were stationed further down the road, so that access to the street could be cut off if the need arose.

Touzin arrived shortly before 7. He read the logbooks, then walked around talking to his staff. Twenty minutes later, he left for a General Managers' meeting in town, which had been called for 8.

Buckolt chaired the morning meeting in Touzin's office.

Jarman reminded everyone that, because the Ballroom was booked for another function, the Koreans would be having both lunch and dinner in the Causerie. Therefore, only the main restaurant would be open for guests. However, the Koreans would be moving to the Ballroom for all their meals during the rest of their stay and the Causerie would reopen, as usual, tomorrow.

That was when Andrew Pierron, the Information Technology

Manager, suggested it might be a good idea to put up a sign for the Koreans to explain where their meals would be served. Something simple, he said, to point the entourage in the right direction. Buckolt casually mentioned that a lot of the entourage didn't appear to speak much English, so Pierron said, "Well, then the sign has to be in Korean." Jarman then went in search of someone to write it for them, which turned out to be easier said than done. None of the Koreans wanted to get involved. It was as if no one dared take responsibility for something that hadn't been agreed upon by someone higher up.

Shortly after 10, Touzin was back at the Hotel. The first thing he did was go upstairs to the Royal Suite where, immediately, a Korean security guard challenged him. He explained who he was. One of the British Diplomatic Protection officers nodded that it was okay and, after the Korean Secret Service guys had a whispered huddle in the corner, Touzin was allowed to inspect the suite.

Seeing that everything was as it should be, he returned to his office to compose a welcoming letter to the President. He always wrote a first draft by hand, with a large, expensive fountain pen. He then gave the letter to his secretary, who checked his English, typed it on the computer and printed it out on Hotel stationery for his signature.

When that was done, he called Roy Barron to ask if all the various security measures were in place. Barron assured him they were, noting that Korean security were operating four command posts and that the Metropolitan Police had one of their own as well.

Touzin then walked out of his office, through the lobby and down the steps to the Hotel entrance, where he personally checked on the luggage porters and the doorman. From there he went downstairs, to poke around in the kitchen. The Chef had prepared several Western dishes for the Koreans' lunch, including beef with onions, chicken with lentils and monk fish *Provençale*, while the Koreans had shipped in various noodle platters and a large selection of sushi. Back upstairs, he stopped in the restaurant to ask Azoulai how many reservations he had for lunch, walked over to the Concierge's desk to chat briefly with Wingrove, wandered into the Reservations office to see how the rest of the week was shaping up, then rang Carole Ronald to ask her if Housekeeping was ready.

Reassured that everything was in place for the Koreans, he asked Buckolt for the arrivals list, so that he could be certain everything was also ready for all his other guests.

By 11 am a buzz started to go around the Hotel.

A dozen young Korean men took up positions in the Front Hall. They were all wearing dark suits, with small gold pins in their lapels. Half of them had wires coming out of their ears. Most of them were talking into radio-phones.

Metropolitan Police Special Branch officers wore white lapel pins. They were standing quietly in pairs.

Some of the Hotel's senior management now appeared in the lobby. Pierron was there. Buckolt joined him. So did Barron and Baxter.

At 11:15 two police officers on motorcycles, members of the special escort detail — which was part of the Diplomatic Protection Group — pulled up in front of the Hotel. They told the uniformed officers waiting there that the Presidential motorcade — 11 cars with police motorcycle outriders — was 20 minutes away.

Upstairs, the nine young Korean men who manned the primary command post were making phone calls, chatting incessantly and assuring each other that the President would be there shortly.

Down the hall, in 148, the Metropolitan Police command post was considerably more relaxed. They'd been through this sort of thing a hundred times before. Although armed officers from Special Branch would sleep at the Hotel, no one seemed to think this visit was anything out of the ordinary.

Roy Barron's worry about demonstrators was unfounded. The street was clear.

Now three buses arrived. There were 70 people in all — the first of the President's entourage — most of them men, most of them dressed in dark suits, most of them bringing with them three or four pieces of luggage, many of them with cameras strapped around their necks.

Next came some officials in a minibus.

Then a van arrived, filled with more luggage.

In all there would be 120 in the President's party, including 50 security personnel. Because rooms had been pre-assigned, none of them stopped to check in. They knew which rooms to go to and only needed to find out where those rooms were.

Suitcases and trunks were already tagged with the owner's room number. As each piece arrived, it was swiftly taken through the luggage room at the side of the entrance and, according to plan, sent down to the basement for sorting and delivery.

By 11:20, the Front Hall was crowded. There were more Korean men in dark suits, and more members of the Hotel's staff — Jarman and Ronald joined the group — and a couple of Korean women in flowery gowns that looked similar to Japanese kimonos.

That's when the Korean Minister for Foreign Affairs arrived. He climbed out of his car, was greeted on the kerb by several people from his London Embassy — commented to someone that there were too many people standing in front of the Hotel — and was escorted inside, where Touzin appeared to welcome him.

Right away, he told Touzin that only the President's closest associates — meaning the Ambassador and himself — together with Korean security, should be outside when the President arrived. He said no one else should be on the pavement and that, if the Hotel staff wanted to greet the President, they should wait inside the front door.

Without explaining that none of his staff were outside — the crowd consisted of seven Korean security men, Mr Lee and four members of his team, two plain clothes Special Branch officers and three uniformed policemen — Touzin said that would be fine. Although he insisted that the Hotel doorman should be waiting at the kerb to open the President's car door.

The lobby continued to fill up.

There were now 65 people waiting for the President to arrive.

Next to arrive was the Korean Ambassador. With him came several members of his immediate staff, most of whom joined the throng on the pavement.

Regular guests staying at the Hotel sidestepped their way in and out, bemused by the crowd and curious about the commotion.

At 11:32, one of the motorcycle officers parked at the kerb received a radio call from an outrider with the motorcade, reporting a minor traffic delay and informing him that the President would arrive in eight minutes. The officer passed along that news. No one seemed to mind, particularly the Koreans, who were all so wound up with excitement that another few minutes merely gave them time to wind up that much tighter.

People stood where they were and checked their watches. Others paced nervously — as best they could in a crowd — then checked their watches, then continued pacing, stopping only a minute later to check their watches again.

When that same motorcycle cop announced to the throng of people waiting on the pavement, "They're a minute away," word came like a wave, breaking through the front door into the lobby.

The pacing stopped.

Everyone hurried to take their places, standing precisely on their marks, waiting nervously, as if a film director was about to scream, "Action."

Then four motorcycles roared to a stop just past the front entrance.

Then the first of the 11-car motorcade pulled up.

Then other cars arrived.

Doors were flung open.

And, from the back seat of a shiny Jaguar, out stepped a short, smiling man in a blue suit with a full head of shiny, black hair — black enough to make him appear considerably younger than his 60 years, shiny enough to have just come out of a bottle.

Now on the pavement, surrounded by nearly two dozen people, Kim Young-sam did what any good politician would do — he began shaking hands.

No one escaped.

There was a lot of bowing from the Koreans and, of course, the President bowed back. But he shook hands with everyone — with the First Lady following in close pursuit — on his short stroll from the car into the lobby.

Touzin smoothly appeared next to him.

Automatically, the President shook his hand.

"We're honoured to have you at the Hotel, your excellency." No one could become the General Manager of a place like this without having mastered the delicate art of benign conversation. "I hope your trip was a comfortable one."

The President shook his hand a second time, while a translator whispered in his ear.

"Thank you," he responded with a smile, his eyes moving beyond Touzin to take in the Front Hall filled with people waiting for him. "May I present my wife."

"François Touzin." The Frenchman bowed and gallantly, almost-but-not-quite kissed her hand.

The First Lady bowed to say thank you.

Knowing the routine, Touzin moved slightly to the side so that the President could walk up to some familiar faces. They bowed and the President bowed and the First Lady bowed and the bowing went on for quite a while. So did the handshaking. And all the time, serious young Koreans in dark suits stayed close to the President, always looking past him at the faces in the crowd.

Finally, someone extended an arm towards the grand staircase, a sign to the President that he should follow Touzin, who led the way up those stairs, around the mezzanine and up the next short flight to the landing with the Royal Suite.

Thirty people followed them.

Guards at the suite bowed and opened the door, allowing the President, the First Lady and Touzin to step inside.

"I hope you will find this to your satisfaction," Touzin said.

The translator whispered in the President's ear and the President smiled to say he was sure this would be all right.

Many, but not all, of the hangers on, plus several stern-faced young men, followed the President into the suite. With 20 people standing around in the living room, the door was shut.

Touzin now guided the President and his wife through the suite — your living room, your dining room, your bedroom, your bathroom — and then, when they were back in the living room, after offering the President and his wife a seat on the couch, he asked if they would like something to drink.

The First Lady admired the flowers.

The President opted for tea.

Magically, two waiters appeared with tea ready to be served.

When the social niceties were over, after everyone had taken two polite sips and Touzin repeated that he hoped the President and his wife would enjoy their stay at the Hotel, he took his leave. The door to the suite was shut behind him and the President was left alone with the closest members of his party and a lot of young men with wires coming out of their ears.

The huge TV set in the corner never got turned on.

The crowd in the Front Hall had dissipated by the time Touzin came downstairs, although a few people returned for an encore an hour later when the President and his entourage were on the move again, this time for a visit to Buckingham Palace to meet the Queen.

Of course, Touzin was waiting in the lobby, along with a few dozen Koreans, to see them off.

And all this time, guests entering the Hotel or leaving the Hotel wondered what was going on.

"Who's here?" an elderly American man asked.

"The President," answered one of the luggage porters.

"Clinton?" The American turned to his wife. "It's President Clinton," he said loudly enough that she could hear him. "The President."

"Of Korea," the luggage porter interjected.

"Korea?" The man looked at the luggage porter.

"Clinton?" his wife asked.

"Korea," her husband corrected.

"Who?" she asked.

"The President . . ." He started to answer.

"Korea," the luggage porter said to the lady, trying to help. "Korea."

She shook her head, "Never heard of him," and walked outside.

Her husband looked at the luggage porter. "Never heard of him either."

Once he was out of the suite, the President's luggage was taken upstairs. There were 75 bags and six large trunks. A maid and a valet unpacked everything, under the supervision of a personal aide assigned to the President's staff. And that was just about the last anyone in the Hotel saw of him.

He stayed away most of the day, coming back late in the evening, going through the lobby very quickly, probably because there wasn't anyone to shake hands with. While the other Koreans breakfasted on kedgeree, bacon, beef sausages, pork sausages, croissants and no eggs, the President's chef used the first-floor pantry to prepare two identical meals for him — orange juice, a three-minute boiled egg, a bowl of cornflakes, a bowl of exotic fruit and a cup of coffee. One was tasted. One was given to the President.

The only people authorized to serve him were Kurt and Enzo, both of whom had been granted security clearance, neither of whom was ever permitted to be in the President's company without his armed security guards there too.

With Korean security crawling all over the Hotel, the meeting in Touzin's office on the second day of the visit had a slightly odd tone. Everyone seemed to feel as if the place was in a mild state of siege.

"Someone rang me at one this morning," Carole Ronald mentioned, slowly taking her place in the chair to the left of Touzin's desk.

"Who did?" he wanted to know.

"One of the Koreans. It was to change some plans for a meeting they were going to have at seven this morning."

"They woke you up at one o'clock?"

"The first time. They rang back half an hour later to say that the meeting would now be held at 5:30."

"Were you supposed to go to this meeting?"

"No."

He stared at her. "What did they want you to do about it?"

"Nothing. They just wanted me to know their plans had changed."

He was genuinely amazed. "Did anyone else get wake-up calls from the Koreans?"

"They didn't have to wake me," Adam Salter volunteered. "Sometime around two this morning they asked me to move some furniture."

"What furniture?"

"In the President's suite."

Touzin said, "Where did you move it to?"

"I didn't," Salter shook his head. "They wouldn't let me in."

"They phoned you to move some furniture at two o'clock in the morning and then wouldn't let you into the suite?"

"That's right, sir, I didn't have the proper security badge."

"So the furniture didn't get moved."

"It did," Salter explained. "They wound up moving it themselves."

"Don't these people ever sleep?" He looked back at Ronald and joked, "Tonight, don't tell them you're staying in the Hotel and don't give them your room number."

"What happens if they need me?"

Touzin pointed to his Night Manager. "Let's get Mr Salter the proper security badge so he can move furniture all night long."

Everyone in the room chuckled and Touzin went for the log-books. "Some guests complained about late breakfasts." He looked at Andrew Jarman. "That shouldn't happen."

"The Room Service supervisor was working out of the first-floor kitchen," Jarman explained, "because of the Koreans. Apparently some guests on the sixth floor had to wait before their call buttons were answered."

"No good," Touzin said. "We must not forget our regular guests. Please tell the Room Service supervisors that someone must be taking care of all our guests on every floor. This is unacceptable."

Jarman said, "I've been onto them."

Touzin read from another entry. "Dr Villarosa in 628 was very upset that his breakfast was late and expressed his anger when he checked out." He looked again at Jarman. "Is this the same complaint?"

"Unfortunately, it's not," Jarman admitted.

"Would you please get me Dr Villarosa's details and I will write him a letter of apology."

Jarman made a note to do that.

"One-thirty am," Touzin read. "Loud drunk on street, shouting. Walked away before the police were called." He wanted to know, "What was he shouting about?"

Salter replied, "Maybe they asked him to move some furniture."
Everyone laughed.

Going around the room, Touzin pointed to each member of his staff to see if they had anything to add.

Ronald wanted everyone to know, "The valets and luggage porters have really been wonderful. They handled 462 pieces of luggage for the Koreans and not one wound up in the wrong room. There wasn't a single hiccup."

Touzin was visibly pleased. "I'll send a note around to thank everyone as soon as the Koreans leave." He jotted down a reminder to do that. "That's very good."

"It's the water company," Rory Purcell volunteered when it was his turn. "They decided to show up early this morning and dig up the road outside the Ballroom entrance. Korean security was in a bit of a tizzy about it, but the British police calmed them down. They've had to cut off water somewhere but the kitchens aren't affected, the guests aren't affected and the Koreans aren't affected."

"Who is?" Touzin asked.

Purcell answered, "I don't know."

"If you can," Touzin said, "please make sure they get their work done quickly and give us back our pavement. As long as the Koreans don't start complaining about something that is out of our control."

"Complaining, no," Purcell said. "But I gather the President gave the water people some strange looks when he saw them."

"What time was that?"

"He went jogging at around five."

"Five this morning?" Touzin was amazed.

Salter said, "Yes, sir, he left with a bunch of Korean security guys and a pair of British policemen."

"Pity the poor British cops," Purcell mumbled, "having to go jogging at that hour."

"Pity the poor British cops," Pierron said, "having to go jogging at all."

"I go jogging," Touzin noted.

Pierron reminded him, "Not at five in the morning, you don't."

The next morning, it was over.

Everyone gathered in the Front Hall to see him leave.

The President and the First Lady, together with their aides and their bodyguards, came briskly down the main staircase, where Touzin was waiting at the bottom. They shook hands — "I hope you have enjoyed your stay with us" — and, after the translator whispered in his ear, the President nodded several times, saying, "Yes, thank you," and shook Touzin's hand again.

Then the President made the rounds, shaking everyone else's hand — first the Koreans who were there, then the Hotel staff who'd formed a semi-circle next to the entrance to the Foyer. He looked to see that he'd said goodbye to everyone and started to leave. But one of his aides quickly informed him that a Hotel photographer wished to take his picture, so the President joined the Hotel staff, standing in the middle next to Touzin, to pose for a photo.

When that was done, he left the Hotel, still bowing and shaking hands.

Outside, car doors opened, car doors were slammed shut, motorcycles roared and just like that he was gone.

The Front Hall returned to normal, except for those few guests who lingered there, still trying to figure out who the man was with the too-black hair and why everyone wanted to shake his hand.

~ 10 ~

No sooner had the Koreans departed than a very high-profile Middle Eastern politician — a household name — moved into the Hotel for one night. The visit was handled with the strictest security. It was unannounced to the press and even Touzin only found out about it at the last minute. This time the threat assessment was high.

The first thing Adam Salter did when he arrived at the Hotel that night at 11 — once he'd changed into his dinner jacket — was to speak with the Duty Manager to find out what had been going on. That's when he learned about the visit. After that, he went into Buckolt's office to see who else was in the Hotel, before running off the day's final statistics so that Touzin would have them at the morning meeting.

On duty with him were the Night Concierge Philip, the Night Auditor, two porters, Abel the night Room Service waiter, and the night chef. There were also two telephone operators, a maintenance man and the cleaning staff — four men in green overalls who polished all the marble floors and three men in orange overalls who scoured every inch of the kitchens. There was also a Timekeeper who doubled as the security man, making two rounds of the Hotel every night, carrying a key with a clock to guarantee that he made the necessary fire safety checks, seeing to it that doors which should be shut were shut, and that the Hotel was secure.

For many people, working nights took a lot of getting used to. Salter had been on Reception for six months before becoming Night Auditor, a job he held for nine months. It wasn't easy for a single guy to adjust to the fact that he was going to sleep when everyone else was waking up and that he was waking up when everyone else was going to sleep. But he'd been Night Manager now for 14 months, and he figured he was as used to it as he was ever going to get. Except on his days off, when he tried to stay awake during the day and sleep at night, and then it wasn't just nights that were tough, it was days too.

A few minutes past midnight, a call came in from a gentleman saying, "I'd like a room."

The Hotel frowned on "off the street" business because there were too many things that could go wrong, too many unknown quantities that could upset regular guests. But as the evening wore on, empty rooms stayed empty, so Touzin instructed his Night Manager to use his discretion. If someone known to the Hotel needed a room, the Hotel should accommodate them. But when someone unknown to the Hotel rang up like that, asking for a room, Salter had only a few seconds to make up his mind. This time, hearing rowdy party noises in the background, he said, "I'm afraid there is nothing available tonight, sir."

The gentleman was insistent. "Come on, all hotels keep rooms just in case . . ."

"Actually we don't," Salter explained, which happened to be the truth. If the Hotel could rent every room in the house, it would. "I'm sorry that we won't be able to help you this time."

Irked, the man slammed down the phone.

Seven minutes later, a gentleman arrived at the front door, carrying a suitcase. He rang the bell and was well dressed enough that Philip let him in.

"I don't have a reservation," he said with an American accent, "but I'm hoping you've got a room for the night . . ."

Salter said, "Let me check to see, sir. May I have your name, please? Have you stayed with us before?"

The man replied, "My name is Prendergast and no, I've not stayed here before."

"Just a moment, sir." Salter left him to wait with Philip while he looked to see that there was no one called Prendergast listed in the NTBT ledger, then to see which room he might have available. He came back to offer the gentleman a single at £220.

The man blenched, "Two hundred and twenty for the night? Thanks anyway," picked up his bag and left.

Every night around 1, the Timekeeper locked the back door and Philip locked the front door. Salter then took the lift to the sixth floor and made the rounds of every corridor, working his way down, closing the fire doors. There were 42. He also checked the lights in the hallway and looked to see if call lights were on in any room.

By the time he came down, the function in the Ballroom was just drawing to a close. A couple stumbled up to him. "Room please," the man said in a drunken slur. "Room for the night."

Seeing that the lady was even more drunk than the gentleman — she was slumped against him — Salter was apologetic. "I'm terribly sorry, sir, but I'm afraid the Hotel is full tonight."

"Don't give me any rubbish," the man said. "We want a room. Hotels are never full. There are always rooms. Please give us a room."

Salter put on his most rueful face. "I'm terribly sorry, sir, but there is nothing I can do."

The man barked, "Let me speak to the manager."

"I am the Night Manager, sir. Perhaps you would allow me to get a taxi for you."

The man didn't move.

Salter offered his arm to the woman, then realized that she was unconscious. "Is the lady all right?"

"Of course not," the man complained. "Now can we have a room?"

Immediately, Salter took her in both his arms and gently lowered her to the floor. Then he summoned an ambulance. By the time it arrived, the woman's eyes were open. The paramedics wanted her to go to the hospital, but she refused. "No hospital."

Everyone pleaded with her to go.

"No hospital," she kept saying. "No hospital."

The medics couldn't convince her. Salter couldn't convince her. And the gentleman with her didn't bother to try. So eventually, once the ambulance crew gave up and left, Salter asked Philip to find a taxi for her. When one came, they helped her into the cab.

That's when she threw up and passed out again.

The furious driver gave Salter hell for shoving her into his taxi.

With the woman fast asleep on the back seat, Salter got one of the night cleaners to help wash out the taxi.

As that was being done, a second cab pulled up to the front of the Hotel and a guest got out. Salter recognized him as a doctor and went up to him to explain the situation.

The doctor agreed to look at the woman and, after a very hasty check, he told Salter that, from what he could tell, the woman was simply drunk and needed to sleep it off.

Her escort, who didn't seem to know her name or where she lived, now climbed into the cab and gave the driver the name of another hotel. The driver was still angry, but the man assured him he had plenty of money. Salter shut the door and, as the taxi pulled away, he thought to himself, so much for one night.

But it wasn't to be.

Mrs Amadou in room 318 rang to complain that someone had removed a large empty cardboard box from her room. Not having any idea what she intended to do with a large empty cardboard box at that hour, Salter apologized and said he would bring another up straight away. It took him 20 minutes of rummaging around the basement before he found one. He delivered it to her — she was bizarrely gleeful to have it — and wished her a good evening.

Then a call came in from a woman who introduced herself as Mrs Bishop. She told Salter she was phoning from Chicago because she was extremely worried about her husband, whom she hadn't been able to contact since early afternoon London time. "He's supposed to be staying at the Hotel."

Salter checked to see that, in fact, Mr Roy Bishop was registered in room 139. But, for the sake of client discretion, he didn't tell her that. He simply said, "Please let me have your number and I will check to see if your husband is indeed here."

She gave him her number and he promised to ring back.

After confirming that the phone number listed in the guest history matched the number the woman had given him, he dialled the room.

The line was engaged. He waited a few minutes, then tried again. It was still engaged. So he went upstairs and, not knowing what to expect, nervously knocked on the door.

There was no answer.

He knocked again, this time with a little more force, and again there was no answer.

"Please don't be dead," he said out loud.

He tried one more time, to no avail, then took his pass key and put it in the door. He opened it a crack and was about to announce his presence when someone inside demanded, "Who the hell is it?"

Salter whispered, "Thank you, God," and explained to the man, "I'm terribly sorry to bother you, sir, this is the Night Manager."

"What the hell is . . . just a minute." The gentleman came to the door. "Who is it?"

Salter repeated, "The Night Manager, sir. Excuse me for waking you."

Mr Bishop couldn't believe someone was there at this hour. "What do you want?"

"I've had Mrs Bishop on the phone from Chicago saying she's been trying all evening to get through and hasn't been able to contact you."

"Who? What?" He was genuinely confused. "My wife?"

"Yes, sir. She's worried about you because she couldn't get through . . ."

The man glanced towards the bed, made a face then said, embarrassedly, "It's off the hook."

Salter withdrew as Mr Bishop promised to ring his wife immediately.

Next came a call from someone in room 427, asking him to come upstairs right away. He was greeted at the room by a young couple — they were registered as Mr and Mrs Rice — and a young gentleman, whom he did not know. A woman was passed out on the bed. Rice explained that she was the young gentleman's lady friend, that the four of them had been dining in the restaurant, had come back up to the room and she had simply passed out. He wanted to know, "Can we get her a room?"

Salter suggested, "I think we should get her a doctor."

"She just needs some sleep," Rice insisted.

"I think it would be wise if we rang for a doctor," Salter said with authority, and reached for the phone at the side of the bed to dial the house physician.

On call every night for situations just like this, the doctor asked Salter to describe the woman's condition and whether or not he knew what she'd eaten. At that point, the woman stirred. The easiest thing seemed to be to let the doctor speak directly to her, so Salter handed her the phone. The two talked for only a few seconds, until she motioned to Salter that the doctor wanted him. The Night Manager got on the line and the doctor said, "Ring for an ambulance and get her to an emergency room."

Hanging up with the doctor, Salter dialled the Emergency Services to ask for an ambulance. While he was still on the phone, the woman went into some sort of fit.

The Rices and the other fellow decided — over Salter's strenuous objections — to wait for the ambulance downstairs. They struggled to get her off the bed, along the corridor and into the lift. By the time they reached the lobby, she was screaming and totally out of control.

From their sentry post on the first floor, outside the Royal Suite, two Special Branch officers came racing down to see what was going on. Salter reassured them that there was nothing to be concerned about, that an ambulance was on the way.

It wasn't until the ambulance arrived and the paramedics took over that the woman finally calmed down.

Except now she started demanding, "My other shoe."

One of the paramedics asked, "What other shoe?"

"My other shoe," she repeated. "I need my other shoe."

Seeing that she was, in fact, wearing only one shoe, Salter said he'd get it for her. But when he looked around room 427 there was no shoe to be found.

Nor was there any luggage.

Apparently, Mr and Mrs Rice had moved into the room without any personal belongings.

He now began to wonder if perhaps drugs might somehow be involved.

Downstairs, he apologized to the woman that he couldn't find her shoe and asked to speak to Mr Rice privately. "Do you know, sir, if she has a history of drug use?"

He, rather off-handedly, insisted she didn't. "Look old man, why not put her in a room for the night, and put the bill on my room?"

Maybe if Rice's room hadn't been so empty . . . "I'm sorry," Salter said. "I think she's much too ill. I think she should go to hospital."

The woman must have heard him because suddenly, like the woman a few hours earlier, she too began screaming, "No hospital."

The ambulance crew said they couldn't take her if she refused to go while Rice insisted that Salter give her a room.

Now Salter announced, "I'm afraid that if she won't go to hospital with the ambulance, I will have to insist that you escort her out of the Hotel."

While Rice and the other fellow conferred, one of the Special Branch officers told Salter that if he wanted them out of the Hotel he would escort them out.

A few minutes later, Rice sent the paramedics away. They got the woman on her feet and, with the help of the two officers, took her to a car parked down the street. The second gentleman got in and drove her away. Mr and Mrs Rice returned to their room. They checked out, luggage-less, early the next morning.

The Night Manager at the Ritz called to ask for a box of eggs as his chef did not have enough.

Salter asked, "How many do you need?"

The man said, "Thirty dozen."

So at 2:20 in the morning, Salter loaned somebody 360 eggs.

Since he was in the kitchen anyway, Salter asked the night chef what he had handy. He ordered chicken and some pasta. Half an hour later, when it was ready, he went downstairs to fetch it, then took it back on a tray into the restaurant where he sat at a table on the mezzanine, near the entrance to the Orangerie.

The Hotel

For the first time in several nights, no guest rang down during his meal to ask for extra pillows or extra blankets, or toothpaste or soap or an ironing board. Unfortunately, being Night Manager also meant being night maid, and when someone came back to the Hotel late to find that, somehow, their room had not been serviced or that their bed had not been made, it was left to him to do that too.

Just as he was finishing his meal, the front door bell rang.

The gentleman staying in room 332 — a deluxe single — accompanied by another gentleman and three ladies came into the Front Hall and seemed as if they intended to stay there. At least they stayed there until Philip turned his back. When he looked again, they were gone. A few moments later, a call came down from room 332 asking that a bottle of champagne be sent up.

The law governing hotel registration was quite specific — all guests had to be registered. If a guest arrived back at the Hotel with a newly acquired friend, intending that the friend would spend the night, the Hotel was obliged to insist that the friend also register. If they were in a single room, the Hotel would insist on moving them to a double. Failure to register a guest, or false registration, was especially serious, as far as Salter was concerned, because the law did not punish the Hotel. Instead, it levied fines on whoever should have registered the guest and failed to do so.

What's more, the Hotel did not permit visitors in rooms after 11 pm. That was policy. So Salter went up to room 332, knocked on the door and asked to speak to the gentleman who was registered there.

He stepped out into the hallway, closing the door behind himself — so that Salter couldn't see in — and wondered what the problem could possibly be.

Salter politely explained, "Unfortunately, sir, no one is permitted to visit the rooms at this hour. If you would like, however, drinks could be served in the Foyer."

The gentleman told Salter, "That's all right. My guests will be leaving."

Thanking him for his understanding — and quietly grateful that the man hadn't caused an embarrassing scene — Salter returned to the Front Hall and related the conversation to Philip.

Half an hour later, no one had yet come down from room 332.

Now, Salter dialled the room. The gentleman answered on the first ring. Salter informed him, "I'm afraid I will have to insist that your guests leave the room." This was the delicate part, because, in the end, there really wasn't much he could do other than ring the police and possibly create a disturbance.

"Yes," the gentleman answered. "Of course. I understand. No problem."

Salter hung up, thinking he'd handled it well.

However, five minutes later, the gentleman was on the phone again. He wanted to know, "Why must the ladies leave?"

"Because it is strictly against hotel policy for unregistered guests to visit the rooms at this hour."

The gentleman responded, "But I am with my very best client. All he wishes to do is have a drink and a little nap with the ladies. So perhaps we should take an additional room."

Salter responded, "I'm afraid there is nothing else available."

The gentleman abruptly changed his tack. "If that is the case, I am afraid that I shall be forced to make a formal complaint about you to the management."

"As you like, sir. But I will have to ask again that your guests leave."

"They will be leaving," the gentleman confirmed, and slammed down the phone.

Some 25 minutes later, the gentleman from 332, his best client and their three lady friends arrived in the lobby. The gentleman announced, "I will be checking out," tapped his toe while Salter prepared his bill, and when it was ready, paid it. Salter asked if they required a taxi. The gentleman said no and, with the other four, walked away into the night.

To many hotels, allowing unregistered guests upstairs doesn't matter. Their feeling is that, as long as someone pays for a room, he or she is entitled to do whatever they want. Some of those same hotels don't mind if prostitutes work the bar or sit around the lobby. It is, in a way, all part of the service.

But not here.

If someone didn't like the local ground rules, they were free to go elsewhere. The Hotel made no bones about it. Right or wrong, this was the way they played the game.

Of course, some clients figured it was a pretty good game, and were more creative than others. One fellow in particular used to introduce his lady friends to Salter. "She's my chiropodist." It never worked. But it amused the client to keep trying.

A Special Branch officer, staying in room 633, had gone off duty, gone back to his room, taken a nap and then decided to go out for a few hours. Carelessly — and absolutely in violation of all regulations — he opted to hide his gun and holster under his unmade bed.

When he returned to the Hotel, the gun was gone.

He couldn't admit this to anyone on the security team — losing his gun meant losing his job — but he needed someone who could help him find it, so he confided in Adam Salter. "I went out at around midnight and the gun was under my bed. I came back, the bed was turned down and the gun wasn't there."

Salter instantly knew something was amiss because there were no maids on duty at that hour. There wasn't anyone in the Hotel to turn down the bed. He went to the computer and printed out the key log, which showed that the floor maid had gone into the room at 7:25 pm — while the officer was still on duty — and that no one else had gone into the room until 2:49 am, which was when the officer returned.

Except that the card used at 2:49 that morning was not the card issued for room 633. It was a pass key. That suggested to Salter someone on the staff had been in there. But the only staff members who had pass keys at that hour were the night waiter, the Duty Manager and himself. Even more oddly, the code on the card that was used to open the door did not correspond to the code on any of their pass keys.

He asked for the card that the officer had, and the moment he saw it he had a hunch he knew what must have happened. Checking the computer log again, he saw that a pass key had been used to enter room 533 — a vacant room — at the same time the officer claimed to have gone into his room.

Salter asked the officer, "Could you have somehow gone to the wrong room?"

And when the two of them went to 533, there was an unmade bed, with the gun and holster under it.

Abel the Portuguese night waiter — a short, stocky man with very broad shoulders and powerful forearms, the kind of fellow you'd want to have on your side if there was any trouble — also came on duty at 11.

He collected his pantry keys from the Timekeeper and signed for a room pass key at the Cashier's office, where it was kept in a safe. He then inventoried his stock of alcohol — wine, champagne and whiskies — although, these days, he didn't sell as much alcohol as he used to because every room had a mini bar. But then, some people were put off by the mini bar — everything there was expensive, like the small jar of jellybeans that cost £5.50 — and only felt they got their money's worth when they had personal service.

Room Service was busy until around 2 am or so, then stayed quiet until breakfast orders began trickling in, usually between 5 and 6 am. Twice a night he collected the order cards on which clients ticked off coffee or tea, hot cereal or cornflakes, toast or pastry, and that they hung on their door before they went to sleep. He picked them up at 1 and then again at 3:30, not so much for the clients' convenience — because clients could always ring for the floor waiter when they woke up — but because it gave him a chance to get the orders prepared before the rush started at 7.

Dressed in a blue dinner jacket with black trousers and a black tie, he'd been on nights for nine years, and the routine suited him just fine. He was home every morning in time to take his kids to school, slept from 10 to 2, got up for a few hours, then cat-napped for another couple before coming back to the Hotel.

Working out of the pantry on the third floor, he served a few light dinners — two couples came back from the theatre and there was one very late arrival. Then nothing happened until 3 when a client rang and ordered, "A dozen Yorkshire puddings, please."

"Yes, sir." Abel waited for the next line. "A dozen Yorkshire puddings . . ." When the client didn't say anything, he added, "Is that all?"

"No, of course not." The client looked at Abel as if he'd said something foolish. "I'd like a bottle of water too."

Half an hour later, a guest staggered in — he'd obviously been drinking — got to his room and rang for Room Service. Abel came in and the fellow chose a full dinner off the menu. However, when Abel returned with it there was no answer at the man's door. He knocked a second time, waited as he was supposed to, then gently opened the door and looked inside. The man was passed out in bed, clutching a bottle of beer. Abel decided he wasn't going to take the dinner away — there was nothing else he could do with it — so he took the trolley in, put it next to the bed and announced, "Dinner is served."

By 5, he was preparing the first round of morning coffee in each pantry. Beginning with the top floor and working his way down — because it was always easier to walk down rather than the other way — he also checked to see that enough trolleys were ready, with tablecloths, cups and saucers, sugar bowls, silverware and napkins.

Going through the breakfast cards, he rang the chef to get bread, croissants, brioches, rolls, and whatever else he needed to set up each pantry for the morning shift. Just as he was finished with that, an American client ordered something called shredded eggs.

Abel said, "Certainly sir," although he wasn't sure what it was and had to ask the chef.

Except the chef didn't know it either. "Never heard of it."

It sounded vaguely familiar to Abel — he was positive he'd served it to someone before — and he tried to recall what it was. Taking a wild guess, he told the chef, "Eggs fried in butter in a small dish, where the white is hard and the yellow is soft."

The order came up from the kitchen just like that, and Abel delivered it to the room.

Seeing it, the client broke into a wide grin. "You are probably the only hotel in the world that knows how to do this."

The two young men who worked as night porters gathered any shoes that had been left outside the rooms to be polished, took them to the luggage porters' room and polished them. Later, they went back through the Hotel, leaving the shoes where they belonged and distributing the morning newspapers, which arrived at the front door by 6.

The two women in the switchboard room on the mezzanine floor had a television to watch throughout the night — although there wasn't much on — and one of them liked to knit. If they weren't answering phones, they were talking, or just staring at the wall where six clocks showed the time in London, Paris, New York, Sydney, Tokyo and San Francisco.

The maintenance man spent the night in his basement office and only appeared if there was some sort of emergency.

◆

A limousine pulled up.

The driver opened the rear door. An extremely attractive, well-dressed woman in her early 20s with long blonde hair stepped out. The driver then rang the Hotel's bell.

Sliding across the rear seat was a guy about her age, with a slightly dishevelled look. He was wearing an old raincoat, jeans and well-worn loafers with no socks.

Philip unlocked the door to let them in.

She motioned to the young man to take care of the driver, and stepped inside, moving quickly through the Front Hall. Without waiting for him, she hurried past the Concierge's desk, past the main lift and past Reception, turned the corner into the side corridor where there was a smaller elevator — traditionally referred to as the Ladies' Lift — and disappeared inside, on her way up to her room.

The staff knew her well. She'd been a regular at the Hotel for years. She claimed to be some sort of model or actress — it depended on whom she was speaking to — but she never seemed to do anything when she was at the Hotel, except sleep all day and party all night. She'd leave around 11 and invariably come back by 4. More often than not, there was a limo. More often than not, there was a young man left at the door to pay the driver.

Now he wandered in, but only got as far as the Front Hall. "May I help you?" Philip asked.

Looking around, puzzled by the fact that his new friend wasn't anywhere to be seen, he announced, "I'm with Miss Rhodes."

"Are you registered at the Hotel, sir?"

"Ah . . . no I'm not." He couldn't figure out where she'd gone. "What room is she in, please?"

Salter walked up to say, "Good evening, sir. I'm terribly sorry, but no guests are permitted in the rooms after 11 pm."

The young man looked at these two. "Can I just ring her room . . . ?"

"It might be better," Salter suggested, "if you rang back in the morning."

"But you see . . . I mean, she . . ."

"I'm terribly sorry, sir," Salter said, "but if you're not a registered guest . . ."

The fellow stood there for several moments, his mouth open, as it dawned on him that he'd been had. "Can I just use the house phone . . . ?"

Salter offered, "May I ring for a cab for you, sir?"

"A taxi, sir?" Philip repeated.

It took another few moments before the man gave up.

Once he was gone, Salter and Philip looked at each other. Neither of them had any idea how much the man had blown at the club and then on the limousine, but both of them could imagine what he was thinking on the ride back to the Hotel, his mind filled with visions of Miss Rhodes and Room Service.

Salter raised his eyebrows and Philip merely shrugged.

Miss Rhodes did this all the time.

Throughout the night, Philip quietly recorded in a log the name of everyone who came in and everyone who went out, and all the number plates of the cars parked out front. It was one of those things that the Hotel did for no specific reason, except that someone decided a long time ago that someday it might be important to have such information.

At 4:30, an Aston Martin DB-7 pulled up to the front of the Hotel. The driver did not switch off the engine, he simply sat at the wheel,

trying to peer inside the Hotel. Philip walked outside to see what was happening. The car window rolled down and the man at the wheel called out, "I want your best suite. The Royal Suite."

Bending down to look inside the car — he didn't recognize the man, who was alone — Philip said, "Certainly sir. May I have your name please? I'll see if it's available."

The man introduced himself.

His name rang a vague bell to Philip, but he didn't know why.

"If you can't help me," the man said, "I'll try some other places." He reeled off the names of three well-known hotels.

"I'll speak with the Manager and see if we can sort something out, sir."

The man waved, "I can't wait," put the car in gear, shouted, "I'll be back," and pulled away.

Philip related the story to Salter — who also said the name sounded familiar — and together they went to check. Sure enough, there his name was — on the NTBT ledger!

Apparently, some years ago, this gentleman had checked into the Hotel, taken a large suite and spent more than a week there, refusing to let the maids service the room. He ran up a huge Room Service bill — money didn't seem to be an object because he paid in full — but he destroyed the bed, ruined several pieces of furniture and smoked so many cigars that the two rooms on either side couldn't be used for several days because they smelled so bad. He was promptly awarded a place on the banned list.

Now here he was again.

"If he comes back," Salter said, "we won't open the door."

Philip agreed.

A dozen minutes later, the Aston Martin pulled up at the front door. The driver waited for someone to come out — Philip and Salter peeked around the corner and saw that he was still alone — and then he started honking his horn.

When no one came to see what he wanted after more than five minutes of constant noise, he threw his car into gear and, obviously annoyed, sped away.

Immediately, Salter got on the phone and rang the three hotels the man had mentioned to Philip, to tell the night staff there that a potential problem was heading their way.

Salter was still on the line when a call came in to the switchboard at 4:40 from a man who said that he wished to book the entire hotel for a wedding the following week. The operator explained the nature of the call, so Salter took it. "The entire hotel, sir? I'm afraid that is impossible."

The caller snapped, "Do you realize how much money you're turning down?"

"Sir, I'm afraid there is no way I can take that booking. May I suggest you ring back after eight am and ask to speak to the General Manager. I'm sure he will do everything he can to help you."

"I want the entire hotel. I will ring back."

But he never did.

No sooner had Salter hung up than a man arrived at the front door, wearing overalls, saying that he was the contract plasterer. Because it seemed like such a strange hour for someone to show up for work, Salter asked him to wait outside while he checked to see if anyone was expecting him. Unable to find any instructions to say that a plasterer would be working in the Hotel that morning, he explained to the man that he could not allow him inside, and suggested he return later. The supposed plasterer went away. No one ever saw him again.

The front bell rang again at 5. Two police officers from West End Central were there to report that they'd just arrested a drunk in the alley behind the Hotel. He'd identified himself as an employee of the Hotel. Bizarrely, the police explained, the man had two fresh trout stuffed down the front of his trousers. Salter took the details. Needless to say, the man's employment was terminated by 9 am.

At 5:15, the front bell rang yet again.

A fairly tall man wearing a shabby sports jacket asked to see his friend Susan who was staying, he said, in 601–602. Without unlocking the door, Philip wondered, "Do you have the lady's surname?"

The man thought for a moment, "Maybe it's Bakersfield."

Philip said, "You're not sure?"

"Yes," he answered. "It's Bakersfield. She's in 601 and 602."

The name didn't ring a bell, at least he didn't recall having seen it when he checked the guest register earlier that evening, so he left the gentleman standing on the pavement while he went to inform Salter. Together they went through the guest list. There was a woman in 601–602, but her name wasn't Bakersfield. Nor was there anyone in the Hotel with an even slightly similar name.

Returning to the front door, Philip informed the man that his friend was not a guest at the Hotel.

Without saying anything more, the man walked away.

However, five minutes later he was back, now demanding to be taken to 601–602 because his friend Susan was waiting for him.

Philip apologized that he could not allow the gentleman into the Hotel.

But the man was insistent. "That's the correct room number. Now let me in."

"I'm sorry, sir." Philip turned and walked away.

The man eventually left, only to return ten minutes later, wanting to use the telephone because he was absolutely sure that Susan was staying at the Hotel.

Salter explained that non-residents were not permitted to enter the Hotel at such an early hour and that even if his friend Susan were there — which he insisted she wasn't — there would have to be instructions from her to allow a guest in. As there were no such instructions, Salter said, "I'm afraid there is nothing I can do."

The gentleman went away.

Half an hour later, a call came in to the switchboard asking to be connected to Rooms 601–602.

Unaware that a man had been refused entry at the front door three times, the operator nevertheless followed strict instructions and requested, "May I have the name of the guest you're calling, please."

The man on the other end of the line told her, "Susan."

She said, "Susan who?"

He said, "It's . . . my friend Susan . . . er, Bakersfield."

Sensing that something was wrong — after 20 years at the Hotel switchboard, she could tell which calls were legitimate and which ones were suspect — she glanced at her computer screen to see that there was no one named Bakersfield registered at the Hotel. "I'm sorry, sir, but I'm unable to put you through."

He hung up, but rang back right away, now ordering her to put him through to 601–602.

Again she politely refused. And this time when he hung up, she called Salter to tell him.

Enough was enough, he decided, and phoned the police. He informed them that they had a nuisance problem and described the man. The desk sergeant promised to notify the patrol, who would keep an eye out for him. "If he comes back, ring us straight away."

But the man did not return. Nor did he ever phone again.

The only thing Salter could do now was to make a point of leaving a note in his log so that Touzin could bring it up at his morning meeting, and remind all the hall porters, everyone working the front desk and all of the telephone operators that someday the man might return.

By 6, Salter was beginning to think about early arrivals and early departures. He'd just finished putting all the morning reports together for Touzin when Mr Saunders in Room 522 rang to ask for a lot of extra towels. Salter said, "Certainly sir," fetched some from a supply cupboard and brought them to the room. When he got there, he found Mr Saunders holding bloodied towels to his face. Salter asked what happened.

Saunders said, "I fell over a chair and I think I've broken my nose."

"I'll call a doctor, sir, right away."

Saunders said, "I am a doctor."

"Oh." That stopped him. "Is there anything I can do?"

Just then, Abel arrived with a bucket of ice.

Taking the extra towels from Salter and the ice from Abel, Saunders said, "You've done it, thank you," and shut the door.

A few minutes later, a very well-dressed Middle Eastern gentleman rang the bell and asked to see the manager. Philip escorted him into the Front Hall where Salter greeted him. The gentleman explained, "I would like a deluxe room."

Salter asked, "Have you a reservation, sir?"

"No."

"Certainly sir. May I have your name, please. I'll check if anything's available. Have you ever stayed with us before?"

He gave Salter his name and answered, "Yes. I have stayed here often."

The gentleman had no luggage, which was a bad sign. But Salter wanted to see the guest history before he made a decision.

Except the gentleman didn't have a guest history.

Nor was there a deluxe room available. Salter returned to the Front Hall and was just about to explain that, unfortunately, the Hotel could not accommodate him, when the gentleman began name dropping. He asked about certain members of staff — "Are they still here? I haven't seen them in a while" — and also about the previous manager. "I haven't met the new one."

Worried that he might have made a mistake in checking the guest history — there was always the possibility he'd not spelled the man's name properly — and not wanting to insult a guest who clearly knew people at the Hotel, Salter confessed that he didn't have a deluxe room available. "I'm afraid sir, all I have left are suites . . ."

"That will be fine," the gentleman said.

Salter quoted him full rack.

Without blinking, the gentleman produced £1000 in cash and handed it to him. "As a deposit."

In exchange, Salter handed the man a registration card. "Welcome back to the Hotel."

Once the gentleman had filled in the card, Salter escorted him to his suite. It seemed straightforward enough, except that, unbeknownst to Salter, the gentleman would check out by 1 that same afternoon.

There were no charges on his bill. He didn't make any phone calls. He didn't use the mini bar. He didn't order anything from Room Service.

And later, when Salter mentioned the gentleman's name to those members of staff whom he'd claimed to know, they said they'd never heard of him.

"How was your night, Adam?" Touzin asked cheerfully as he stepped into the lobby at 7:15.

An exhausted Salter handed over his logbook. "Nothing much happens here at night."

~ 11 ~

$\mathcal{D}$ANIEL AZOULAI HAD JUST COME to work when the Chef phoned to say he wanted to show him the new selection of bread. Making a face — "He always rings at the wrong time" — Azoulai walked downstairs to the Chef's office, where Lesnik went through each item.

There were three different white rolls, a semi-brown, a sourdough and a raisin. Lesnik had already taken colour photos of the bread so that Azoulai could explain the new selection to his staff.

"We'll monitor how many of each the clients take over the next few weeks so that we'll have a better idea of how many to bake each day."

Azoulai said, "Fine."

"All of them should be served slightly warm, except the sourdough."

He said, "Fine," again.

The Chef went on with his speech.

Azoulai began studying one of the rolls.

Oddly shaped, it looked like branches coming off the trunk of a tree. It also struck Azoulai as being much too big for one portion. He broke one in half. "Either the client has to get one whole piece or, if he takes it like this" . . . he held up both halves . . . "the next client will think he's getting someone else's bread."

Lesnik answered, "Let the waiter explain to the client . . ."

Azoulai snapped, "The waiters don't have time to explain the bread to everyone . . ."

"If it's properly presented the customer himself will ask."

"They don't have time . . ." He let it drop because he didn't want to get into an argument.

When Lesnik was finished, Azoulai headed upstairs. Stopping in the restaurant kitchen, he asked, "What's the soup of the day?"

Christian told him, "Pea and mint, slightly chilled."

"Consommé?"

"Chicken."

"Anything missing from the menu?"

"No."

With that in mind, still thinking about the oddly shaped bread, he began preparing the restaurant.

Half an hour later, once all the waiters were in, the Chef interrupted him again, this time to assemble everyone in the restaurant kitchen to show them the new dishes for the weekly menu.

Lesnik had reluctantly given in to Krenzer over changing from a daily to a weekly menu — in the end, he didn't have much choice — but had only half-agreed that it made some economic sense to do it that way. He remained adamant that a weekly menu limited his ability to cook with the markets.

He'd also lost the dessert battle.

There used to be a daily dessert special on the set-price menu, but the waiters quietly put an end to that. Because the special dessert was made to order in the pastry kitchen, whenever anyone asked for it the waiters had to go downstairs to fetch it. Desserts on the trolley were more convenient — no stairs to climb — so the trolley desserts were the ones they preferred. Lesnik understood why the waiters sold fewer and fewer specials, but here too Krenzer seemed to be on their side, so Lesnik threw up his hands in defeat and the daily dessert special was stopped.

Now he had six plates laid out on a serving table. One of the younger cooks was perched on a stepladder to take photos of the new dishes, while the waiters jostled for position to see them.

Going through every item, one by one, Lesnik told the waiters precisely what it was, how it was described on the menu and how it should look when they served it.

Azoulai studied everything very carefully, making notes on a copy of the menu.

The Chef was concluding his discourse with the bread — "Never offer less than four different varieties" — when Azoulai interrupted, pointing to one dish in particular that bothered him. "It needs vegetables."

Lesnik stopped long enough to respond, "Vegetables should be served separately."

"Then it takes two people to serve the dish."

"It looks better this way."

Azoulai shook his head. "It still takes two people to serve it."

Secured permanently onto the wall in François Touzin's office, in between the two curtained windows that look out onto the street, just beyond his reach, was a small black panel — someone must have put it there ages ago when General Managers could, with self-possessed grandeur, push a button to summon an employee — and two rather ugly light bulbs.

One was green. The other was supposed to be red, except that it was orange. When the green one flashed, it was a sign from the doorman or from the Front Hall porter that a VIP was arriving. When the orange one flashed — pretending to be the "red alert" signal — it meant a royal, or at least someone who should be considered a V-VIP, was arriving. For the green light, Touzin tried to make himself available. For the orange one, he believed he didn't have a choice.

And it was the orange one that went off a little after noon.

He jumped up from his desk and walked out to the Front Hall, getting there just in time to welcome the Princess of Wales. She was having lunch with her step-mother in the restaurant. Touzin escorted her in and wished her a pleasant meal.

Azoulai now took over, squiring her to table 107 — near the front in the corner on the right. He pulled a chair out for her and held it while she sat. He purposely had her facing the restaurant, because she liked that and, anyway, he figured it couldn't hurt the Hotel's reputation when other customers came in and saw her there.

In the kitchen, word went out, "Diana's here."

But Christian had other things on his mind. He was annoyed that some of his cooks were forgetting to season dishes properly. So he took a salt carton, cut out the side of it — where the word SALT was written in big letters — and tied a string to it. "Anyone who forgets to season a dish," he warned, "wears this around his neck for the rest of the day."

The dozen cooks working there with him grumbled in unison.

He shoved the kitchen equivalent of a dunce's cap aside just as the first orders came in from the restaurant. Taking each pink slip in turn, he reeled off the orders loudly enough that everyone in the kitchen could hear him. Two soups of the day. Two terrines. Two sea bass. One sole. One tournedos. Two raviolis. One salmon.

Each station — sauce, fish, meat, salad and vegetables — answered, "Oui chef," telling him that the orders had been received.

After punching the time on the pink slips, he clipped each one onto the highest of three racks — just above the hot table where the waiters arrived to fetch their orders — leaving it there until the entrée came out. When a cook delivered a plate to him, Christian inspected it before passing it along to the waiters. Then he took the pink slip and lowered it to the next rack, waiting for the main course to come.

A waiter appeared with the order for table 107. The Princess of Wales was having asparagus and grilled Dover sole. No vegetables. No dessert.

After calling out her order, Christian fetched an asparagus tray but didn't like the way it looked. He glanced up, to the far side of the kitchen where dishes were washed. Someone should have been polishing silver. Finding no one there, he cursed and shouted, "Back of House?"

No answer.

Now he yelled over the intercom that carried his voice downstairs, "Back of House?"

After a few minutes a young man in overalls came upstairs.

"You work right over there," Christian berated him. "When I'm here, you're there. Now polish this."

The fellow sheepishly took the platter.

A salesman showed up to see the Chef. He had to wait for half an hour — because the Chef was busy and, anyway, salesmen were always showing up to sell something — but eventually he was shown in.

The product was an oven timer and for the first few minutes the man went through a lot of bowing and scraping. He obviously thought that, if he scored here, the Hotel could become one of his major clients. When he finally got around to setting up the small device — it looked like a Geiger counter, complete with all sorts of lights that were supposed to blink and bells that were supposed to chime — he bragged about how it would help the pastry chef make the perfect soufflé.

Lesnik nodded politely.

The salesman plugged it in and punched the button to begin his demonstration.

Absolutely nothing happened.

He tried again.

Still nothing.

There was a lot of embarrassed chatter from the salesman about how there must be something wrong with the plug while he fumbled with it. He got it working for a few seconds, before it stopped again. His face flushed as he made more excuses. "This is our test model. Although the actual timer looks like this, once you plug it in . . ."

The Chef shuffled his feet.

"You see, it's programmed, there's a key . . ." He spoke quickly, knowing that he was losing the sale. "Once you've got it programmed to your recipe, you turn the key and then no one can change it. You will always get it done the way you want it . . ."

In the nick of time, the machine started to work.

Lesnik was courteous enough to let the man go through his pitch.

"This will guarantee that it is always done your way . . ."

When the man was finished, the Chef thanked him for dropping in. The salesman apologized again for the faulty test model, handed the Chef a pile of brochures and assured him that the real thing never failed. The Chef asked Marie to see the salesman out and, when he was gone, Lesnik took the brochures and tossed them away.

The Chef and his sous-chefs met for a meal every day after the luncheon service was finished, sitting around the table in Lesnik's private dining room.

"We didn't have any sorrel," William said.

Henry told him, "I've ordered it."

"Pumpkin seed oil." Lesnik pointed at Henry. "We need that too."

Christian brought in a platter of chicken breasts with an herb crust.

"They eating this upstairs too?" the Chef asked, referring to the waiters.

Christian said they were.

"Good." He was pleased because the dish had been prepared for a banquet, except that Jarman was told at the last minute there were 30 fewer covers than originally ordered. It meant there were now 30 extra pieces of chicken. Instead of letting the waiters order anything they wanted off the menu, the Chef decided they'd have to eat this like everyone else.

When their meal was finished, the Chef went straight into his menu meeting.

They all had a copy of the seasonal menu, on which they noted dishes they wanted to remove, or highlighted dishes they wanted to keep. Each of them had a vote. Lesnik had a veto.

The restaurant staff had a vote too, but Lesnik tended to go with his chefs' opinions before he'd seriously entertain any other suggestions. The way he saw it, the waiters only came up with ideas that satisfied themselves and a few of their regular clients. They never saw the big picture. But then, Lesnik reminded everybody often, this wasn't about democracy.

"The grilled wild salmon stays," he announced. "But we'll change the presentation."

"What about the scallops and langoustines?" Henry asked. "It's a colourful dish and it sells well."

"The baked sole sells well too," he said, "but it's been on the menu long enough. We need to put something else there. I think we'll keep the steamed turbot."

Prepared with spinach, roasted scallops and langoustines, Henry reminded him, "Scallops again."

"It took a long time to get it right. We'll keep it."

"It's a good dish," Christian volunteered.

The Chef agreed. "It's good for at least one more menu. Maybe two." He pointed to a pair of starters. "But these both go." One was goose liver ravioli served with wild mushrooms and lobster. The other was risotto of fresh truffles with shellfish. "They're out. Your tagliatelle dish . . . we'll see about putting it here."

Christian grinned triumphantly.

However, before Lesnik would put it on the menu, he'd serve it to the waiters. It wasn't so much that he was looking for their opinions, more catering to their egos. Getting their approval for a new dish was important if the dish was ever going to succeed. If they didn't think it would sell, they wouldn't feature it and the dish would become a self-fulfilling failure. The opposite was also true. If they liked it, they'd recommend it and sell a lot of it, reconfirming their own opinions that it was a good dish.

He knew how waiters thought that because the Chef rarely if ever saw clients he never had to take any heat from the guests. He knew how waiters believed that, when someone was unhappy with the food, they were the ones who got hell for it. He'd heard waiters say, so many times, when we complain to the Chef, he shoots the messenger.

But that wasn't the way Lesnik saw it.

Waiters were an uphill battle.

Waiters, he figured, always had two people to blame. The clients. And the chef. Never themselves.

The Kuwaiti Ambassador's wife came to see Jarman and Lesnik, bringing with her two menus that had been proposed by the chef at Buckingham Palace for the Queen's State Banquet.

Sitting around the table in the Chef's dining room, she stressed that it was important that he not duplicate any dish the palace was serving. But he already knew that.

The first menu consisted of something called Glengarry Paté — he guessed that was a cold game paté — chicken breast with tarragon in an herb sauce, leeks in butter, squash, potato croquettes, a beet salad and an apple crêpe dessert. The second started with a cream of pea soup, went on to fillet of brill, then duck breast, with poached asparagus, carrots, potatoes and a green salad, before ending with guava ice cream for dessert. Neither struck Lesnik as being very adventurous. But then, the kitchens at Buckingham Palace, although professional, had never been known for particularly adventurous cooking.

Both menus had been approved by the Queen and would be presented to the Amir to choose one. Because this was the return match, the menu discussed at the Hotel would first be presented to the Amir for his approval and then sent to the Queen for hers. And unless there was something totally out of order on either menu — an unlikely possibility — the Amir would, presumably, be too polite to refuse the Queen's offering and the Queen would, presumably, be too polite to refuse the Amir's.

The Chef needed to know, "What is the Amir's preference? What does he like? What does he dislike?"

The Ambassador's wife described something with an unpronounceable name that he was especially fond of, consisting of boiled milk infused with cardamom.

"What do you do with it?" Lesnik asked.

She told him, "You thicken it a little with some starch and pour it into a cup."

"Oh," he smiled politely. "What else does he like?"

She answered, "Dates and chocolate and yogurt and pumpkin."

That was better. "All right, why don't we begin with pumpkin soup? Yes, pumpkin soup thickened with Greek yogurt and seasoned with saffron. It would be very light, and garnished with little pearls of pumpkin, some bay leaves and thyme. How does that sound?"

She liked that.

Next came the fish course. He said, since Buckingham Palace didn't have a salmon dish, perhaps he could do something with wild salmon.

"No," she said. "We would like to supply the fish ourselves. There is a very special fish that is found only in our waters. In Arabic it is called *hamoor*."

"What's the name in English?"

"I don't know."

He asked her to describe the fish, but "Something like a sea bass" wasn't much help. "How does the Amir like it served?"

She told him, "With a red sauce."

"What kind of red sauce?"

"Like a tomato soup."

He forced a smile, sensing all the potential problems that a dish like this could cause. "I think that before I could come up with any suggestions, I should see the fish. Perhaps I could also ask that one of the Embassy's chefs show me how he cooks it."

"A very good idea," she said, and promised to have a sample of the fish delivered to him. "We will also supply the plates and cutlery for the banquet. There will be one set for the head table, and another for the rest of the room."

Here, too, the Chef envisaged problems. In some cases what was served, and in all cases how much he prepared, depended on the size and the shapes of the dinner service. "Would it be possible for me to see the plates while I am still preparing the menu?"

She promised to get samples of those to him as well. "Oh, by the way, the Embassy will supply two chefs to prepare the rice, because rice in our part of the world is prepared in a special manner."

Without hesitation, Lesnik said, "That will be fine." But he wasn't going to have chefs he didn't know cooking in his kitchen.

"They will be most welcome to use the staff kitchen to cook anything they want."

She must have thought he was being very gracious. "For the main course," she went on, "we were wondering if you could do a typical dish, such as a whole stuffed lamb."

"For a small dinner," he explained, "that would be possible. But with a banquet for so many people, it would be very difficult. May I suggest that, if you want roast lamb, we bring it out already sliced on each plate." He was thinking of ways to simplify the service. "And I would like to cook it medium, you know, lightly pink." He'd forgotten that the Queen liked her lamb well done, to the point of being overcooked.

"Yes, lamb," she said. Then suddenly remembered, "You know, there is supposed to be a dinner on the Wednesday in the City, possibly at Mansion House. They might serve lamb there."

If they did, Lesnik would have to rethink the main course. "We can hold off on that for now. And when we decide on the main course, we can then choose the vegetables."

"The Amir likes desert truffles."

Knowing this to be a very starchy fungus with no particular taste, Lesnik skilfully talked her out of that, in favour of more standard Western vegetables such as carrots, tomatoes and leeks.

They moved on to dessert.

"The Amir likes chocolate, honey, cardamom, coconut, strawberries and pears."

"All right." He thought about that for a moment. "How about a roasted caramelized pear with honey and cardamom ice cream, wild strawberries and spun sugar?"

It sounded fine to her.

Jarman asked about wine. Normally there wouldn't be any alcohol because Muslims weren't supposed to drink and Kuwait was officially dry. Whether or not wine would be served only to the European guests, she said, was something she'd have to check on.

However, she was sure that the Arab guests would have only water and fruit juice. Jarman then suggested that coffee would be served in the French Salon and the Drawing Room because he knew the Queen liked that. The Ambassador's wife said the Embassy would supply their own coffee. The Chef said he would prepare *petits fours* to go along with it, probably using fruit and nuts typical of the region — dates, nougat and pistachios.

The menu started to take shape.

Towards the end of the afternoon, each sous-chef made up his market list for the next day, filling in preprinted forms on which there was room to add quantities and the name of a preferred supplier.

Two boxes of cucumbers. Six bunches of radishes. Two boxes of curly endive. A kilo of *foie gras*. 125g of Beluga caviar. Meat. Fish. Fruit. Vegetables.

The forms were compiled and handed to the Chef for his approval. Once that was done, he sent them on to Purchasing.

Huddled into a small office in the basement, not far from the Timekeeper, the Purchasing staff of two bought everything the Hotel needed, from bath gel to toilet paper, from pens, pads, sheets and blankets to milk, eggs, flour and butter. On behalf of the kitchen alone, they spent £3000 a day.

They used to buy a lot of cheeses for the restaurant because Lesnik believed that his clients wanted them. A couple of thousand pounds each month was spent importing cheese from throughout Europe. But the restaurant sold only a small portion of it every week, and Lesnik had to admit that the cheese course was a loss. His orders were reduced to six different French cheeses and four different English cheeses, and left at that.

Every market order out was recorded in detail, and every delivery in was checked against the market list. Someone from Purchasing actually stood at the back door inspecting everything — counting quantities, checking weights, looking at quality.

When the orders arrived in the kitchen — in the reception area in front of the pastry station — either Lesnik or one of his sous-chefs re-inspected everything, particularly for quality — size, colour, smell, texture and taste. And if something wasn't absolutely right, it went straight back to the supplier.

From there, meat, fish and game were taken to the various cold rooms where they were labelled — which included the name of the supplier and the date it came in — then stored on large stainless steel trays. In the old days, there used to be a qualified butcher working in the kitchen who'd cut meat as it came in. But after the old butcher retired and the Chef fired his replacement, some accountant reviewing the budgets decided Lesnik would have to make do without a butcher. So now he required his suppliers to pre-cut most meat — which they did, reluctantly. When they forgot, or simply wouldn't, or when the Chef wanted it butchered in a special way, he had to assign a sous-chef to do it — a major annoyance, because it tied up one of his staff for however long that took. Being under-staffed — at least Lesnik thought they were — meant no one had time to waste.

The night before, William had decided he needed some fresh morel mushrooms, so he had got on the phone and had found a supplier who stocked them. Pampering the Hotel, the supplier told William that his van driver would drop them off on his way home. The mushrooms did, indeed, show up as promised, but the bill for them only appeared on the next day's invoice.

Purchasing examined the delivery against the invoice and couldn't find the mushrooms. The driver who brought the morning shipment wasn't the same driver who'd brought the mushrooms, and didn't know they'd already been delivered. So he got angry that someone had forgotten to load them on his van. That's when Purchasing discovered that an order of pears was missing too.

A hasty phone call was made to the supplier, who explained that the morels had already been delivered and insisted that the pears must have come with the mushrooms.

Riffling through a stack of orders, Purchasing found one for the mushrooms, but there was nothing for the pears. So the driver was sent back to get them. However, before he left, he handed Purchasing an invoice to sign. They refused to do it, knowing that if someone signed an order before it was complete that might be the last anyone would ever see of that order.

The disgruntled driver mumbled that he'd be back.

William then walked into Purchasing and asked them to check the price of blueberries.

Someone announced, "Five-fifty a punnet."

He shook his head, "Too expensive. Send them back. Also, send the flat mushrooms back. They're too big. I need them smaller. And the raspberries. They're too soft. They go back too."

When the driver returned later that morning with the pears, he was handed the goods William would not accept. A "goods returned" note went with it, which the driver had to sign. Purchasing kept a copy. Either the items would be exchanged or a credit would be issued against them.

There was a time when wines and spirits were the only things that didn't go through Purchasing. They were ordered through a Group office because someone decided that, by ordering in bulk, they'd get a better deal. But, after a while, the *sommeliers* started complaining and, when the accountants looked into it, they discovered the Group wasn't actually saving any money.

The Hotel's wine cellar was nothing more than a storeroom in the basement, with a lot of standard warehouse metal shelving. They stocked 10 different mineral waters, but only 5 different beers, because the clientele wasn't a beer-drinking crowd. However, they had 15 different scotches and 10 different malt whiskies. The oldest vintage wine they held was 1970. Touzin would have personally appreciated more depth to the wine stock, but he knew that most clients wouldn't pay the price for old wines. Anyway, if someone wanted older vintages, the Hotel could always get them with very little notice.

Most suppliers and shippers were happy to deal directly with the Hotel, although many of them admittedly found the Hotel a very tough customer. And the kitchen was the toughest of all. Every time a supplier changed his sources, the Chef insisted on a sample which he could cook and taste, so that he could make certain it was what it was supposed to be. The Chef also reserved the right to change his mind at any time, to send back anything he didn't want. On top of that, the Hotel categorically refused to pay delivery charges.

Occasionally a supplier tried to sneak delivery charges through, putting carriage onto the bill and hoping no one would notice. But Purchasing always noticed — they got their kicks finding mistakes in bills — and, when Purchasing found something, word shot out to the accountants, don't pay this. Some suppliers only learned the hard way that, these days, someone at the Hotel was paying attention to every penny.

~ 12 ~

N American guest named Goodman, who'd checked into the Hotel without any luggage because British Airways had managed to lose it for him, spotted Rory Purcell standing in the corridor outside his room. He stared at him for a long time, then asked, "By any chance, do you work here?"

"Yes, sir."

Purcell was just about to introduce himself when the man cut in, "Listen. I've got a problem. My luggage got lost by some genius at British Airways. All I have with me are the clothes on my back. I wore them on the flight over and they're pretty gamy. How can I get all my clothes laundered right away so that I can get out of here sometime today. I've got an appointment for dinner. Otherwise I'm stuck in this room."

"Have you tried ringing for the valet? Usually he can help . . ."

"I did, I did. But he told me he couldn't get my clothes back in an hour and I've got to get out of here."

Purcell looked at the man, decided they were about the same size, and tried to recall what he had hanging in the cupboard in his office. "I'll be right back."

Fifteen minutes later, the man was on the way to dinner, dressed in Purcell's clothes.

Maintenance was a daily routine that, at least to the uninitiated, bordered on being repetitively dull. A maid's call button was not working. A glass shelf was broken. A door lock stuck. An armchair had to be taken away because the leg was cracked or the upholstery was ripped. A window handle was broken. A television didn't work. A towel rail didn't heat. A shower leaked. But, to a maintenance man, all that added up to a great day. Purcell was constantly hoping for something to break — as long as it didn't reflect poor maintenance — so that he could install a better one.

Two dozen people worked for him, including engineers, painters, plumbers, carpenters and electricians. His most common headache was bath overflows. They were all the more annoying because they inconvenienced the person in the room below. Frequently they were caused by Japanese guests, because they bathed in running water.

Despite his Irish brogue, Purcell was born in Massachusetts. His parents had left Tipperary to make their fortune there, but in 1963, when he was two, they went back to Cork. He trained as a marine engineer and, although he spent time at sea, he wound up plying his trade in hotels. Touzin discovered him at the Inn on the Park. He was perhaps the "youngest" Chief Engineer in the business.

At that place, the guys in the workshops had installed an infrared beam on the stairs to tip them off when the boss was coming. It gave them time to look busy. When he came to the Hotel, Purcell discovered that his predecessor had a different, less forceful personality which was reflected in the way that he played his part on the senior management team. It was the opposite of Purcell's style. Purcell was a more "in your face" sort of guy.

Touzin recognized right from the start that the old engineer — who'd been at the Hotel for years — couldn't get the resources he needed. Purcell, on the other hand, would fight for his territory. So Touzin brought him into months of meetings with architects and builders. Together they drew up plans for the Hotel's refurbishment and came up with an estimate of costs. Then they met for several more months with the company to get the best value for the money.

Meetings that went into excruciating detail were held between the Hotel's management, the company's accountants and the various professionals they were about to employ — architects, quantity surveyors, designers, project managers and contractors — and at each step along the way, it was as if the Hotel's guests were also at those discussions. Because at each step along the way, the question was endlessly repeated, how will this affect our guests.

A budget was finally agreed at just over £30 million. That included the air-conditioning and plumbing refit throughout the Hotel, the refurbishment of the sixth and seventh floors, maintenance work on the roof, and the creation of new staff areas in the basement. There was to be a new staff entrance and, Touzin insisted, a modern, well equipped and considerably more comfortable office for the Timekeepers. There were other changes Purcell wanted to make, but he understood he wasn't going to get anywhere if the company thought he was wasting money. So he planned everything in such a way that he maximized revenue during the renovation. He would do all the work while guests were still in residence, even though that meant he couldn't just worry about the room he was working in, he also had to worry about people sleeping next door.

General Managers, he knew, never gave the Chief Engineer the opportunity to say, I don't have the resources. When a job needed to be done, they wanted it done. The simplistic view was that a good Chief Engineer was someone who could do for 50p what any idiot could do for £1. He looked at it in another way. Anyone can build something that crosses a river. One guy throws enough rocks into it to get across. Another guy comes up with a suspension bridge. The trick is not to let them budget for rocks. So he pulled out his "good news, bad news" routine. It had always worked in other hotels. "I've got good news," he'd announce. "I just renegotiated a new gas price." The boss's guard would drop. Then he'd just happen to mention, "Oh, by the way, I need some money to rewire the lighting in the main ballroom."

He was counting on it working with Touzin.

"The good news," he declared, "is that I've devised a way to re-plumb a bathroom from the room below that is less costly than doing it the usual way."

Touzin liked that.

"The bad news," he added, "is that it's more expensive."

"Huh?"

Without giving Touzin too long to think about that, Purcell explained that to replumb a bathroom in normal circumstances he'd have to remove everything inside it. The bath, the toilet, the basin, the taps and the heated towel rails would all have to go. That took the room out of service for a long time, inconvenienced guests next door and maximized breakages. Because many of the Hotel's bathrooms were pure art deco, they were protected by English Heritage, who required the Hotel to save all the original fixtures and fittings. Breakages displeased them. Lose an historic basin and they'd create all sorts of red tape to protect everything else in the Hotel.

What he wanted to do instead was to remove the bathroom ceiling in the room below, bore through the structural slab and re-plumb the existing fittings from underneath. It was a more complicated way of working and, consequently, more expensive. It would also mean that two rooms would have to be taken out of service for each bathroom refit.

But it would get the work done faster, inconvenience fewer people and minimize breakages.

In the long run, he needed Touzin to believe that the more expensive method was actually the less costly.

Touzin knew he needed to bring in new blood, not to produce change simply for the sake of change, but to improve on the way the Hotel functioned. That's what the fellow from Euro Disney was supposed to be about.

A tall, fair-haired 41-year-old who was born in Denmark to a Danish mother and an American diplomat father, his name was Michael Duncan.

The new Assistant General Manager got to the Hotel every morning by 6:30 and spent two hours in his tiny, upstairs office going through the arrivals list, checking names against guest histories and sending a handwritten welcome to all repeat clients. Reception knew to bleep him whenever regular guests arrived, so that he could greet them personally.

He walked around saying hello, not just to the guests, but to the staff as well. That both he and Touzin knew everyone's name was also a surprise to the staff. Then, he ate breakfast every morning in the canteen. Before he arrived, senior management used to breakfast in the restaurant with the guests. But Touzin put an end to that. He also ate lunch in the staff canteen. And after his first few weeks, one of the staff came up to him and confessed that it was the first time any of them had ever seen senior management there.

One problem with this place, Duncan quickly sensed, was that many people on the staff were afraid to make decisions. It was a vestige of the past, when none of them was allowed to make decisions. That's the way all hotels used to be run. Employees had been encouraged to leave their brains at the door. But it couldn't be like that any more.

This was the modern equivalent of the 18th-century stately home. It operated much along the same lines. Although it needed to look crisp and clean, and to respond to clients' needs with that traditional feel, it was nevertheless self-contained. Guests had, or could have, everything they needed.

Much of the outside world was deliberately shut off — there were men in liveried uniforms and string orchestras and servants who arrived in your room at the push of a button — because the Hotel was all about old-English standards, old-English values and old-English manners. It was an illusion of another time. But that too was a great British tradition.

Funny, Duncan thought, with a couple of Frenchmen, a Danish-American, a Yugoslav, an Irishman, a load of Brits who were born outside the country and at least 30 different nationalities working there, the Hotel retained an essential British character.

Duncan kept one of those little portable computers in the inside jacket pocket of his morning suit — his appointment diary was on it, as was his phone book and all the notes he'd write to himself throughout the day — and the instant Andrew Pierron spotted that, he reckoned he'd found a comrade.

Information Technology had not been rapidly embraced by the hotel industry. There were still too many people who honestly believed that, because computers replaced human beings, what you inevitably wound up with when you computerized a hotel was a nameless and faceless product. Many of the large chains were proof positive of that. Even something as basic as backing up the Hotel's entire computer system four times a day was seen by most of the staff as a chore instead of a necessity.

Getting them to understand wasn't easy.

When Pierron first started talking computers, and tried to explain what computers could do for the Hotel — how they could set people free from their desks to spend more time being a name and a face to the guests — his claims were greeted with scepticism as deeply rooted as the Hotel's tradition for service.

Now, there was an Assistant General Manager with his own tiny computer.

Standing six foot three, and with a quirky sense of humour, Pierron had a certain air of confidence about him, the sort of self-assurance that comes with always being taller than everyone else. His office was on the second floor, in an oddly shaped room where the back wall was considerably narrower than the front wall and the side walls sloped in to connect them. He filled the room with computers. Shelves were covered with boxes and software manuals. There was a large printer and a couple of strange contraptions that just sat on a table with wires coming out of the sides.

In many ways, people into computers are like folks who restore vintage aircraft and fly them at shows. It is never enough just to take off and land. They have to do inside loops and figures-of-eight and skim the ground upside-down. So Pierron tinkered with the Hotel's computer system and tweaked the software to do inside loops. He could push a few buttons and the computer showed, in graph form, occupancies and room rates and yield. It displayed critical factors geographically, so that within a few seconds anyone could see exactly how much money the Hotel had made over the past six months with guests arriving from Uruguay or Finland, or how many guests they'd had over the past year from Uzbekistan.

Willing to concede that it was as much for his own amusement as anything else, he'd also put the guest lists, arrivals, billing and the accounting system onto the computer. However, because not everybody had access to everything, the computer was still thought of as a slightly elitist contraption. Touzin could check to see arrivals on the screen at his desk, and he could get into the guest history files as well. But he couldn't make changes to the guest histories. He could see accounts receivable but he couldn't change anything there either.

Access to view and access to change were on a need-to-know basis, and it was Pierron who decided need to know.

He'd designated 45 employees, each of whom had their own password, for entry into the first level of access. Fewer than half had a second password that could take them into level two. The master password was known only to Pierron. He was the only person who could access and change everything on the computer — although Touzin insisted, just in case Pierron got hit by a bus, that somewhere in the building there had to be a sealed envelope, locked away, with the master password. But only a handful of the senior managers knew where it was.

Pierron felt he was winning, little by little. There were now computers in the front office, the back office, at the Concierges' desk and in the accounting office. But it wasn't going fast enough for his liking. He wanted to connect the Concierges to the Internet, giving them direct access to airline and train timetables and restaurant listings. In the back of his mind, he was already formulating plans for a very advanced information technology system that would, in effect, put the entire business — every aspect of it — within a keyboard's reach.

He knew that, with so much funding already committed to the refurbishment, his dreams were pie in the sky. But he saw a day when there would be computers throughout the Hotel, maybe even in the guests' rooms. If Pierron ever got his way, the world would be wired up.

Then again, it already was.

When American guests first began asking about using their laptop computers in the rooms, the Concierges and the maids didn't know what they were talking about. Eventually the call would be passed to Pierron, who had to explain that, because British telephone sockets were incompatible with American sockets, they would unfortunately not be able to use their modems. He quickly grew tired of having to make excuses. Realizing that the budget committee then knew as much about computers as the maids, Pierron took it upon himself to buy 20 adapters. Even then it was a struggle to get anyone to approve the purchase because the accountants refused to believe that these things were important.

Change, he reasoned, was all about gentle persuasion. So he decided it was finally time to play that game.

He'd heard about a group in the States called the Hotel Information Technology Association, understood what a good idea it was and formed the first European branch. Not surprisingly, he got himself named chairman. The next thing he did was to schedule the first annual HITA–European Branch luncheon at the Hotel. He invited Touzin and Duncan, both of whom said they would be there. Then he asked the company's MD to be the inaugural speaker.

Pierron was determined to get some heavyweights on his side.

Purcell was standing in the Head Cashier's office, admiring the old pigeonhole cupboard mounted on the rear wall — the panel of small boxes where keys and post were once kept for every room — when he turned around and happened to notice a large aluminium duct running up from the floor and through the skylight. "What the hell is this?"

Horvath answered, "Good question." He explained how one day, a few years ago, the floor in the office started to shake and the room started filling with dust. The cashiers, understandably concerned, looked down, and found a drill coming through the floor. No one in engineering had bothered to say anything to them about this. A few days later, the duct was in place. For the next few weeks, Horvath asked everybody he could find, what's this for? But no one ever gave him an explanation. No one seemed to know.

Inspecting it closely, following it with his eyes up through the skylight, Purcell had to admit, "I don't think it goes anywhere." He promised Horvath he'd find out what it was and why it was. He walked away thinking to himself, over the years so many bits and pieces have been added that none of it works properly now. In fact, it turned out that the aluminium duct didn't go anywhere.

Purcell stopped in the side corridor, near the Ladies' Lift, to write himself a note about the duct when a woman said to him, "You're part of the staff here, aren't you?"

Looking up, he recognised Mrs Daniel, a flamboyant old lady who flitted around in ostrich feathers and lace.

"Yes, ma'am, I am."

"Well, it's my air-conditioning," she complained. "It's not working. Why not? It should be working. But it's not. My beau won't come to the room because he says it's too hot."

"Your beau?" He guessed she had to be on the far side of 85.

"That's none of your business, young man. Your business is my air-conditioner."

He told her, "Madam, I assure you that the Chief Engineer will personally take care of it right away."

"He'd better," she warned. "I'm inclined to tell all my wealthy American friends about this and they'll stop coming here."

He smiled, "No you won't."

She retorted, "Oh yes I will."

"No, you won't," he repeated. "And the reason you won't tell all your wealthy American friends about this is because you'll give us a chance to fix it."

"Just one chance," she warned. "I'll be out for a few hours." She left him standing there.

By the time she came back, her air-conditioning was fixed, although he was still wondering about her beau.

He wrote up the incident in his log. Touzin read it the next morning and commented, at the meeting, that he'd done well. In response, Purcell reminded everyone on the staff, "The Chief Engineer should be the reason why a guest recalls a great plumbing experience."

~ 13 ~

HERE WAS SOMETHING SOLID AND reassuring about the Foyer when the string ensemble was playing in the corner. Seven old men in green waistcoats and black bow ties carefully wandering their way through the greatest hits of Ivor Novello, while waiters in full livery served champagne cocktails to men in expensive suits.

And in the room, women come and go, speaking of David Hockney.

♣

It was Officer of the Day in the Air Force and the Army, and Officer of the Deck in the Navy. Like the military, the Duty Manager shift at the Hotel was assigned on a rota basis — all senior managers, except Touzin, pulled the chore every 12–14 days. It meant being on call, resident in the Hotel, for a 24-hour stretch.

For Andrew Pierron, to be stuck there over a Friday night and all day Saturday was not his idea of a great start to the weekend. Still, the Hotel at the weekend was a pleasant enough place to be — slower, more relaxed, more like that 18th-century stately home.

He spent a good part of the early evening strolling around the lobby, greeting guests on their way in, saying good evening to guests on their way out, making his presence felt. His height and his black tails reinforced for clients the impression that the Hotel had stationed someone there to do their bidding.

A couple were asking the Concierge about a dinner reservation and a well-dressed young man was sitting in one of the armchairs in front of the Foyer, obviously waiting for someone to join him. The orchestra had just begun another set. Pierron checked his watch and thought for a moment about ringing the kitchen to order his meal, when a woman hurried in, carrying four large carrier bags from shops along Bond Street.

He smiled. "Let me get someone to help you with those."

She stopped, hesitated, stared at him, then grinned, "Thank you."

An American from California, somewhere in her late 30s or early 40s, this was her first visit to the Hotel. She'd come in on Thursday morning and was due to leave on Monday. Her stay had been booked through her company and the room had been paid for, in advance, with a company cheque. She was alone, in a single room. No one knew anything about her.

Taking the bags from her, Pierron nodded towards the Concierge and Wingrove called for one of the pages. The boy appeared, hurried over to the Duty Manager and took the shopping bags from him.

"Mrs Thomas is in 302," Pierron said.

After putting two of the white-braided rope-handled bags over his shoulder and grasping the others in his left hand, the porter escorted Mrs Thomas to the lift.

"Have a pleasant evening," Pierron said.

She looked back over her shoulder, smiled, "You too," and disappeared into the lift.

A gentleman came up to ask directions to Oxford Street, so he took the man to the front door and pointed to the corner. "Turn right there and you'll come to it." A couple wanted to know where the restaurant was, so he walked them into the restaurant and introduced them to Daniel Azoulai. Then one of the Foyer waiters presented him to a guest who'd been waiting, along with several other people, to be seated. "The gentleman does not have a tie."

"Certainly," Pierron said, leading the gentleman to the cloakroom, where the attendant opened a small cupboard. Stored there were collar studs, dinner suits, bow ties, shirts, ties and cufflinks. "I'm sorry the choice isn't all that extensive . . ."

The man helped himself to a tie and rejoined his party in the Foyer.

Now Pierron's bleeper sounded. He went to Reception and picked up one of the house phones. The operator asked him to wait a moment while she put through a call from Mr Ettinger in 318–319. "Where is my snowboard?"

"Your what, sir?"

"My snowboard. I'd like to know where it is."

"I'm sorry, sir," Pierron confessed, "I don't know what a snowboard is. Where did you leave it?"

"It's like a surfboard," Ettinger said impatiently. "Except it's for snow. I had it shipped over from New York yesterday. It was supposed to be delivered today. Where is it?"

"I don't know. But if you'll allow me to make some enquiries . . . If it's been delivered to the Hotel today, sir, I'll find it."

"It's been delivered," Ettinger insisted. "Trust me. It's just that it hasn't been delivered to me."

Pierron asked Reception if they knew anything about it — they didn't know what a snowboard was either — then checked with the Concierge, who hadn't seen anything that even closely resembled a snowboard. But when he poked his head into the luggage porters' room and asked there, one of them nodded, "A snowboard? Sure, I saw it."

"Where?"

He pointed to an empty space against the wall. "Right there."

"And where did you take it?"

"I gave it to Mr Bridgeman's driver. The bloke who arrived yesterday without a reservation."

Pierron realized he meant Peter Bridgeman, a long-standing client. "Why did you give it to his chauffeur?"

"Mr Bridgeman left his luggage and a carton to be picked up. The snowboard was on top of it. There wasn't anybody's name or anything on it. The driver came by this afternoon and I even asked him, is this for you? He said, it must be for Mr Bridgeman's children, so he took it."

"Where was the driver going?"

"To the airport."

"With Mr Bridgeman?"

"He was on a flight to New York."

"Terrific," Pierron mumbled, thought for a moment, then went to the back office where he sat down at Buckolt's desk and tapped into Mr Bridgeman's guest history. He found a number in New York, figured it was worth a shot, dialled it and got Mr Bridgeman's secretary on the line. He introduced himself and explained the situation. She knew what a snowboard was but said that Mr Bridgeman hadn't landed yet and probably wouldn't bother coming to the office until Monday.

"Would it be possible for you to reach him sometime this evening and, assuming that he has the snowboard with him, explain to him this is our error? If he would be kind enough to hold onto it, I'll make whatever arrangements are necessary to retrieve it."

She promised to do what she could.

Pierron then went to see Mr Ettinger. "I think, sir, that we've found your snowboard. Unfortunately, at the moment, it seems to be going to New York."

"New York?" Ettinger wasn't amused. "How the hell did that happen?"

"It is totally our fault, sir. And we will do everything we can to get it back to you right away. I've already contacted Mr Bridgeman's secretary in New York . . ."

"Bridgeman? Peter Bridgeman? I know Peter Bridgeman. How did he get my snowboard?"

Pierron told him the story.

Now Ettinger started to chuckle. "I'll tell you what. My wife is coming to London on Sunday. She's in New York now. Can you reach Bridgeman? If Peter can get the snowboard to her . . ."

So Pierron called Mr Bridgeman's secretary again and she eventually called Mr Bridgeman, who subsequently called Mrs Ettinger and, for the third time in as many days, the snowboard crossed the Atlantic.

Before long, Pierron's thoughts turned back to his stomach.

The best thing about being Duty Manager was that you could order anything you wanted off the menu and have it served in your room. So, once he decided that life in the Front Hall had slowed down enough that he could make an exit, he told the Concierge what room he'd be in, left a note for Adam Salter to say what room he'd be in and phoned the operator to let her know as well. He checked to make sure that his mobile phone was well charged — the Duty Manager had to carry a mobile with him at all times in case the Hotel phone system crashed — then he went to his own office to fetch his small overnight bag. From there, he walked upstairs to room 419.

As soon as he got inside, he took off his jacket, fell into the armchair, grabbed the Room Service menu and went through it — slowly and with pleasure — before ordering soup, lamb chops and a soufflé dessert.

The luxury of Room Service was a definite perk. But staying overnight didn't mean he could think of himself as a guest in the

Hotel. He was on call. If he was lucky, the phone wouldn't ring until 7 am when the operator woke him. Even though it was the Night Manager's watch — he had the bridge — the Duty Manager was there, just in case, representing the Admiral.

Now he went through what he hoped would be his final chore of the evening — "snagging" the room.

He inspected it for dust behind the mirrors and opened the magazines on the end table to see that no kids had drawn black teeth or spectacles on the pictures. One of the pre-set stations on the radio needed tuning — he retuned it — but the pre-set stations on the television remote were okay. He found an ink mark inside a lamp-shade, looked at the stock of stationery and counted the postcards. One window seemed stuck, so he gave it a tug and unstuck it. He then opened the mini bar to see that no seals were broken on the spirits. It seems some people drink the vodka, then refill the bottle with water or drink the Scotch and refill the bottle with tea. He also checked the sell-by date on the jar of mixed nuts and, sure enough, it had passed.

Because a hotel room didn't always "work," it was necessary for someone who knew how it was supposed to be to sleep in the bed, to take a shower in the bathroom, to push the floor waiter button, to look for draughts, to check if any furniture needed to be repaired. By design, the Duty Manager slept in a different room each night. It meant that, over the course of six or seven months, someone from the senior staff snagged every room of the Hotel. Any redecorated room was snagged within a week of the work being finished. The more exigent the Duty Managers were, the sooner faults showed up. And as long as it was the staff who found those faults — before a paying guest did — Touzin believed the room would always be up to standard.

Having found those things, Pierron honed in on the rest of the room. The paint work below the wardrobe door was chipped. Paint was flaking high up on one wall in the bathroom. There was no on–off knob for the towel rail.

Everything was recorded in his log for Touzin's attention. Minor faults would find their way into a memo from the General Manager to the Chief Engineer or the Executive Housekeeper. Major flaws would be discussed at the morning meeting. And nothing ever seemed to fall by the wayside. Touzin followed up on everything.

If a guest discovered that the radiator wasn't turned on, or the air-conditioning didn't work, or the shower curtain didn't keep the water off the floor, or the lights above the mirror were not bright enough, or the phone was too far from the desk to reach, or there wasn't a waste paper basket under the dressing table or there weren't any notepads next to the phone — Touzin figured that was directly down to Housekeeping not doing their job or Engineering not doing theirs or the Duty Manager not doing his.

When guests were paying for a room, Touzin insisted, guests had a right to find it in perfect condition and the Hotel had an obligation to make certain that they did.

A knock on the door broke into Pierron's thoughts. The waiter was there with a trolley. He wheeled it into the middle of the room, Pierron switched on the television, and the phone started to ring.

"Thanks," he said, motioning to the waiter to leave the food right there, and took the call.

"Mr Pierron," a woman said, "this is the operator. Mrs Thomas in 302 would like to speak to you."

He said, "Put her through, please."

"No sir. She would like to speak with you. Can you please go to her room."

He groaned, "All right," hung up, slipped on his jacket, checked to see that his shirt was tucked in and that his tie was straight, and headed for the stairs.

When he got to 302, he knocked loudly twice, then waited. He thought he heard a woman say something, but he wasn't sure whether it was "Come in" or "Just a moment," so he announced, "It's the Duty Manager."

Now she said more clearly, "It's open."

He turned the knob and pushed the door just enough that he could poke his head inside the room. "Good evening, Mrs Thomas. May I help you?"

"Yes, you can." She came around the corner, holding her dress up to the front of her. "Come in. Come in."

He stepped inside, but left the door ajar. "What can I do for you?"

"It's this dress. I can't get it closed. Can you zip it for me?" She turned her bare back to him and waited.

The dress was falling off her shoulders and it was obvious that she wasn't wearing a bra. He hesitated for a fraction of a second too long.

"Don't be afraid," she said. "I don't normally bite."

"Of course not," he said politely and opened the door a little wider before walking into the room to reach for her dress.

"You could have shut the door," she said, not looking at him.

"Let me help you with that." He tried to sound cheerful, as if this sort of thing happened all the time, as if he never once doubted her good intentions. "Here." He took the zip and pulled it up the back of the dress. "How's that?"

"Do you think you could just hook it on top, please?"

"Certainly." He did, then stepped back. "Will there be anything else?" Immediately he hated himself for asking such a dumb question. "Have a pleasant evening, ma'am." He retreated to the door.

She turned to grin at him.

He smiled nervously, bowed slightly, left her room and shut the door.

She needed someone to zip up her dress, he kept telling himself. That's all. She's alone and couldn't get her dress zipped up. Not that it would have been so difficult for her to do . . .

Just in case, before he sat down to his now lukewarm soup and quickly chilling lamb chops, he took the Duty Manager's log and wrote, "8:20: Mrs Thomas in 302 called to ask the Duty Manager to zip up her dress. I went to her room, she was alone, and helped her. The door stayed open."

To protect himself further, when he'd finished his meal, he put his jacket on and went downstairs into the Front Hall, to wait for the Night Manager and explain it to him.

Later, Adam Salter wrote in his log, "11:10 pm. Mr Pierron the Duty Manager informed me that Mrs Thomas in 302 had requested he come to her room to zip up her dress. He says that he went to Mrs Thomas's room at around 8:20 and kept the door open. He zipped up her dress and left right away."

Touzin read both log entries the next morning but chose not to comment on either at the meeting. Instead, he spoke privately to Pierron and then privately to Salter, telling them both they'd done the right thing. Just about the last problem he wanted was a sexual harassment suit. Anything of this nature had to be logged and kept on record.

"Perhaps," Pierron offered, "she just needed to have her dress zipped."

"Perhaps," Touzin said. "Perhaps."

On Saturday morning, Pierron ate breakfast in the staff canteen and when he was finished he wandered upstairs to welcome the first of the early check-ins.

As soon as she spotted him, one of the Hotel's older regular clients — one of those women of a certain age who had, for years, been on Carole Ronald's "special care" list — hurried up to him. Without bothering to say hello, she demanded, "I need another key."

"Yes, certainly, milady," he bowed and motioned towards Reception where he could cut a new door card for her.

"Not that sort of key," she snapped. "A key for my safe deposit box. Do you have a spare key for my safe deposit box?"

He suggested, "Milady, it wouldn't be very safe if we did."

She challenged him, as if all this was somehow his fault, "Well, I've lost mine."

"I'm afraid . . ." he knew her well enough to understand that he had to explain this very gently . . . "if the key is lost, we will need to call our locksmiths to drill into the box for you. Unfortunately, there will be a charge of £197.25."

"How much?" She raised her eyebrows. "That's a terrible imposition. Outlandish." She turned on her heels and headed back to her room. "I shall keep looking for mine."

Although there was a safe in every room to store passports, money and small valuables, many clients wanted bank vault-like protection both for their own safety and for insurance purposes. So the Hotel maintained permanent safe deposit boxes in a cramped room behind a locked door between the Front Hall and the Cashier's office made available to any guest on request.

Reinforced into two walls, running floor to ceiling and covered in thick, polished bronze, the boxes came in different sizes. The biggest of them could hold several large travelling cases. Each box had twin locks, and required that both the client's private key and the Cashier's master key be used at the same time. Access to the safe deposit room was so restricted, and limited to one guest at a time, that simply having a key wasn't enough. Every guest had to sign a card when they were allocated a box and then had to sign in — the signatures had to match — each time they wanted to open it. The Cashier's master key was stored in a safe and not everyone working in that office had access to it. At the same time, the cashiers were expected to know their guests. They were under strict instructions that if they didn't recognize a guest — irrespective of whether or not signatures matched — they were to make discreet but scrupulous checks on the person's identity before allowing anyone past the locked door.

Granted, most places were duly cautious with their safe deposit boxes. But not all of them took the same rigorously vigilant approach as the Hotel. A prime example of how even minor laxity can create disaster occurred some years ago, in another hotel, when an unscrutinized employee was able to make clay impressions, one by one, of every key. On the night he copied the last one, he emptied all the safe deposit boxes. Taken totally by surprise, the management learned something was amiss only when guests complained the next morning that they'd been robbed. The police didn't even have a suspect until that evening, when the employee didn't show up for work.

Inasmuch as space was limited, guests at the Hotel were expected to clear their safe deposit box when they checked out. However, a couple of dozen long-standing clients retained boxes, not necessarily because they had stuff to leave, but because they wanted to have the same box whenever they returned. Supposedly, the most desirable ones were the most accessible ones — those at eye level. At least, that's what guests believed. Except that guests never had to reach for a box — no matter where it was — because the Cashier always unlocked it, took it out of the wall and handed it to the guest.

Pierron learned a few days later that the lady had found her key. Clearly, the idea of shelling out £197.25 had concentrated her mind on where she'd hidden it. However, while no one liked to mention such things at the Hotel, at one point there were spare keys to the safe deposit boxes.

They were hidden in a locked safe, and only five staff members knew of their existence. And then, not all five had access to them. But on those very rare occasions when a spare key was brought out, it saved guests from missing flights. None of those guests seemed to mind.

However, Touzin minded.

When he heard that there were spare keys, he took it up with the Hotel's insurance company. And they minded too.

Faced with all sorts of possible problems — not the least of which was nightmarish litigation — Touzin personally destroyed every one of them.

His Lordship came to the Hotel for one Saturday every month. He was now past 80. But his routine never changed. He arrived at the end of the morning, alone and beautifully dressed, and went to his suite.

An hour or so later, his lady friend joined him. She too was always beautifully dressed.

They had Room Service lunch and, later, Room Service tea.

Then she left.

Then he left.

It had been going on like that — two old friends meeting discreetly one afternoon a month — for more than 40 years.

An American gentleman came down to the Concierge. "I've brought a group of clients in from the States and I want to make certain that each of them gets the Sunday *New York Times* tomorrow. Can you arrange that?"

"No problem," Wingrove said. "How many do you need?"

"Six will be fine."

Writing himself a note, Wingrove assured the gentleman, "I'll reserve them now. We usually receive them around noon on Monday . . ."

"No, no, no. I'd like them to have the paper tomorrow."

Wingrove shook his head. "They leave New York on Sunday, sir, on the night flight, so they don't actually get to London until Monday morning . . ."

"That's the point," the gentleman said. "I want my guests to have the Sunday paper on Sunday."

"Well . . ." Never one to say no without first trying everything, Wingrove promised, "I'll see what I can do."

The gentleman said he would appreciate it and walked away.

It was just 5 pm in London, which was noon in New York. Wingrove picked up the phone and rang the Concierge at the Carlyle Hotel to explain the problem. The Concierge there said he could easily buy the newspapers late that evening and shove them into a taxi, which would get them to Kennedy Airport an hour later.

"But," the American Concierge wanted to know, "then what?"

So Wingrove rang a friend at British Airways.

At 11 o'clock Saturday night New York time — which was 4 am Sunday morning in London — the Carlyle's Concierge purchased six copies of the Sunday *New York Times*, and dispatched them to Kennedy Airport, where they were held at British Airways for the morning Concorde.

The plane landed at Heathrow Airport on Sunday afternoon, at 5:25.

The Hotel's airport representative was there to meet it.

Six copies of the Sunday *New York Times* were hand delivered to the gentleman's guests on Sunday evening at 7.

With only a couple of hours left of his shift, Pierron took a long inspection stroll around the Hotel. Jotting down everything he saw in his logbook, he decided that the Ballroom fire exit needed to be tidied, discovered plates stacked in the corridor outside room 218, and noticed that a light bulb needed to be replaced in the corridor outside room 108. He noted that 20 white napkins had been issued to the restaurant and that 20 grey tablecloths plus 20 grey napkins had been issued to the Room Service supervisor. He learned that the restaurant coffee machine was blocked and, after fumbling with it for a minute, found that he couldn't unblock it.

When his time was up, he waited in the Front Hall for the new Duty Manager to come on — it was Philippe Krenzer. Pierron briefed him on what had happened over the previous 24 hours, handed him the logbook and, with the string ensemble playing softly in the Foyer, headed home to start his weekend.

On Sunday morning, a newspaper columnist criticized the Hotel for not having a doorman on duty to take his car when he pulled up. All four doormen read the article and they were furious. One of them decided that, given half a chance, he'd be happy to punch the columnist on the nose.

Touzin had seen it too, but didn't say anything about it to the doorman when he walked in on Monday morning because he hadn't yet decided how he would deal with it, if at all.

Nor did the doorman mention it. He just tipped his hat, as usual, and said, "Good morning, Mr Touzin."

A copy of the article was waiting, neatly cut from the newspaper, in the centre of his desk. Touzin pushed it to one side. The columnist was difficult, all the more so because being exigent was a reputation he apparently enjoyed. But Touzin felt that the man's opinions shouldn't take away from the fact that he was still a client. And any hotel or restaurant that couldn't properly deal with such clients absolutely wasn't doing its job very well.

Without acknowledging that the columnist was right, Touzin ruled that there should be a second doorman at the front of the Hotel during peak periods. So he announced at the morning meeting, from now on the Duty Manager must pay special attention to the front door, particularly in the early morning. "If you see that the doorman is busy, put someone else out there."

Over the next several mornings, Touzin made a point of standing near the fireplace at the side of the Front Hall, where he could watch the door. Arguably, the tone of the column was that of a man with a strong personal point of view. But Touzin could live with that. He was more concerned that the front of the Hotel had to be properly attended. He needed to be sure that no one else could find fault.

After a few days of watching, and thinking about what he was seeing, Touzin decided to have a little bell installed that the doorman could ring to summon help from the Concierge and the luggage porters when he was busy.

Now all Touzin had to do was persuade the doormen to use it, without making it look as if he was agreeing with the columnist.

~ 14 ~

*T*HE DECISION, MADE BY THE Ambassador and his wife, was that lamb would be the main course.

The Amir himself ruled out wine.

To get the pumpkin soup right, Henry made four variations, each time changing the consistency, each time making slight alterations to the spices. He brought four bowls into the Chef and, when Lesnik asked which was which, Henry smirked, "I'm not telling you."

Lesnik took a spoon and stirred, then tasted the first one. "Too much pimento." He found the second more true to the pumpkin taste but a little too creamy. He tasted the third, shoved the bowl away — "Forget it" — and didn't even bother to taste the fourth. "No. The colour is all wrong."

Returning to the first two, he stirred and tasted them again. "The soup should be thick enough that it looks almost like a mousse. It should look almost set. This one . . ." He lingered over it. "Cut down on the pimento. It should have just a hint of pimento. And I'd like a little more colour. The texture is lovely. But it should be fine sieved."

Leaving Henry to try it again, he walked through the kitchen, stopping at each station, speaking to his cooks, checking on what they were doing.

At the fish station, he spotted some trays sitting on one of the stainless steel counters. "Trays go away," he called out.

No one answered.

He said it again, this time louder.

Still no answer.

Grabbing the trays — they were labelled "red mullet" — he carried them into the cold room and put them on a shelf. While he was there, he found another tray sitting off to the side — this one unlabelled — and tossed that onto a shelf too.

"Trays go away," he bellowed, shutting the heavy cold room door.

A young cook suddenly appeared. "Sorry Chef."

"They go away," he barked. "Trays go away."

"Sorry Chef," the boy repeated.

Moving past the young cook, Lesnik went upstairs to watch Christian at work in the restaurant kitchen — he tasted the sauces and showed the fellow at the salad station how he wanted a dish decorated — then came back downstairs to speak to his pastry chef.

"Preparation of the banquet dessert is going to be a problem," Derek said, just finishing a tray of small lemon tarts. "The timing is going to be very tight."

Lesnik watched a young woman cook cutting dough for croissants, then opened a fridge to peek at the chocolate mousse. "The ice cream should be pre-scooped and the pears pre-glazed."

"We can't do that here for 180 people," Derek said.

"No, we can't." He thought about that. "We want the dishes all ready and laid out well in advance. The easiest place would be upstairs. Glaze the pears here and then take them up to decorate the plates there. Then, at the very last minute, you take up the ice cream. How's that sound?"

"It's going to have to be a big space, and I'll need help."

"I'll get a space for you," the Chef promised. "And as soon as we finish with the main course, we'll all come up to help you."

Marie hurried over to him. "The Embassy is on the phone."

Lesnik went back to his office and took the call. "Chef speaking."

"Good morning," a gentleman said. "I am calling on behalf of the Kuwait Embassy to inform you that four chefs are arriving from Kuwait for the banquet and would like to speak with you. Perhaps tomorrow. Would 4:30 be all right?"

"That would be fine," Lesnik said, writing it in his appointments diary. But when he hung up, he mumbled, "Just what I need, people to get in the way."

The Back of House Manager, a young fellow who darted around the kitchen in a white smock with BOH printed in large letters on the back, brought in a carton filled with china. They were the plates the Embassy planned on using. Gold-rimmed Minton with the Kuwaiti seal for the top table. Gold-rimmed Limoges without the state seal for the rest of the room.

The Chef studied them one by one and decided they were okay. Then he turned his attention to the very wide-rimmed glass plates, in three different colours, that the Embassy wanted to use for dessert. He hated those. It wasn't just a matter of taste, the colours were wrong for his glazed pears.

"What about the Queen's peach melba?" William broke into his thoughts.

He handed one of the dessert plates to William. "Not this time."

"She likes that." William held the plate up to the light, then shook his head. "No good."

"Why make a peach melba for the Queen when she isn't going to have it?" He took the plate back and put it in the box.

"Because it's tradition. The Queen comes, a peach melba is ready for her. We've always done that."

"Not this time. If she wants it, she can ask for it. But she won't. This is a State Banquet. If she was dining in the restaurant, or if this was a private dinner for her, that would be different. This time, why bother?"

Henry showed up just in time to volunteer, "I'll eat it for her." He had two more versions of the soup — one with yogurt, the other with sour cream.

Lesnik said no to both. "Too heavy."

William tasted the soup and agreed with the Chef. Then Henry saw the dessert plates and agreed with William. "No good."

They both wanted to know, "What about the fish?"

Lesnik confessed, "Not a clue," and when they left, he went to look at the posters in the corridor. He'd already checked in several books. "You only find it in the waters around Kuwait," the Ambassador's wife had insisted. So, for the third time, he ran his eyes down every name listed under every picture of every fish on the poster titled "Fish From The Gulf." But there wasn't anything anywhere called "*hamoor.*"

Two fish, however, had similar names. Perhaps, he thought, he'd misspelled the word, having written it phonetically from the way he thought the Ambassador's wife had pronounced it. The first was "*hamer*" — goatfish. The second was "*hamrah*" — red snapper. The problem was, she'd described *hamoor* as being like sea bass. That definitely ruled out both goatfish and snapper.

He felt frustrated because there were too many variables in this equation. The fish they were supplying could be too small, or too bony, or too tough for Western palates. It was impossible to plan a meal around a fish he didn't know and had never cooked. Seeing it for the first time only two days before the banquet could be too late. If the fish wasn't right, there might not be enough time to do anything about it.

The Gulf prawns posed less of a problem because he'd cooked them before. The Embassy said they'd come fresh, packed in ice, and that was exactly the way he wanted them. But the Ambassador's wife wanted a sauce to suit the Amir. She wanted the Amir to recognize the taste and also the colours. She said she wanted the sauce to have a yellow base and lots of green.

Lesnik was also concerned about those Kuwaiti chefs. He didn't know them, didn't know what they could do and didn't want to be in a position where he might have to depend on them for anything. There was enough confusion already built in to cooking a banquet like this, he didn't need any outsiders adding to it. So, after wondering whether or not he should mention it, he decided the direct approach was best, and rang the Ambassador's wife to let her know that he was worried about them.

"Do not give in to them," she answered right away. "No matter what they say. Except for their advice on spices, because they know how the Amir likes certain spices, do not let them make any changes. Do not take any of their suggestions. They will cook a small dish of veal and tomatoes which is then thickened with wheat and they will cook the rice that goes with it. Our traditional rice. But that is all."

Lesnik couldn't promise her fast enough, "I will do exactly what you say."

The moment he hung up, Marie tapped on the sliding window. He opened it and she told him, "It's here. The fish."

"The *hamoor?*" Delighted, he jumped up from his desk and went to the fish station to find a small tray of John Dory. "What's this?" It had nothing to do with the banquet. "What's this for?" No one knew. He shouted, "William?"

"Yes Chef." William poked his head around the corner, spotted the John Dory and said, "Oh, it's here."

"What's it for?"

"The dinner in the French Salon tonight."

"The dinner tonight?" He pointed to the tray. "It's nowhere near enough for the dinner tonight."

William weighed the fish at just under 4 kilos. "Is this all?"

In a panic, the two of them checked the original order to see that it should have been 8 kilos.

"Purchasing should have caught this." Angrily, Lesnik grabbed the phone to see if he could get more at the last minute. But there didn't seem to be a fishmonger within 50 miles who had any John Dory. "Why didn't someone check the order when it came in?" He didn't give William a chance to answer. "Wait a minute." He suddenly remembered the unlabelled tray he'd shoved on a shelf, and hurried back to the fish cold storage room. "What's this?" He tossed the tray on a table. "John Dory!"

William mumbled, "Thank God."

"Now the question is, who forgot to label the fish?" He screamed at the cooks, "We have procedures . . . who did not follow procedures? I want to know, now."

No one came forward.

"Dammit." He'd reached the end of his tether. Bringing William, Henry and Christian into his office, he slammed the door and gave them hell. Out of earshot of the rest of the kitchen, he yelled that people weren't following procedures and if he hadn't recalled seeing that John Dory in the cold room, they would have had a real problem on their hands.

Each of the three sous-chefs tried to explain that they didn't know anything about it, but Lesnik didn't want excuses. "Find out who screwed up and let me know."

They sheepishly promised they would.

And as fast as his temper came to the boil, that's how fast it came off. He looked at his three sous-chefs and demanded, "What the hell is *hamoor?*"

With less than one week to go, Andrew Jarman arranged a briefing for Touzin, bringing together all the senior staff and all the department heads, in a large, windowless, basement room behind the kitchens, where there was just enough space to push tables and chairs together to seat 24.

Jarman began, "There will be 172 guests based on one top table of 28 and 12 rounds of 12. The top table seating is being coordinated between the Palace and the Embassy. The Queen and the Amir will sit on thrones in the middle. Everyone else will spread out from there in descending order of rank, with husbands and wives on opposite sides."

Some people took notes. Most simply stared back at him and listened.

"No red carpets are required," Jarman went on. "The themers are providing deep burgundy carpets which will run from the pavement at the front of the Ballroom entrance, up the steps, through the Rotunda and into the Ballroom Reception. All the Hotel's hallway carpets will be removed the night before because the Ambassador's wife likes our black and white tiled floors and wants them left uncovered. However, we will have our own red carpets clean and on standby, just in case."

He stopped, checked his notes and announced the next item. "Royal retirement rooms."

Ronald took that as her cue. "The Royal Suite will be kept aside for the Queen's personal use. It will be stocked with flowers, extra towels, unwrapped soap, plus those special silver hair brushes and clothes brushes that we hold just for her."

By not letting the Royal Suite for that night, they were, in effect, making available to the Queen a £2000 bathroom, which she might never use.

"The suite next door," Ronald explained, "rooms 114–115 will be set aside as a powder room for any other senior ladies, just in case."

The bathroom bill jumped to £3500.

Touzin asked, "What about the gentlemen?"

She told him, "They're on their own."

Jarman moved on to staff uniforms. "All management, plus

head waiters, will be wearing evening tails with a white waistcoat and white tie. All waiting staff will be in black tails with black waistcoats and black ties. Uniforms have been ordered and will arrive the day before." He turned again to Ronald. "Ladies' uniforms?"

"Long sleeves with jackets," she said. "No elbows showing. Arab custom. And only ladies will accompany ladies. The cloakroom is briefed. There will be footmen to pull chairs out for the Queen and the Amir." She asked Touzin, "Do you want them to wear wigs?"

He made a face. "Wigs are too smelly."

"All right," she said. "No wigs."

The procedure for the evening, Jarman said, was fairly straightforward. Guests would be greeted by the Amir and the Ambassador in the Reception Room, immediately in front of the main entrance to the Ballroom. Non-top-table guests would be handed a seating plan inside a specially designed programme, then escorted by Hotel staff through the tiny Painted Room, at the side of the Reception, down the hallway and into the French Salon and Drawing Room where fruit juice would be served. Top-table guests would stay in the Reception Room waiting for the Queen. She and Prince Philip would be the last to arrive. Their timetable was fixed, down to the minute, by her ADC. They would leave Buckingham Palace at 8:20. It would take five minutes to get to the Hotel. She would be stepping out of her car at exactly 8:25. Touzin would greet them at the kerb and escort them into the Reception Room. Once they were inside, the curtain at the entrance to the Rotunda would be dropped so that no one could see in from the street. After the Queen had greeted the Amir and his top-table guests, dinner would be called precisely at 8:35. Non-top-table guests would have already been taken into the Ballroom, where they would remain standing at their seats while the top table filed in — the Amir and the Queen being the final pair.

"We still don't know," Jarman added, "if someone will say Grace. The question has arisen because a Christian prayer may not be in keeping with a State Banquet hosted by a Muslim ruler. It's the Amir's decision."

After dinner, he continued from his notes, coffee and *petits fours* would be served in both the French Salon and the Drawing Room because the Queen preferred that. The Mirror Room would be used as the corridor between the Ballroom and the other two, with a red carpet laid down to guide them.

"When the Queen gives her aide the signal that she wants to leave, he will inform the Amir and the Amir will escort the Queen down the marbled corridor to her car. The rest of the Royal Family will then leave in order of rank."

Pausing to make certain that everyone understood everything so far, Jarman proceeded through his list. Flowers are being handled by the themer. Furniture is also the themer. Flags are us.

"Who is sending us the Kuwaiti flag," Joe the upholsterer wanted to know.

Jarman said, "The Embassy."

"Well, then, please make certain this time they send us a four-yarder."

"A four-yarder?"

"That's right. Last time they sent us a twelve-yarder and it fell all the way down to the pavement."

Jarman jotted that down. "At the Ballroom entrance, we should fold the revolving doors flat so they don't keep swinging around. This way, people can just walk through."

Touzin asked, "What happens if it's cold?"

Ronald said, "If we use the revolving doors, it presents a problem for any ladies in large dresses because the doors at the side are too small."

"Then let's hope it's not cold," Touzin gave in. "What about music?"

"We don't know yet," Jarman said. "But I have a string orchestra standing by, just in case."

Touzin wondered, "Speeches?"

"There will be no toasts and no speeches," Jarman said, "at the request of Her Majesty. However I also have a toastmaster on standby."

"Photos?"

"It's up to the Embassy. We haven't been told yet."

"Fire safety?"

Purcell took up this point. "The tent is fire-proofed. No exits will be blocked. The organizer understands that."

"There is only one special request," Jarman said. "A gentleman who will be at the top table . . . I can't remember his name . . . he's way down towards the end . . . he needs a cushion for his back."

Ronald promised to arrange that.

Touzin again. "Lighting in the room?"

Jarman told him, "We'll be able to gauge that better on the day when the tent is up," then turned to the Chef, "The menu?"

"So far," Lesnik said, "the menu is, pumpkin soup with yogurt and saffron. Baked fish with shrimp and a sauce served separately. Then there is fillet of lamb with a ragout of vegetables. There is saffron rice which will be made by some Kuwaiti chefs. In every course there will be their spices, notably saffron and turmeric, and there will be yogurt. Dessert will be caramelized pear. The Embassy will prepare an extra dessert. All of the dishes have been designed to be server friendly because the service will be tight."

Jarman interjected that six Kuwaiti waiters would offer Kuwaiti coffee to all guests when they left, as a symbolic gesture.

"The Embassy has provided all the china for the evening," Lesnik said. "They have also sent me, to look at, some glass dessert plates." He smiled. "But the rims are too big. They won't physically fit around the table. So we will use our own dessert plates."

"Tasting?" Touzin asked.

"Whenever you want." Now the Chef pleaded Derek's case. "There is just one logistical problem. We need to do the desserts close to the room. We can't prepare them in the kitchen because it's too far away. They are too sensitive to carry any sort of distance. I'd prefer it, too, if they didn't have to be carried up the stairs."

Touzin pondered that. "I suppose we can always close off the Reading Room at the side of the Foyer. Will you have enough room to prepare them in there?"

"I think so. But we'll have to move the furniture out."

"What about afternoon tea?" Jarman asked.

"No problem," Touzin said. "We'll serve it in the Foyer as usual and maybe even in the Causerie, if we need to. The thing to do is set up screens so that no one can see into the Reading Room."

"Very heavy screens," the Chef recommended, "so that no one can hear the chefs cursing."

"What are we supposed to do about all the furniture there?" Ronald asked. "You don't really want to take it all out, do you? As long as no one can see in, can't everything just be pushed to the side?"

The Chef said, "As long as I have enough room to lay out 172 desserts."

Duncan warned, "172 dishes won't be very quiet."

"I'll have to see it," Touzin said. "If we can make enough room there so that the chef can operate, that's probably where we should do it. Now, tell me about that rice dish. Why is it such a big event?"

Having worked in the Middle East, Duncan explained, "It's symbolic. When they bring it out, it looks like gold. Sumptuous. Very traditional. It stands for prosperity."

Jarman returned to his checklist. "There will be food for the security people in the staff restaurant. Carpet cleaning on Monday, although there are functions in the rooms on Tuesday and Wednesday. We've got a cocktail party on Tuesday for 500–600 people, which means we'll have to look at the carpets again on Thursday morning. The themers are coming in at six pm Wednesday. There may be a press corner, but that's not been decided yet. The press are usually permitted to stand off to the side at the entrance, to film people coming in. But they cannot come inside the banquet."

Touzin wanted to know, "Are we supposed to feed the themers?" Jarman said, "No."

"In any case, I will need to know the staff canteen requirements," the Chef reminded him. "And what are we supposed to do for the police?"

"We feed them," Jarman said. "Usually steak and chips."

"Why not set up a little buffet?" Touzin asked.

"We're talking about 40 or 50 people," Jarman confirmed. "Yes, maybe a buffet is right. There's no reason why we should have to serve them."

Touzin then asked if the nurse would be on duty in case someone became ill.

Jarman said she would be, and pointed to Chris Baxter. "Security?"

Baxter announced, "The police tell me that they are expecting some protesters. It seems there is a fundamentalist group who have said that they will demonstrate outside. That won't create any real problems, because the police will keep them far enough away. But some of these groups have been known to book rooms, which brings them inside the Hotel. We'll need to check the guest lists to determine if any of them have managed it."

That worried Touzin. "Are you sure about this demonstration?"

"The police tell me it could happen. They're in contact with the group. It's generally nothing more than people making noise. The usual crowd control barriers will be set up by Thursday morning. Anyway, the banquet is being treated as a high security risk event. Officers will move into the Hotel from Wednesday morning and at six am Thursday, a full hotel search will begin. We will need two engineers on standby, plus a lift engineer, because they go into everything, including the lift shafts. They will also want roof access. They'll be using the gents' cloakroom off the Ballroom as a control centre for their search. They also need a room on the mezzanine where they can store equipment, you know, radios, batteries, chargers, that sort of thing. Dogs will be brought into the Hotel at five on the evening of the banquet to carry out a final sniff of the Royal Suite and 114–115. The retiring rooms will then be double-locked and guarded."

He added that there would be 19 special escorts, 9 officers on fixed posts and 20 others. Three close protection officers would be in the function room, dining with guests at tables near doors, facing the top table so that they could maintain eye contact with the Queen, the Amir and Prince Charles. Security officers would also need to have a guest list. The usual parking restrictions would apply. The street in front of the Hotel and the alley at the back would be cleared. All staff would be required to have little stick-on badges to identify them.

"Good," Jarman said, and began outlining the cleaning schedule — windows, marble, curtains and chandeliers — when something dawned on Touzin.

"Should we avoid selling the first-floor rooms?"

Ronald assured him, "We've already taken the rooms over the Ballroom out of service."

And Duncan piped in with, "What a perfect way to end a perfect evening, a bath overflow."

The Chef at Buckingham Palace was on the phone. "I just realized I don't have enough seven-inch savoury moulds. It's for the banquet here. Help. Can you send us ten?"

"All right," Lesnik agreed. "But if you don't send them back to me the next day, I will personally tell the Queen." He hung up and turned to Henry, who wanted to show off his new asparagus dish. "Let's see."

Surrounding the asparagus was a salad — with chives, spring

onions, three different-coloured peppers and diced cucumber — seasoned with a light vinaigrette sauce. Lesnik looked at it, suggested Henry might cut the vegetables a little finer, then tasted it. "A bit more salt," he said, as Marie opened the sliding glass window to announce, "The Kuwaiti chefs are here."

"Please escort them down." That gave him enough time to get Henry's salad off his desk and tie on a fresh apron.

Expecting four, he got ten.

Marie led the group into his office and for a few minutes it looked as if he was a one-man receiving line. They filed past him, shaking his hand, mumbling their names. He didn't understand a word that any of them said. And except for three cooks and a caterer, he never figured out who the others were or why they were there.

The crowd spilled into his private dining room.

Some of them admired his corkscrew collection. Most of them didn't speak English. It took a few moments before he found one fellow who seemed to be in charge — he was carrying the most expensive looking mobile phone — so Lesnik asked him if he could translate to the others, and the chap with the phone said he would.

"You are all very welcome," the Chef told them. "But I need to be certain that we all understand each other." He intended to set the record straight right from the start. "I will cook the banquet, prepare all the dishes, decorate the plates and have the final say over presentation. I will also cut the fish. I will need you to help with the Arabic sauces and perhaps the actual cooking of the fish. I understand you will be doing a rice dish, and that is fine. You will cook that but I will decide the presentation of it. I am also told that the Embassy chef will provide an extra sweet to be served with dessert."

The fellow with the phone translated, and everyone nodded. But laying down the law like that must have scared a few of them because, as soon as his speech was done, six of the ten — including the fellow with the phone — shook his hand and left.

Lesnik asked for one of his junior cooks to serve coffee and now, with only four, there was space enough to sit around his dining room table. "Which of you is the Amir's personal chef?"

A thin nervous man in his early 50s — who turned out to be a Lebanese who once ran a restaurant in Kuwait — explained, "I oversee special functions for the Royal Family."

Lesnik shook his hand again, before turning to the others. "And you?" Two of the three didn't speak enough English for him to figure out what it was they did, so he focused on the fourth fellow. The oldest of the group — a man in his mid-70s with a thin grey moustache and a gentle face who seemed to understand more English than he was willing to speak. Lesnik asked him, "Are you the Amir's personal chef?"

"Mohammed," the man smiled.

"And you are the Amir's personal chef?"

"No."

The Lebanese caterer finally explained that Mohammed had cooked for the Amir when the Amir was a young man, that they'd known each other for 50 years, and that whenever the Amir needed a special dish he sent for Mohammed. "He isn't exactly the Amir's personal chef; Mohammed is more like the Amir's most trusted chef. I have asked him to prepare the rice dish because I know the Amir will appreciate it that much more when he knows Mohammed is doing it."

With that out of the way, Lesnik started going over the menu, dish by dish. "We have Spanish and Turkish saffron. Which one do you prefer?"

The caterer said, "We will bring Iranian saffron."

"The soup."

"Instead of yogurt, please use sour cream. That is all right."

"Now, the fish." At last, he was going to find out, "What is *hamoor?*"

The caterer shrugged. *"Homooa?"*

"Hamoor . . . Homooa, yes, what does it look like?"

"Homooa?" The caterer asked the other three in Arabic but they didn't seem to know, either. He turned back to Lesnik, "How do you spell it?"

He tried it phonetically but only drew blank stares. "Follow me," he said, and led them into the corridor to look at the posters. Pointing to *hamer,* he wondered, "Is it goatfish?" Pointing to *hamrah,* he asked, "Or is it red snapper?"

"Hamoor!" Mohammed suddenly understood. He reeled off something in Arabic to the caterer, then said, *"Hamoor.* Here. Look." He studied every picture on the chart until he pointed to a brown spotted grouper. "This is *hamoor."*

"Ahhh. Grouper." Lesnik patted the old man gently on the back. "Mohammed, you have saved the day."

"Yes, *hamoor."* Suddenly the other two also understood. "Not *hamer. Hamoor."*

"Hamoor. Yes," the caterer said. "They will come to you fresh and filleted."

"Hamoor," Lesnik repeated, then cautioned, "But they mustn't be broken. How much do they weigh?"

"Three, maybe four kilos." The caterer asked the others in Arabic, waited for their answer, then confirmed, "Yes, maybe four kilos."

Leading them back into his dining room, Lesnik kept his arm around Mohammed. "My friend, you have saved the day."

Now Mohammed warned, "The Amir. No salt. No pepper. No oil. No fat. When you make fish, just lemon."

"And how does the Amir like his lamb?"

"Well done."

"Then it shall be well done." Which was fine with him because that was fine with the Queen. "The ragout of vegetables. I'm planning on using pimentos, all cut in different shapes, celery, carrots, okra, aubergine, courgette and tomatoes."

Mohammed shook his finger. "No okra."

"All right. Tell me about the rice."

"*Machboos*." Mohammed said. "It is dome shaped. Fried onions, raisins, spices that we will bring, and chick peas."

"And that other dish?"

"*Jerish*. Ground meat with wheat that is like a paste."

Without showing as much, Lesnik had serious concerns that these dishes could get in the way of his meal. "We'll need to sort out platters and covers for the rice."

"No covers for rice," Mohammed said. "It is served loose. And there is meat in the rice with bones."

"Bones?" He didn't like that. "No bones."

"Okay," the caterer said without any argument. "No bones."

"What about bread?"

"Lebanese white and brown breads," the caterer said. "For the Amir, some must be toasted, some must be untoasted."

"We will also put our bread rolls on the table."

"There must be dates but we will supply special dates. And a salad," the caterer decided. "Lettuce and cucumber only with lemon. No dressing." Now he leaned forward as if he was about to let Lesnik in on a secret. "Please remember when you are buying your ingredients, money is no object. Whatever it costs is all right. Do not worry about money. The Amir wants to see lots of food on all of the tables."

Lesnik wondered, "How much *hamoor* will there be?"

"Seventy kilos."

"And Gulf prawns?"

"Three jumbo boxes. About 60 kilos."

"Anything else?"

"Yes," the caterer said. "We will make a special dessert . . ."

"Ah . . ." Although Lesnik was polite enough to listen to what they were proposing — a special Middle Eastern pastry that, anyway, struck him as being too unusual for Western palates — he had what he thought was a very diplomatic excuse. "It sounds wonderful but I'm afraid it will not work with our dessert. You see, our dessert must be decorated. That will take us time. Adding an extra course like that will require an additional 15 to 20 minutes of preparation. It will throw off all our timing."

"Then perhaps we shall supply a small pyramid of sweets that will be brought to the table and put in the middle."

Lesnik was very concerned about all this extra food. "The dinner is to start promptly at 8:35 and must be finished by 10:20. Service must be quick."

Obviously someone had warned the caterer that the Chef was in charge. "Yes. Of course. Whatever you want to do."

Lesnik asked Mohammed, "What will you need?"

The old man reeled off his shopping list. "Eighty lambs and 480 kilos of rice. For the *machboos* alone I will need eight baby lambs, about 10 kilos each, *halal* killed, and with the head. For the *jerish*, I will need, maybe, four more lamb."

"Another thing," the caterer recalled, "on the head table, there must be a basket of green apples for the Amir. Personally for him. Maybe there should then be a basket of fruit for the other guests. But only green apples for the Amir. And yogurt for him too."

"Greek yogurt," Mohammed insisted. "No-fat."

"Fine. We'll have his yogurt served to him in a silver bowl . . ."

"No bowl," the caterer said. "The pot."

"What pot?"

"The pot of the yogurt."

"What about the pot of yogurt?"

"Yes, yes," Mohammed confirmed. "The Amir likes to see that it is fresh. The pot must be sealed. Closed."

Lesnik was flabbergasted. "You want me to put a little white plastic pot of Greek no-fat yogurt on the table?"

That's exactly what they said he should do.

♣

The fish arrived in four huge blue and white containers, packed fresh on ice. And he didn't like them. They were much too large. He'd expected each to weigh 6–8 pounds. These came closer to 30 pounds. A third of them were already filleted. The rest were whole. He couldn't figure out why.

Then, instead of three jumbo boxes of Gulf prawns, there were only two. They were in perfect condition, except that they were frozen. He'd been promised fresh and was counting on fresh. Not being in control of the market annoyed him enormously. The market was where any meal had to begin. Being forced to give up control of the market like this put the meal at risk.

That afternoon, he personally cleaned, gutted and filleted one of the fish, then cooked it — to see how it handled, to test the texture and the flavour, to figure out the seasoning. He also wanted to see how it worked with the sauce. Once he had some ideas formulated in his head, he left written instructions for William.

Next, he peeled a few of the prawns and sautéed them. Worried that they might be a little tough, he told one of his cooks that he wanted each one peeled by hand and the tracks taken out of the spine. That would make them easier to chew.

He then drew up a list of special supplies that the Kuwaitis required — dried black lemon, fresh green cardamom, fresh spices imported from India, freshly ground turmeric and whole black cumin seeds. It took him some time, but he eventually found everything. He also ordered extra pimentos, tomatoes, red chillies, green chillies and fresh coriander. A couple of hours later, the caterer rang to say that Mohammed would be cooking his dishes at the Embassy, which meant that — much to his embarrassment — Lesnik now had to get back on the phone to those suppliers and cancel.

The following day, the caterer called to say that they'd decided, after all, they didn't want whole lambs for their dishes, they wanted the meat butchered. The animals had already been shipped from Wales to Birmingham where they'd been slaughtered by a licensed *halal* butcher. Lesnik now had to arrange to have the meat shipped from the slaughterhouse to a butcher he knew, so that he could be present to supervise the butchering.

Meeting with the Back of House Manager, Lesnik went through the platters, soup tureens, sauce boats, meat trays, fish trays and covers. They selected 20 pieces in all, which were then sent 100 miles away to be re-plated. The foundry owner, who stopped everything else he was doing to handle this special order, faithfully promised that everything would be returned to the Hotel by Wednesday.

At the last minute, Lesnik remembered to add one item to the list. He asked the replater to make a small silver bowl with a cover, shaped to fit a 35-pence, plastic pot of no-fat Greek yogurt.

The price for the bowl was £50.

~ 15 ~

$\mathcal{T}$HE DESK SERGEANT AT WEST End Central Police Station phoned Roy Barron to inform him that a gentleman named Patel had just been arrested for leaving unpaid hotel bills and other fraud-related crimes. The suspect had in his possession a number of brochures, including several from the Hotel. He was wondering if perhaps Patel had been a guest there. Barron promised to find out and get back to him right away.

Cooperation between the Hotel and the police was close. The police operated the Hotel Intelligence Unit and, in conjunction with that, a group of 21 hotel security officers formed the Institute of Hotel Security Management. There was also an informal arrangement between security people — they called themselves the Hotel Collation Unit — to keep each other informed about undesirable clients. If someone walked out of a hotel without paying a bill, or was refused a room because they were drunk, or their credit card was no good or they seemed to be otherwise unsuitable, their name was dispatched to the other hotels on the network.

After checking with Robert Buckolt — who went through the guest histories — Barron told the desk sergeant that they had no record of that particular Mr Patel ever having stayed at the Hotel.

217

The policeman said thank you and hung up. Barron rang Buckolt again, this time to suggest that Mr Patel's name be added to the NTBT list.

❖

Aspirin was a headache for Touzin.

The Hotel had always refused to supply aspirin, or any sort of medication, because their lawyers said they couldn't. According to counsel, if the Hotel dispensed medication and someone then became ill, the Hotel could be held liable. So it became Hotel policy — whenever anyone asked for an aspirin — to send someone to fetch it from a nearby pharmacy. But the Hotel could only do that — again according to counsel — on condition that the client was willing to pay for it.

It created some animosity, especially with American clients. They had a headache, they wanted an aspirin. And they couldn't understand why the Hotel wouldn't supply one.

After hearing guests complain, Touzin decided he had to do something about the ill will that the no-aspirin rule was causing. So he sat down with the Hotel's lawyers, who explained to him that their problem was with the word "dispensing." As long as the Hotel was dispensing — or offering — medication, the Hotel was at risk.

He reminded them that he wasn't asking what he couldn't do, he needed them to tell him how he could do it.

Putting their heads together, with the meter clicking, the lawyers eventually determined that, if the Hotel was selling aspirin, then it wasn't dispensing it. They decided that, if a client was paying for medication, then the client was making a conscious decision to take it. In that case, the Hotel's liability was limited.

So now the Hotel stocked a brand of mild buffered aspirin, and had the lawyers' blessing to supply two tablets — up to a maximum of four — on request, for which they were required to charge the guest 10p.

It ended complaints that the Hotel wouldn't help clients out with a couple of aspirin. But it created the problem of having clients say, you're charging me how much for a room and have the nerve to ask me 10p for an aspirin?

♣

Just as Carole Ronald finished her own morning staff meeting, Buckolt phoned to say that Mr Fleischer, who'd been booked into 310, wanted a non-smoking room. It wasn't in his guest history, "But it is now," he said, adding, "He's arriving this afternoon from Berlin."

The third-floor housekeeper had already disappeared down the corridor. So, after checking her computer to see that the room had not yet been serviced, she left her office to speak to the maid there. On her way, she spotted the carpet fitter. "I found you." He stared at her as if he didn't know he'd ever been lost. "Rooms 305–306," she told him. "The carpets are in."

He mumbled, "Okay."

She headed down the back stairs, and bumped into the maid coming out of the third-floor service room. "Three-one-oh is non-smoking."

With her arms full of bedding and towels to go to the laundry, the short, dark-haired Filipino woman responded, "It's not on the chart."

"It is now," Ronald said.

"Okay, madam," the maid nodded.

Later she would take all the ash trays out of 310, leave the windows open for several hours, and then spray everything with Pozium, an aerosol that removed smoke and smoke-related odours.

But first she dumped the bedding and towels into a large aluminium chute.

♣

That chute ran from the top floor to the basement and emptied into a wheeled metal container that only just fitted into a two-by-four cubbyhole. When the container was full, the dirty linen was sorted and counted. Nearly 40 containers were parked along the far wall. Some were waiting to be filled. Some were waiting to be emptied. Twice a day, three in high season, a laundry truck pulled up at the Timekeeper's door. Everything going out was logged, so the Hotel knew what had been sent, and everything coming back in was checked, so the Hotel knew what had been received.

The morning delivery, which had just come in from the laundry, was short of 100 pillow cases. Janet, the woman who ran the linen room, went to her tiny office — where she'd taped pictures from magazines of flowers to the walls — and phoned the laundry manager across town.

Considering the volume of stuff that went back and forth, it was little wonder that only 100 pillow cases were missing.

While she was reminding him that 100 pillow cases didn't simply walk away, a valet arrived with cleaning for Mr Budhrani in room 444. The laundry manager promised he'd personally look for the pillow cases and send them over the minute he found them. She answered, "That's what I'd hoped you'd say," and hung up. The valet, carrying Mr Budhrani's suit, shirts, underwear and socks, told Janet that the gentleman was leaving for India that evening and needed everything back by 3:30 pm. Seeing that it was just 10:30, she mumbled that he was cutting it a bit fine. Still, she special-tagged the order by putting it in a blue box, rang the laundry manager again and asked him to please look out for it when the next delivery got there. He promised her it would be back at the Hotel with the 2:30 delivery.

Most of the linen room — a large, neon-lit space with yellow floors and yellow- and white-tiled walls — was taken up by eight colossal floor-to-ceiling shelves. Running on tracks, each with a ship's steering wheel to move it hydraulically, there was just enough room between the shelves to load them or take supplies from them.

There were sheets, towels, pillow cases, blankets, bathrobes, tablecloths, napkins, doilies, hand towels, cloak room towels, bedside mats, bath mats, bed covers, large banqueting cloths and napperons, which is what they used to cover tables in the Foyer for afternoon tea. Most of it was white. Anything that was pink belonged to the Causerie. Anything that was grey belonged to Room Service. And at the end of one shelf, on the bottom, there were clean, neatly folded discarded bathrobes. Deemed no longer good enough to be used for guests, they were for sale at a discount to the staff.

In all, there was enough flatware on hand to keep the Hotel fully stocked for two days. What would happen if the laundry trucks didn't show up for three, no one knew.

Beyond the linen room was the uniform shop, where staff came in all day throughout the day, left uniforms for cleaning and picked up clean ones for work. In fact, it looked exactly like a neighbour-hood dry cleaners, with clothes in plastic wrapping hanging on long rails. There were uniforms for the chefs, kitchen staff, waiters, hall porters, banqueting staff, Back of House staff, cashiers, maids, door-men, pages and Foyer staff. There was everything that senior man-agement needed too, such as dinner jackets and morning suits. And, like any neighbourhood dry cleaners, everything worked with a ticket.

To the side of the linen room, there was a washer and a dryer and an ironing board, where someone could do a gentleman's shirt or a lady's blouse, or someone's smalls if they absolutely had to. Janet also had a seamstress working here, to make small repairs on staff uniforms and do simple stuff for clients. If a gentleman needed a black band sewn onto his trilby, or a lady ripped a zip on her evening gown, the seamstress obliged. But when a woman sent down several items of school clothing for her children to be hemmed and cuffed, Janet said no. Tailoring wasn't part of the Hotel's service. It took time away from other work. Worse, it was rarely appreciated. She'd lost count of how many times she'd done a client a favour, only to have the client complain that the Hotel's sewing wasn't up to Savile Row standards.

♚

There was good news and there was bad news.

It was Touzin's turn to play that game.

First, he gave Purcell the good news. "Mr Leggett is coming to the Hotel for a month. He's got his family with him. He wanted me to put together a series of rooms, you know, to form a big enough suite for them. I thought to myself, why don't we rent him one of the penthouses? It's got everything he needs. Two bedrooms. A sitting room. A patio. A kitchen. And a dining room. I agreed we'd charge him £800 a night."

"Great idea," Purcell said. "Except the penthouses aren't in any shape to be lived in."

Now he hit him with the bad news. "You've got ten days to put one into shape."

"Ten days?" Purcell stood there for the longest time. At other hotels, he'd learned it was wise to make big jobs appear to be more difficult than they were. It was all about winning brownie points. The solution here was, simply, to throw bodies at the job. Painters. Carpenters. Carpet fitters. Decorators. Just get everybody in there and do it. But if the boss thought it was a near-impossible task . . . "Only ten days?"

"Can you do it? And what will it cost?"

"Can I do it?" He shrugged. "And . . . off the top of my head, £10,000."

"Not bad," Touzin nodded. "We're getting about £25,000 for the month. That's a pretty decent return on our investment."

"Ten days?" He knew where he could get furniture for the penthouse, and it was no trouble to install a TV, a VCR and a CD hi-fi. He'd need an air-conditioning unit in there, but a dealer he knew would sell them one, then buy it back after a month, which would work out cheaper than renting one. The rest of the work was strictly cosmetic. He'd make it suitable for the 1990s with white ceilings and brighter colours on the walls. "Only ten days?"

"Only ten days," Touzin said. "I know, it's a challenge."

Purcell thought to himself, a challenge would be a weekend. Ten days was a luxury. Except, he couldn't tell Touzin.

Zsa Zsa Gabor walked into the Foyer and sat down at a table with a small "Reserved" sign on it.

The waiter came over to her, bowed, said, "Good evening, madam," and politely pointed out, "I'm afraid that the table is being held."

She refused to move. "It is being held for me."

This was not a place where scenes were encouraged.

"Yes, madam," the waiter said, and let her have the table.

When the fire alarm sounded, it wasn't a siren or any sort of bell that rang throughout the hotel, it was a series of beeps that went off on bleepers carried by the senior management team, each floor house-keeper and most of the technical services department.

The Hotel was required to test the alarms regularly. Every six months, the entire staff went through a fire training session. Every four months, the night staff trained for that eventuality as well. But when the alarms actually went off, it was different.

No one ever knew if, this time, it was for real.

Staff members throughout the Hotel read their bleepers — it said the fire was in the kitchen — and raced downstairs. Buckolt left Reservations. Jarman left the Banqueting Office. No one waited for the lift. All the fire doors in the Hotel closed, automatically. Purcell raced down from the sixth floor. Andrew Pierron came running out of his office.

They had exactly four minutes, and not one second more, to take action. If there was a small fire, they had to put it out. If there wasn't a fire, they had to decide why the alarm had sounded and silence it. If they couldn't manage either within that four-minute limit — about the time it would take the average person to pour a glass of milk, grab a biscuit and finish them both — or if the alarm was smashed, or if more than one alarm had gone off to warn of smoke or heat build-up in two different locations, then it was automatically relayed to the fire service. While fire engines were dispatched with their sirens blaring, the senior staff had to go into evacuation mode.

If they didn't solve the problem in four minutes, they had to empty the Hotel.

The first to get to the kitchen was Pierron. Jarman was right behind him. Buckolt and Duncan and Touzin were there seconds later.

"An alarm fault," Pierron called out, as Purcell arrived.

Everyone swept past the chefs and went through the kitchen to make certain that nothing was burning.

"The heat detector," Lesnik said, standing calmly next to William.

"Same story," William shook his head. "Turn on the oven, sear a piece of meat and that one goes off."

The system was reset with one minute to spare.

At the rear of the Hotel there was a locked door, which came to be known as the Company president's entrance. It was put there a long time ago so that certain V-VIPs could visit the Hotel without having to use the front entrance. Some V-VIPs feel all the more important for using it.

The laundry van arrived back at the Hotel at 2:31, without the blue box.

The valet showed up a few minutes later to collect Mr Budhrani's clothes.

Janet was already on the line to the laundry manager. "Well, it's not here."

"Well, I sent it," the laundry manager insisted.

"Please check with the driver."

He said he'd have to ring her back.

Hanging up, she told the valet, "I'm working on it."

He insisted, "Mr Budhrani absolutely must have his clothes."

She repeated, "I'm working on it."

The valet said, "Please page me when it's here," and went back upstairs. Five minutes later, because the laundry manager hadn't yet phoned, she rang him. "The blue box."

"I'm still looking for the van driver."

She threatened, "You'd better find him soon," hung up and thought to herself, I don't want to be the one to explain this to Mr Budhrani.

Three minutes later the van driver rang. "I've just spoken to the laundry who says something about some missing shirts."

"No," she screamed in exasperation. "A blue box." She read off the number on her receipt. He insisted he never got anything of the kind from the laundry. So she hung up on him and dialled the laundry manager again. "Where is my blue box?"

"I'm still waiting to hear from the driver," he said right away.

"I've already spoken to the driver . . ." She was furious. "I'm going to take this up with the Housekeeper and ask her to take it up with Mr Touzin . . ."

That's when he cut in, "Hold on. I've got the driver on the other line now."

She tapped her foot against the side of her desk until he came back on the phone.

"We found it," he announced, as if he'd done her a favour. "The driver said it was on his manifest after all. He had it."

"Where is it? Why don't I have it? What did he do with it?"

The laundry manager answered meekly, "He ah . . . he delivered it to the wrong hotel."

She warned him, "You'd better get him to deliver it to the right hotel in 15 minutes." And slammed down the phone.

The blue box was on Janet's desk at 3:10.

She phoned the valet, who fetched it, checked it and took it to Mr Budhrani, who now had clean underwear and socks for the flight to India, and who never knew that it took three people and half a dozen phone calls to make certain that he did.

Some people are born in hotels, some people spend their lives living in hotels, and some people die in hotels too.

During World War II, the King of Yugoslavia moved into the Hotel. At the time, seven exiled Kings were living there. When the Queen of Yugoslavia gave birth to the heir apparent, Crown Prince Aleksander, she did that at the Hotel too. For the event, the King summoned some earth from his native country and put it under the bed in which his son was born. The Hotel allowed him to proclaim that room to be Yugoslavian territory, so that the prince and future king would be born on his own soil, forever preserving his right of succession.

The last permanent resident of the Hotel moved out some years ago, although people often come to stay for six months at a time.

As for death, that was a subject people in the hotel business superstitiously avoided. They feared that the mere mention of it would bring about the reality of it. The last death at the Hotel was several years ago, when one of its elderly live-in clients succumbed. His nurse was with him at the time, so there was no real drama. The man was taken out of the hotel by undertakers, through the back door, without any of the other guests ever knowing.

Still, it was guaranteed to happen every now and then — there was no way they could beat the actuarial tables — and, even though everyone on the staff was supposed to be able to cope with it, just the thought of death threw many of them off their stride.

One evening, a call came in to the Duty Manager from a guest in 223 that water was pouring down from the ceiling above. The Duty Manager checked to see who was staying in 323 and was quite surprised that, at least according to the computer, the room was vacant. So he rushed upstairs, banged on the door several times, got no response and let himself in.

Lying on his back in the bath was a totally naked man, his eyes shut. The taps were on full and the floor was awash with the overflow.

First, the Duty Manager turned off the taps. Then he reached into the bath to feel the side of the man's throat. Several people at the Hotel were trained in first aid, including all of the senior staff and everyone on the Duty Manager rota.

There was a pulse.

He decided the man was passed out drunk.

Fearing that he might drown, the Duty Manager emptied the bath, took off the coat of his morning suit — but soaked himself anyway — to lift the man out and into his bed. He then rang the Housekeeper to move the lady in 223 into another room and to get the engineer to begin the repairs on 223 and 323.

He never discovered how the fellow, who should have been staying in 423, got into 323.

The next morning, when the Duty Manager saw him and asked him how he slept, all the man had to say was, "I had a horrible nightmare."

The Duty Manager added, "Me too."

There was a party of 45 dining in the restaurant, and the host had ordered Lobster Thermidor for all of his guests. The Chef personally supervised the meal and the waiters made a big entrance with the dish, presenting the lobsters on their trays before serving them. Everyone applauded.

Azoulai watched his waiters parade in and stood there for a few seconds, listening to the applause, when he sensed there was something very wrong.

He made a fast count of the waiters. Someone was missing. He was 12 lobsters short.

Racing into the kitchen, he told the Chef, "Send out the next tray."

The Chef looked at him quizzically. "What do you mean?"

"We need 12 more."

"Your waiters took them."

"We're 12 short."

The Chef got angry. "Impossible." He swung around to ask one of the cooks, "Did you bring all the trays up?"

The boy said he had.

Hoping he hadn't, Lesnik darted down the steps and into the fish preparation station. Sure enough, there on a shelf were the last 12 lobsters. His cursing could be heard at the other end of the kitchen.

A young luggage porter had just been hired, and was working his first day when a Rolls-Royce pulled up. The chauffeur got out and told him to take everything out of the boot and take it up to room 131. He did. Later that evening, when the guest who was staying in 131 came back to the Hotel, he found his luggage sitting waiting for him, next to a jack and spare tyre.

When the attendant working in the Gentlemen's Cloakroom came on duty, he found a handsome black leather briefcase sitting on the floor at the rear of the cloakroom. There was no identification on it, except for three tiny gold-lettered initials under the handle — PAR. And because he had no way of telling to whom it belonged, he asked Robert Buckolt to come and take a look at it.

If it had been something more sinister — an unidentified wrapped package, for example — Buckolt would have followed standard procedure for that sort of event and phoned the police. But this was clearly a matter of someone having forgotten to collect their briefcase. So he carried it back to his office and checked his guest list to see if there was anyone staying in the Hotel with those initials.

There wasn't.

So he rang Security.

When Baxter got there, the two of them tried to open the case, but it was locked. Baxter assured Buckolt that someone would soon be ringing for it, and took it up to his office, where he locked it in a cupboard. Buckolt made a note to himself to mention it at Touzin's next meeting, so that everyone on the staff knew that someone named PAR had lost a briefcase.

It stayed in Baxter's cupboard for three days.

When no one had claimed it by then, he duly logged it into Lost and Found — a secure storage room in the basement   and left it there for safe keeping. The law required that any property found in the Hotel had to stay on the premises for six months. If, after that time, it was not claimed by the rightful owner, it could be given either to the person who found it, or to charity.

In most cases, however, when something was found the owner was known.

If someone forgot to pack a raincoat when they checked out of their room, the maid would know. If someone left a Filofax on a table in the restaurant, the waiter would find it. If someone forgot they'd sent a suit to the laundry and left the Hotel before it came back, the valet would know.

It happened often and it was, usually, easy to trace the owner.

The real problem was how to tell the owner. That was part of Baxter's job. And the unalterable policy was, be discreet.

He'd phone the guest and always insist on speaking directly to him or her. Although he didn't necessarily hide the fact that he was ringing from the Hotel, he never explained the nature of his call. Nor did he ever leave a message.

It was all too obvious why.

In the normal course of their business, the Hotel went to considerable lengths to protect their clients. Baxter figured it was, therefore, the least he could do never to say something like, "Please tell your husband that we found his cufflinks, and oh, by the way, you left your underwear in the bathroom too."

Reservations was a cramped room off the main Reception, with three computer screens and a lot of filing cabinets, two fax machines, a computer printer, a telex machine, a link to the Utell Reservation System, and a lot of traffic moving through the room because it was the way into Buckolt's office.

The staff of two answered all the phones, retrieved all the faxes and took all the bookings. Reservations came in from individuals, from travel agents, from booking agencies — such as Leading Hotels of the World — and from the airlines, which had enormous power when it came to channelling their clients into hotels. Not surprisingly, reservations from individuals were the most interesting, because the Hotel didn't have to pay anyone a 10 per cent commission on the room rate.

While Friday afternoon was their busiest time — many people wanted to confirm their booking before the weekend — reservations in general tended to be "event" sensitive. They dropped dramatically during the Gulf War, when Americans stopped travelling. They increased dramatically every time Sotheby's or Christie's held a major art auction. They went up during Wimbledon, the Chelsea Flower

Show, the polo season and the hunting season. They went down in summer when every tourist seemed to be on a package deal. And they boomed, unlike Barings Bank, when Barings crashed and it seemed as if every foreign businessman in the world was circling above London to see what bits could be picked off Barings' bones. There were already 19 bedrooms confirmed for New Year's Eve 1999–2000.

At least half the Hotel's guests requested a specific room. Which was what Mr Farouch wanted when he insisted on 204–205 for three nights.

The clerk said, politely, yes, they had rooms for those three nights, but explained that he could merely take a request for the specific room, although he promised the Hotel would do its best to meet that request.

Farouch said that wasn't good enough. "If you don't want my business . . ."

Without blinking, the Reservations clerk said, "Sir, let me see what I can do. Would you please be kind enough to hold on for just a moment . . ." And he instantly passed the call on to Buckolt.

Recognizing the man's name and knowing that he needed to be treated with kid gloves, Buckolt stroked his client by saying, "Yes, of course, sir, we would be delighted to have you back at the Hotel. And if those rooms are available, I will be more than glad to hold them for you. But I can see that we have someone in there who has suggested that he might not be checking out the night before you arrive. Obviously if he doesn't, I would like to propose a better suite for you, of course, at the same rate."

It was enough to pacify Farouch. "That would be fine."

Buckolt quoted the rack rate — Farouch accepted it — and then he asked, "Would you please be kind enough to confirm the reservation by fax."

"What are you talking about? I never confirm by fax. I have been staying there for a dozen years . . ."

Buckolt could tell from the guest history that Farouch had only stayed two other times, and both times were last year. "If you would rather not, sir, I can only hold the reservation until six that evening."

That gave them both a way out.

"Fine," the man said.

When he hung up, Buckolt added a note to the man's guest history that, if he didn't show up, they would require confirmation by fax from now on.

King Hassan II of Morocco checked in with his own bed, brought from one of his palaces. But he was having trouble sleeping, so someone on the staff suggested that they put one of the Hotel's own handmade mattresses on his bed. The King agreed, and slept so well that he placed an order with the Hotel to buy a palace-worth of their mattresses.

Lunch time was when Carole Ronald could sit down in her office for a few minutes.

First she did her weekly rota. Floor housekeepers worked until 6 pm, with one staying on until 11 to handle any evening problems that arose. A maid stayed on until 11 as well. Then she did her weekly requisition order for bathroom and cleaning supplies, and her bi-weekly stationery and pencil requisition. After that, she hurried through the arrivals list for the next day, writing out instructions for each floor housekeeper and posting them on the "Specials" board in her office. It was vital, she knew, to keep her floor housekeepers aware of those clients who throw tantrums when they don't get the extra attention they demand. The floor housekeepers, in turn, would post their instructions on a bulletin board in the maids' rooms, which were just behind the service stairs on each floor.

In other hotels, clients were made to feel anonymous. Here,

that was not the case. Until Ronald came along, staff addressed clients as Sir and Madam. She changed that, telling her maids, when you know a client and when it is appropriate, refer to the client by name. Then she put a sign in every maid service room reminding her staff, "You must always address a client by Sir or Madam. If you know their name, use their name."

It was a change that was slow in coming.

There was a time when the Back of House personnel — especially the housekeeping staff — were invisible. The only sign anyone ever saw of a maid servicing a room was her cart outside. But there were no maids' carts at the Hotel because Ronald felt they looked messy, and anything as unsightly as a messy trolley would detract from the overall effect.

As soon as she was finished with her "Specials" board, she was on her way out the door — back on her feet, moving around the Hotel — trying to solve problems before they became a problem, trying to stay ahead of a game that never ended.

~ 16 ~

$\mathcal{D}$ESSERTS HAD BEEN ON FRANÇOIS Touzin's mind since he got up that morning. He stood in the Front Hall, looking closely at the huge flower arrangements there, and thought about desserts. He continued thinking about desserts as he read through the logs. He wrote the word in English on a slip of paper, promising himself to bring it up at the morning meeting — "D-e-s-s-e-r-t-s," then realized it was the same word in French.

The meeting began, as it always did, with the statistics.

"Last night's occupancy was 89 per cent, we're getting there, with an average room rate of £265. The month-to-date occupancy is 70 per cent with an average room rate of £249.75. Last year-to-date's occupancy is 73 per cent with an average room rate of £223.90." He looked at Buckolt. "What did you think we'd end the month with?"

"Just over 70."

Touzin pulled an envelope out from his top drawer. "I'm going to win."

"Did you say 70?"

"Better," he bragged and, without opening it, put the envelope away. He pulled a log off the top of the pile. "Chief Engineer: Radiator covers in front of the lifts."

"They need changing," Purcell said.

"I agree. Let's replace the wire mesh with copper mesh because it looks better." As Purcell wrote himself a note about copper mesh, Touzin went on to the next item, "Boiler."

Purcell reported, "Our number three boiler went down last night. They worked on it overnight and it's up again now."

"If all our boilers go," Touzin wondered, "is there some place we store enough hot water for an hour or two?"

"No."

"So what do we do?"

Purcell told him, "Pray it never happens."

Touzin took the Rooms Division log: "Mr Tcherna in 302 originally said he'd be leaving today but has decided to stay on. However, the room has been let, so the guest has agreed to move to 412."

Buckolt acknowledged, "Taken care of."

He moved on to the Housekeeper's log. "Five-two-eight. Overflow."

Ronald said, "Last night at about 10."

"Bad?"

She shrugged, as if to say, are any of them good? "Average."

He read, "Lady Bancroft in 229 complained that the chairs which have been in the room for the past 40 years are not there any longer, and she wants them put back."

"Obviously," Ronald suggested, "Lady Bancroft hasn't stayed there for 40 years because the whole suite has been redecorated."

"Do you know what chairs she's talking about?"

"Yes."

"All right." It seemed simple enough to him. "Please get them and give them back to her." Then he said, "Shirts. Mr Christofi in 337, except he's already checked out."

"You'll like this one," Ronald said. "Mr Christofi handed two shirts to the maid for the laundry a week ago Thursday. By the time he left, the following day, the shirts had not come back. He only noticed they were missing when he got home. So he rang me first thing Monday morning, to ask that they be given to his friend Mr Georgio in 144 who would be leaving at the end of last week. I said I would. That same day, which was last Monday, one of the receptionists was taking a client up to 131 and found two white shirts sitting neatly folded on the chest of drawers. Not knowing the story of Mr Christofi's shirts, he took them to the valet, who brought them to me. I sent them to 144 with a little note explaining the situation. Mr Georgio, obviously wanting to pass the good news on to Christofi, phoned him to say he had the shirts. But after a short discussion, where Mr Georgio must have described the shirts, Mr Christofi decided these weren't his."

"Oh." Touzin wanted to know, "Whose were they?"

"The plot thickens." She said, "Mr Georgio returned the shirts to me. At that point, Mr Youngblood in 132 called the valet to ask where his shirts were. So I sent the two white shirts to Mr Youngblood, who took them from the valet, packed them and went home." She stopped there.

Touzin waited. When nothing more was forthcoming, he asked, "So where are Mr Christofi's shirts?"

Ronald shrugged, "I was hoping you knew."

"They've never shown up?"

She confirmed, "They've never showed up."

Taking a deep breath, he dared, "How much?"

"I'm still waiting to hear about that from Mr Christofi."

"Just once," he said, "I'd like to lose a Marks and Spencer's shirt that only cost £10."

Pierron volunteered, "It's been a long time since you've shopped at Marks and Spencer."

Grinning, he closed Ronald's log and took the Night Manager's. "Mr Fredericks, 516–517, ordered a bottle of house champagne from Room Service last night. After he opened it, he complained that it was too dry." He turned to Salter, "The house champagne is Pol Roger, no?"

"Yes, sir."

"That's not very dry." He made a face. "What did he want?"

"He was shown the wine list and chose Laurent Perrier Brut."

"Laurent Perrier Brut?" Touzin couldn't believe it. "That's much drier than Pol Roger."

"He loved it."

"As long as the guest is happy," Touzin laughed, jotting down a note to himself to see that Mr Fredericks' guest history was updated to note his preference for Laurent Perrier Brut. "Duty Manager: At 17:30 a passerby informed the doorman that there was a dead body lying on the street just up the road. The doorman called for an ambulance. The dead man was revived and taken to hospital." He had to know, "Was he one of our clients?"

Purcell, who'd been Duty Manager, assured him, "No."

"That's good. Otherwise it would have affected our yield." He nodded. "Mrs Lerner, 323, complained that the phone in her bedroom didn't ring. Only the extension in the bathroom rings. She was very upset."

"I found out about that this morning," Pierron said, "and went to her room. Apparently someone had turned down the volume on the ringer. I fixed it and apologized."

The logbooks finished, Touzin went around the room.

Ronald said, "Nothing," but he said to her, "You know, we are very lucky. Our flowers in the Front Hall are very well behaved."

She stared at him wondering what he was talking about.

"Very well behaved," he repeated. "They don't bother anyone. All they ask for is a little water."

She nodded, "I get the message."

Purcell said, "Nothing," but Pierron had something to discuss. "The switchboard is not being told who's gone home. They need to know that so they can turn off that person's bleeper. Please, when you leave, tell the switchboard you've gone."

"Good point," Touzin agreed.

Krenzer had nothing, but Jarman did. "There is a dinner in the Ballroom tonight at nine for 96 people. The workmen will come in after midnight to start on the room for the banquet. They'll be in the Hotel all night."

"Ah." Touzin raised his index finger, suddenly remembering, "Desserts." He paused, but it was one beat too long because, as he sat there with his finger pointing towards the ceiling, no one in the room had a clue what he was talking about. "Desserts." He asked Jarman, "When we do a buffet, how do we present the desserts?"

"If you're referring to a sitting buffet, we do a wonderful dessert selection. But for a standing buffet we only do finger desserts. Otherwise people have to juggle too many plates. They run out of hands."

He nodded several times, then leaned back in his chair. "I went to a cocktail party last night and they did à la carte desserts. Each waiter carried a large round tray and served one dessert after another onto a tea plate with a spoon. It was perfect. They had apple tart, cassata, bread and butter pudding and crêpes. It all came out of the kitchen. It was very impressive."

Jarman was fast to say, "We can do that sort of thing . . ."

"Of course, we can. I know that. But we didn't think of it. And when I saw it, I said to myself, we're not being innovative enough. We can't allow ourselves to get stale. We've got to keep coming up with new ideas. So, when any of you go somewhere, watch the competition. If the bill is reasonable and we learn something from it, I'll pay for the evening. How's that?"

"What else did they do?" Jarman wanted to know.

"They did cold canapés but ours are better than theirs. Although they had some wonderful sushi. We also beat them on the hot side. I must say, I didn't like their waiters. But I did like their desserts. And it bothered me because I know we can do them better. So I'd like you to take a closer look at the way we do it. Look at everything, even the china we're using."

"All right." Jarman made some notes.

"Are you really going to pay our bills?" Purcell asked mischievously.

Touzin knew what he was thinking. "No, you cannot go to Hong Kong and check into the Mandarin for five days." Everyone laughed. "But we can't allow ourselves to become complacent. We've got to keep beating the competition, so let's get out there and find out what they're doing."

Buckolt said, "Four days in Hong Kong?"

Again everyone laughed.

"I'll tell you what else I saw last night. I checked out their restaurant. I didn't like the colour of their tablecloths. Much too dark for that room. Then I walked across the street, and you know what struck me when I walked into that lobby? Reception was two desks with laptop computers. You know, the sort that fold down, so that you can't see a computer screen when no one is using it. Very elegant."

Pierron volunteered, "I'd love it but you wouldn't when you saw the bill. Changing over to something like that would cost a fortune."

"I liked it because it was discreet. It was well thought out. And elegant." He looked around the room. "We need to get out more." Then he said, "Michael?"

Duncan announced, "The Princess Royal will be in for lunch today. She will arrive at 11:30 at the front door." He asked Touzin, "Will you be in tails to greet her?"

He said he would.

Now it was Buckolt's turn. "We need to get 407 straightened out."

Purcell assured him, "I can do it, but you have to give me the room."

"How long do you need?"

"Overnight."

"I'll get it to you this week." Then he said, "I need a CD player to go into 510 for Mr O'Mally."

Pierron answered, "I've got three but two are out."

Buckolt said, "That leaves one."

"Anyway," Pierron reminded him, "he has his own in storage. He left it here last time."

Ronald corrected, "He took it with him."

"Then why is it still in the guest history?" Pierron wondered.

She shrugged, "It should be deleted, but I can't delete it."

Pierron gloated, jokingly, "Rightfully so."

Touzin asked, "Arrivals?"

"The big one is Mr Al-Turki." Buckolt said, "He's coming into 528, 529 and 530 for six weeks, with his family. He complained last time that the room was hot, so Mrs Ronald, could you check please to make certain the air-conditioning is on before he gets here this afternoon. He's due in around five. Also, you'll see in his guest history that he wants the desk moved in 528."

"If I remember right," Touzin said, "he complained last time that there weren't enough vegetarian dishes on the menu. I'm sure it's in his guest history. What are we doing for him this time?"

"We have a special file on him," Buckolt said, "which I'll bring to you after the meeting. He mentioned the food to me as well when he booked. I passed it along to Mr Krenzer and he's arranged for the Chef to do a special menu for him. It will be changed every week as long as he's here."

"All six weeks?"

"The Chef knows and doesn't see any problem with doing new dishes every week."

"We have to handle him very carefully," Touzin warned.

"That's another thing," Buckolt said. "There's also a note in his file that he wishes to be addressed as Your Excellency. So please," he looked around the room, "if you see him, don't call him Mr Al-Turki. Address him as Your Excellency." He nodded to show Touzin he was finished with that. "Ambassador and Mrs Nicholson are due back, arriving at 11 am, staying in 423–424. Will you please greet them?"

Touzin noted their arrival. "I will make myself available."

"Mr and Mrs Ralph Roberts, in 320, are due in this morning. They were here for a week last winter. And they're staying a week again this time. It's Mrs Roberts' birthday on Saturday . . ." He stopped and looked at Touzin.

He picked up the cue immediately. "Yes, please arrange for a small cake to be sent to their room."

Buckolt scribbled that down. "We have a honeymoon couple coming into 107–108 for two nights . . ." He stopped again.

Touzin nodded.

And he wrote himself another note, this time to see that a bottle of champagne was waiting in the suite for them.

"Mr and Mrs Lassiter have requested 114–115 for three nights and have been warned that it might not be available. It isn't. So I've put them in 401–402. The artist Christo and his wife are in for five days . . ."

Touzin, knowing that Christo was famous for wrapping bridges in Paris, islands in Florida and the Reichstag in Berlin asked, "Shall we leave the room unwrapped?"

There were polite smiles around the room.

Buckolt covered the silence. "Mr and Mrs Pickford are on the London Greeting Program, arriving today for two nights in 141. Mr and Mrs Sonnenberg are honeymooners coming in around noon for one week. I've put them in 312–314 and arranged for a bottle of champagne, if that's all right."

Touzin said it was.

Ronald cut in, "There's a small problem in 312–314 with the wallpaper. It's being repaired now but won't be ready for their arrival."

Buckolt wondered, "Why wasn't the room blocked?"

"It was," she said.

"If it had been taken out of service, I wouldn't have let it."

Touzin asked, "Is 412–414 available?"

"I can do that," Buckolt said, "but I'm concerned that the room didn't show up on the computer as out of service."

"I'll check," Pierron offered. "We can discuss it right after the meeting."

Buckolt continued. "Mr Howard, 631, two nights. He liked that the last time. Mr and Mrs Jensen are in 627, their favourite room, for two nights, full rack. Mr Figiero is here for his third visit this year in 401–402. I've put Mr and Mrs Peters in 220 for two nights. They're lovely people who have stayed here for years. But he's getting very old and doesn't hear very well. Just to warn people. And we've got Mr and Mrs Keating with their daughter coming into 127–128 for three nights . . ."

Ronald asked, "How old is the daughter?"

Buckolt checked his notes. "Nine."

"Thanks," she said, and wrote, "127–128, one child's bathrobe."

Touzin wanted to know, "What do we charge for extra beds?"

"You mean to put an extra bed in a room?" Buckolt told him, "Five pounds. I assume you're referring to a bed for a child."

"Yes. And I think it's not enough."

"We never used to charge . . ."

"Let's add five more."

Buckolt had his doubts. "That's doubling it."

"That's right. Make it £10. Don't start with the Keatings, but from now on."

He shrugged, obviously unsure it was the right thing to do. "All right."

"That all?" Touzin looked around the room and, seeing that no one had anything else to say, reminded his staff, "Parking restrictions for the Return State Banquet will go into effect tomorrow morning in the front of the Hotel. Parking at the rear of the Hotel is already blocked off as of today. Okay? Have a good day."

The meeting broke up, but Salter stayed to speak to Touzin. "Are we going to continue keeping cigar boxes on the floors? People ask for cigars after the restaurant closes, and the restaurant won't let us use their cigars."

"Do you know why they won't let you use their stock?" Touzin explained, "Because it's a losing business. Shelf life is too short, turnover is too small and stock control is a nightmare. Nobody will let you use their stock. I don't blame them. You shouldn't let them use your stock, either."

"Then you want me to keep some on the floors?"

"Maybe two or three of each kind, and preferably those in tubes because they last longer. We want to continue serving the guests but . . . well, maybe when they ask for a cigar we should remind them that smoking isn't good for their health."

"Tell them what, sir? Are you serious?"

Touzin grinned — "Two or three of each kind, preferably in tubes, should be fine" — seeing that a week of nights had taken its toll.

~ 17 ~

*M*ONDAY, WORKMEN POURED INTO the function rooms. The walls were painted, the carpets were shampooed, the chandeliers were cleaned, the marble was polished and the curtains were vacuumed. Jarman phoned the Assistant Master of the Household at Buckingham Palace — for all intents and purposes he was the Queen's Food and Beverage Manager — to go over the menu and ask if there was anything else Her Majesty wanted. He also rang the Queen's ADC to ask, "Is there anything I should know?" The ADC assured Jarman that everything would be fine.

On Tuesday, the Amir of Kuwait — Sheikh Jabar al-Ahmad al-Jabar al-Sabah — arrived at Buckingham Palace, taking up residence in the Belgian Suite on the north side, not far from the Queen's private apartments, overlooking Constitution Hill. Jarman rang the Queen's ADC again, this time to ask, "Is there anything I should tell you?" The ADC reassured Jarman that everything was going according to plan.

On Wednesday, Jarman got to the Hotel just after dawn, convinced that there weren't enough hours left in the day and a half that remained to get everything done. He sat at his desk, oblivious to the

Hotel waking up around him, going over the seating arrangements and sorting out place cards.

Downstairs, at the rear door, while fruit and vegetables and bread were coming in from suppliers, the silver arrived from the re-plater. An hour later, plates, cutlery and glasses for the State Banquet — every piece brand new — were also delivered. The Back of House Manager counted them and reported to the Chef, "They've sent 180 covers. More than enough for 172 guests." But Lesnik saw it differently. That many covers for that many guests meant there was very little leeway for breakage. The Back of House Manager spent the rest of the morning polishing the silver.

The company hired by the Embassy to create the theme for the State Banquet had designed a huge tent which they intended to construct inside the Ballroom. They'd gone through months of meetings with the Ambassador and his wife, a task completely separate from anything that involved the Hotel. The original plan was to use a dark cherry colour, and at first the Kuwaitis liked that, but they changed their minds and opted for something lighter. At the last minute, they also asked to have a gilded cage set up at the entrance to the Ballroom, with a live falcon inside.

Although the themers and their designer came to look at the Ballroom, discussing some of their plans with Jarman, it wasn't until 5:30 on Wednesday afternoon — when the crews arrived to start building the tent — that he, or anyone at the Hotel, realized how massive an effort this was going to be. It took 30 workmen just to bring all of the equipment into the Reception Room (where everything had to be hand-searched by the police), eight electricians to wire the function rooms and 12 florists to help decorate them.

Throughout the evening, as they were setting up, Jarman constantly had to remind the workers not to make any noise because there was a dinner going on in the Ballroom. But the moment that dinner ended, the noise was turned on, and stayed loud, for the rest of the night.

On Thursday morning, somewhere around 3:30, Jarman simply gave up. He'd been running on little more than nervous energy for the past three days and had finally reached the point where he couldn't keep his eyes open any longer. He went upstairs to an empty room and tried to get some sleep. He was back in the Ballroom by 5:30.

The sides of the tent were up, casting a glow of billowing golden beige silk. The ceiling was covered in silk too, crested at the top so that no one could miss the desert effect. But the tent — constructed on supports fixed against the walls — narrowed the room by 2½ feet. The head table was in place — running the entire length of the far wall — and a dozen large round wooden tables were being rolled in. He watched as they were set up, then as chairs were carried in, stacked three and four together. Then came four thrones, to seat the Queen, the Amir, Prince Philip and, Jarman presumed, the Amir's senior wife.

And now the room felt cramped. There wasn't a lot of spread between the tables and only a few feet separated the back of the thrones and the wall of the tent. He began to worry that it didn't leave the waiters a lot of space to manoeuvre behind the top table.

He noticed that someone had placed a large chair, slightly hidden, just at the rear of the thrones. Obviously intended for a translator — because the Queen didn't speak Arabic and the Amir didn't speak English — it completely blocked the way.

That can't stay there, he mumbled, went behind the top table and carried it away. Then he went in search of something to take its place. Eventually, he settled on a piano stool. It didn't look very elegant, but it would have to do.

At exactly 6 that morning, 22 uniformed officers, together with two sniffer dogs, arrived at the Hotel to carry out a search.

They scoured the place — going over every inch of the basement, the ground floor, the first floor and the roof — and looked in

ventilation shafts, lift shafts and roof voids. They found some interesting stuff — a couple of wallets that had, long ago, been stolen
from some members of staff — but nothing that worried them for
this visit. In the past, the police had occasionally put marksmen on
the roof of the Hotel, but that wasn't going to happen this time.
They were mainly concerned with explosives.

Just after 9, once most of the guests were awake and finished
with their breakfasts, Baxter took the dog handlers, the dogs and a
few officers along the first-floor corridor. He knocked on doors,
waited for guests to respond and politely explained the situation.
"We have a very important banquet in the Hotel tonight, with members of the Royal Family attending, including Her Majesty the
Queen. If it's not too inconvenient for you at this time, may we
please bring the sniffer dogs in to check your room?"

Almost everyone seemed amused by the idea, especially the
Americans, who were only too happy to let the dogs in because it
gave them a story to take home — "Let me tell you about the time I
personally protected the Queen of England!" In one room, however,
a European gentleman appeared a bit unsure about the sniffer
dogs, and tried to talk Baxter out of it. But the officer in charge was
quite insistent — he didn't have to smile the way Baxter did — so
the guest moved out of the way to allow one of the dogs into the
room. After checking the bed, under the bed and behind the curtains, the dog sniffed the television set, started to walk away, seemed
a little unsure, and came back to it. His tail wagged to show his interest in the television, but it wasn't the reaction his handler knew
the dog would have if he'd found explosives. So, after the handler
had taken him through the rest of the room, he proclaimed it clean.
At least, there were no explosives. Baxter said thank you, the group
moved on to the next room and the guest was plainly relieved to see
them go.

The search went on until 3 that afternoon. The final area to be
swept was the banqueting rooms. When the dogs had finished there,

Special Branch designated the rooms "Red" — which meant that anyone now coming into that part of the Hotel needed a pass to get by the police.

At the same time, Special Branch set up a command post in room 52, on the mezzanine floor, to coordinate radio communications.

There was still no word on whether or not the fundamentalist group would show up, but the police were planning that they would, and barricaded the street. There was no parking anywhere along the block, except by police vehicles. The large, uniformed presence that was already in place efficiently discouraged anyone who even thought about parking near the Hotel.

Baxter asked two Intelligence officers to glance through the Hotel's guest list, but no names stood out. So he reported to Touzin that, at least according to the police, no one from the fundamentalist group had got inside. Still, two plain clothes cops were stationed in the Front Hall, to look at everyone coming and going.

The main contingent of protection officers arrived at the Hotel by 5. Backup cars were put in place. Everyone was briefed on escape routes, just in case the Queen and Prince Charles — as heir to the throne — had to be evacuated. A "safe" room was also designated, in the centre of the building, should the Hotel come under attack and the royals couldn't be taken out safely.

Jarman was still concerned about the waiters. With chairs in place around the tables, the space between them seemed as tight as it was behind the top table. So he pulled one chair away from a table in the centre of the room — approximating where it would be when someone was sitting on it — and sat in a chair at the table next to it.

He was still sitting there, worried, when one of the Food and Beverage secretaries appeared carrying a package of shop-bought muffins and a cup of coffee. He swallowed a muffin and gulped some coffee. That's when Sally — the Food and Beverage Sales Coordinator — ran up to inform him that some of the rented uniforms didn't fit. He asked her if she would please handle it. But the woman at the formal-wear hire shop only wanted to argue with Sally — insisting that everyone had been properly measured — and nothing Sally said could make her understand that that wasn't the point. So Sally persuaded Jarman to ring her. He went up to the Food and Beverage office, got the woman on the line and repeated to her that two trousers and one jacket didn't fit. The woman maintained she'd sent the correct sizes. He didn't think he had the energy for this and he knew he didn't have the time for this, but he stayed calm and after a while got her to agree to replace the ill-fitting items.

A few minutes later, Reception rang to say that there was someone downstairs to see him. He asked, who is it? Reception said, a man who'd come to see the function rooms for a banquet next week.

Afraid that he'd somehow forgotten an appointment, he checked his diary. Nothing was written down. His first thought was to say, I just don't have time. The man didn't have an appointment and Jarman was annoyed that someone should just show up like that, at exactly the wrong time. But the State Banquet wasn't the only event he'd booked for the year and, after thinking about it for a moment, he decided he also owed this client some of his time. He told Reception, "I'll be right there."

Pulling himself wearily out from behind his desk, he told himself, if the man really wants to see what the Hotel can do for him, I'll show him. He walked into the Front Hall, found the man waiting there, greeted him, said, "I'm not supposed to do this, but . . ." and escorted him into the Ballroom.

The tent, the flowers, the workmen moving in every direction, the police guarding the doors — the effect was astonishing.

Impressed beyond words, the man just stood there with his mouth open.

As soon as he politely could, Jarman escorted the gentleman to the Front Hall, said he looked forward to next week's function, shook his hand, and hurried back to the Ballroom.

It never even dawned on him that he should go to Touzin's morning meeting.

"Duty Manager," Touzin read, "Mr and Mrs Cresswell, 221–222, are not happy because the room for their children is not connecting with their suite."

Buckolt explained, "It wasn't reserved as a connecting room. The best I could do was to put them across the corridor, just opposite."

"Can you rearrange it?"

"I'm already trying."

"One of the night switchboard operators was ill." Touzin looked at Pierron. "I'd like to make certain that we always have two people on the switchboard overnight. It's not just for clients but also for security in case of an emergency."

Pierron nodded.

He continued. "Mr Boyer, due in yesterday, had asked that we put a fax machine in his room. All ours were being used, so I hired one for him. Late last night, he cancelled his reservation."

Buckolt shrugged.

"Mrs Zeeman," Touzin said, then explained, "There was some confusion six months ago when Dr and Mrs Zeeman stayed with us. The afternoon they were leaving, Mrs Zeeman saw another guest, who was also leaving, being presented with a bouquet of flowers. Dr Zeeman wrote me a note about it and I added a note to their guest history. Well, the Zeemans are coming in tomorrow."

Right away Buckolt said, "I will arrange the flowers for her."

Touzin grinned and picked up the Food and Beverage logbook: "Someone complained about having to wait too long in the Foyer for a drink." He told Krenzer, "When the Foyer gets busy, I want the Hall Porter or the Duty Manager, or whoever notices that it's busy, to notify the restaurant so that they can send a second waiter in to help. There is no reason for anyone to complain about not getting prompt service."

Krenzer said he would speak to Azoulai.

"Housekeeping: At 16:45, yesterday, a woman fainted in front of the lift. The Nursing Sister was called immediately. Her husband has a virus and the woman was simply fatigued."

Buckolt again. "I have spoken to them this morning and they're both feeling better."

"Good." Finished with the logs, Touzin pointed around the room.

Buckolt wanted everyone to know, "Mr Halpern is due in from New York on Concorde. You all know how difficult he can be."

"That's right." Touzin warned, "He's got to be treated with kid gloves. Please make certain that everyone knows."

It was Krenzer's turn. "The uniforms for tonight have arrived. Everyone must try them on before noon, so that if something doesn't fit, they can go back."

"What about the retiring rooms?"

Ronald answered, "They're ready."

"I'll want to look at them," Touzin said. "As you all know, the event is dry. No alcohol will be served at the banquet. However, the lounge is open just in case some of our honoured guests would like to have something to drink or somewhere to sit before the banquet starts."

Krenzer said, "Everyone in tails by 5:30, please. Andrew will brief the staff then, but there won't be any separate briefings for the managers."

"Where is Andrew?" Touzin suddenly realized he wasn't there. "Will someone please tell him I would like another briefing." He checked his calendar. "Let's do it at 11:30."

✠

It was just what Jarman didn't want to hear.

There was too much happening. He didn't have the time. Anyway, there wasn't much he could say that Touzin didn't already know.

He was busy going through a long list of things he needed to discuss with the Banqueting maîue d', a short, wiry guy in his early 50s named Joe Domingues. Jarman was about to ask if there was enough space between the tables for the waiters to serve, when Domingues said something about the waiters making their entrance through the three doors at the side of the Ballroom. That's when Krenzer appeared, needing to know right away where the briefing would be.

Jarman answered with the first place that popped into his head, "The Drawing Room." But when Krenzer insisted that the two of them go there to have a look, they found that the florists had taken over. Boxes and crates and flowers were spread out everywhere. Wherever they turned, another florist said, "Excuse me, please," and made them get out of the way.

So Jarman had to go off in search of somewhere to hold the briefing. The room behind the kitchen was available. He asked Lesnik's secretary to ring Krenzer and tell him, then rushed back to the Ballroom to find Domingues.

Between the themers, the florists, the carpenters, the carpet fitters, the painters, the waiters and the uniformed cops who packed the function rooms, it was as if a 75-headed monster had taken over the Hotel. Worse still, it was as if everyone on the staff was being sacrificed in order to feed that monster.

The Hotel was 83 per cent full. Guests checked in and guests checked out and guests wanted Room Service. The kitchen couldn't stop. Housekeeping couldn't stop.

Nor was there a halt to the stream of people who, throughout the morning, kept walking up to Jarman to tell him their problems. I

don't know where these flowers go. Ask the florist. Where am I supposed to put these chairs? Ask the themer. I can't come to the briefing. Too bad for you.

At 11:15, he made his way to his office to get his notes. Phones
were ringing and bleepers were going off. Sally was sitting at the side
of his desk, trying to match place cards with the seating chart.

A man came up to Jarman carrying a fistful of pens and pencils.
"Are there any pads in here?"

Jarman snapped, "This isn't W H Smiths."

Duncan opened the door, spotted Jarman and explained that
his jacket was one size too large.

Jarman told him, "Take it to the valet and he'll alter it for you."

Seeing the unfinished box of muffins, Duncan helped himself
to one, bit into it and mumbled, "These are even moister than the
blueberry muffins we make."

No one wanted to know.

The Embassy rang to say that they would not be sending four
waiters to serve the Amir and the Queen, as previously planned. Jarman wondered out loud, what else can go wrong? He grabbed a few
place cards to help Sally. But the name on the card didn't match any
on the list. "Who's this?"

Sally answered, "I don't have a clue."

He put it aside to worry about later.

"Here's a name spelled one way on the guest list and another
way on the place card."

She took it from him and put it aside as well.

A television producer from an Arabic station called to ask if he
could film the banquet. Jarman told them, "No. It's not permitted.
You can check with the Embassy but they'll tell you the same thing."
The producer mumbled something, giving Jarman the impression
that he'd already checked with the Embassy and been told no. "It has
nothing to do with the Hotel. You'll have to take it up with the Embassy." He hung up, too spent to explain how royal protocol dictated

that the Queen must never be filmed or photographed while she's eating.

Purcell came in carrying a pair of trousers. "These are too long."

"The valet," Jarman said.

Sally handed him more place cards.

"The valet?" Purcell waited for someone to explain which valet. But no one did. So he shrugged and went to find any valet.

Now Domingues was on the phone. "What am I supposed to do with a box of sugared almonds that was just delivered me?"

"Send it to the Chef."

Five minutes later, one of the cooks called. "There's a box of sugared almonds here. Chef wants to know what we're supposed to do with it?"

"Serve them tonight," Jarman snapped, hung up, checked his watch and realized he was late. He told Sally, "Leave the cards right where they are," and hurried down to the briefing.

He rushed into the room. But most of the people who should have been there were not yet there. "Where is everybody?" He checked his watch again. It was 11:40. The Queen's ADC was due in at 12:10 to look around and Jarman didn't want to keep him waiting.

Then Touzin showed up. The others walked in behind him. So Jarman began. He told the staff how the themers had come in last night and that the tent was now done. He suggested everyone be in their formal gear by 5:30 and said that there would be an order-of-service briefing at 6:30. He also outlined everyone's jobs for the night. It was fairly straightforward, he reminded them. "We've been over it all before. Does anyone have any questions, or anything they want to add?"

Baxter raised his hand. "The police have just confirmed that an Islamic student organization will be protesting against the Amir's visit tonight."

Collectively, everyone in the room groaned.

"The police are not expecting any trouble," Baxter said. "But it could get noisy. They'll be kept across the street and well away from the Queen and the Amir."

It was easy to see from Jarman's expression that he was thinking, I could have done without this.

"There was a demonstration in front of the Guildhall last night protesting against the Amir's visit," Baxter went on. "It was 30 to 50 students. They were well organized and well behaved, except that they were noisy. Please, if anyone sees an early build-up of demonstrators, let me know."

Buckolt asked, "Are we going to close the side entrance?"

Touzin said, "We can if we have to."

"I'll see what the police say." Baxter took note of that. "We're expecting 45 officers on fixed-post duty, which includes the side entrance, so it may not be necessary."

"Anything else?" Jarman said impatiently.

Baxter again. "I have little stick-on dots which everyone will have to wear this evening. Red for management. Yellow for supervisors. Blue for the rest of the staff, including all the waiters. Anyone who doesn't have one on his or her lapel will be challenged by the police. I'll hand them out later. Please remember to wear them. Please make sure they don't fall off."

"You know what?" Touzin had a thought. "We should send a note to every guest in the Hotel, explaining that we're having a Royal State Banquet here tonight and apologizing for any noise or inconvenience." He pointed to Buckolt. "Don't scare anyone. Just explain all the extra security."

Buckolt said he would do that.

"Oh," Touzin added, "I want an extra Foyer waiter in the lounge this evening."

Jarman looked around the room to see if anyone else wanted to say something.

Baxter showed that he wasn't yet finished. "Once everyone sits down to dinner, we're going to put a table in the Painted Room for eight of the police officers to eat. And there will be dinner for 40 in the staff canteen, which will include the chauffeurs, the uniformed guys, and so forth."

Ronald wanted to know, "Will the Queen have a cape?"

No one knew.

"The Queen usually leaves her cape in the car," she said. "But just in case, one of my girls will be in the Ladies' Cloakroom, so if she walks in with a cape, she can leave it there. In fact, there will be two people in the Ladies' Cloakroom and two people in the Gents'. The retirement rooms are now closed. Remember, the Royal Suite is for the Queen. The other royal ladies will use 114–115."

"The dogs haven't been in there yet," Baxter said. "They won't be in until five, although there is an officer at the door now. We've given keys to the Royal Suite to the Queen's close protection officer. And some of the other officers have keys too."

Touzin wanted everyone to remember, "Mr Jarman will control the service. If you have any questions, go to him. And the Chef will only take instructions from Mr Jarman."

Jarman nodded, as if to emphasize that's the way it had to be, then read from a printed list. "Seven pm the fitted red carpet goes down; 8:20 the Queen leaves Buckingham Palace. All the guests will be in the Hotel by that time. Eight-twenty-five she arrives here, to be greeted on the pavement by Mr Touzin. She and Prince Philip are the last people to arrive. Her aide will organize the top-table entrance. There will be no toasts and no speeches. There will be two TV crews here, by invitation of the Embassy. One will be in the street to film the arrival of the Amir and the Queen. The other will be behind the stanchions in the Ballroom Reception to film them coming into the reception. Then they will leave." He stopped, waited, then dared, "Anyone else?"

The Chef wanted everyone to know, "There will be Lebanese bread in addition to the Hotel's dinner rolls. Ours will be served at the beginning of the meal. The Lebanese bread won't be served until the lamb is served."

"Good." It wasn't that Jarman could have cared less about bread, it was just that he had too many other things on his mind. "Anyone else?"

Touzin asked, "Which route will the Queen take when she leaves the French Salon?"

"She'll go down the Painted Corridor," Jarman explained. "She and Prince Philip and their close protection officer will be escorted by the Amir back to the Ballroom entrance. Cars will just appear. Her aide arranges all that. The entire evening should last no more than two hours. Although, if the Queen is enjoying herself, she has been known to stay a little while longer." He glanced at his watch and saw that it was just 12:10. "Nothing else?" He didn't leave a lot of time for anyone to think about it. "Thank you." He dashed away, hoping that the Queen's ADC hadn't yet arrived.

Touzin pulled himself out of his chair and, leaving the room, said matter of factly to Duncan, "So far so good."

Duncan wondered, "You ever hear of Murphy's Law?"

He stopped at the pastry kitchen to see what was happening.

Derek, working at the far end, pointed towards a side counter. "That's what it should look like. We'll add the ice cream at the last minute."

Touzin studied the caramelized pear. "I'll come back when there's one for me with the ice cream." He said hello to some of the young cooks, who were too busy to pay him any attention, turned out of the pastry kitchen and walked up the steps towards the Chef's office.

Lesnik, who was standing just inside the door of the main kitchen, spotted him. "Come and taste this."

Ambling over, Touzin put his hand on the Chef's shoulder. "I'm hungry."

"Get me a spoon please," Lesnik called to a cook, then led Touzin towards a small pot on the stove. "We're just finalizing the soup." A cook arrived with two spoons.

Touzin took them, stared into the pot, stirred the soup gently — "What a beautiful colour" — then lifted out just enough for one taste. "Hmmmm." He started nodding with the spoon still in his mouth. "I love it. The saffron taste is just right." He dipped the second spoon in for a second taste. "The texture is right too. Wonderful."

"Now look at these." The Chef escorted him into the fish station, opened one of the cold storage cabinets and brought out a tray with the fillets. "You like that?"

"What did *hamoor* turn out to be?"

"Grouper."

Touzin inspected the fillets. "I think I owe it to the Queen to come back at around seven this evening, just to have a taste. How's that?" He left the Chef, taking the long way around the back corridor to the Ballroom stairs.

Someone had taped large cardboard arrows on the floor near the staff canteen with the words "Tea Room" so that the police could find the place.

In the hallway, just in front of the staff kitchen, sat a 30-foot steam table. With a flat surface on top and cupboards underneath, a large valve opened to let steam run through it. If the Chef left the steam on for just half an hour, the table and the cupboards stayed hot for up to four hours.

Facing the steam table were two staircases, both strictly one-way. Right was always up, left was always down, because in the commotion caused by cooks working a banquet, waiters needed to serve food quickly, and there could never be any confusion about the stairs.

There was also a large clock facing the steam table, to help keep the chefs on schedule. Ten minutes to first course, 25 minutes to second course, 45 minutes to dessert. Nearby was a large combination oven — convection and steam — which they used mainly for soufflés.

At the top of the stairs there was a small room where the waiters could get plates and table service, and then another set of double doors — again, one to go out, one to come in — at the side of the Mirror Room.

That's where the waiters would assemble before serving each course in the Ballroom.

Now upstairs, Touzin went to see what the French Salon and the Drawing Room looked like. The Hotel's furniture had been taken out and the rooms were restocked with chairs from a supplier who did film sets. In the Drawing Room, two very ornate chairs, with a small table separating them, were set up so that the Queen and the Amir could take their coffee together. Although there were other chairs in both those rooms, everyone else would be expected to stand.

Touzin liked what he was seeing.

In the Ballroom, dozens of people were scurrying about, setting up tables, hanging flowers, running wires along the floor, standing in the corner watching the others work.

Jarman was deep in conversation with the ADC, showing him where the Queen would come into the room and how the doors at the side would be opened when the meal was over and that the Mirror Room would be the corridor she'd use to go into the other two rooms where coffee would be served.

The tables were in place, but chairs were scattered everywhere. The room hadn't yet taken shape. It would be another three hours before every chair was covered in beige silk — to match the tent — and waiters would start to set the tables.

Still, the tent made the room feel warm and intimate. Touzin admired it for quite a while, before walking behind the head table to look at the room the way the Queen would see it. He leaned on one of the four thrones.

Suddenly, a workman came by and literally moved that throne out from under him. "Sorry, guv."

Now there were only three throne chairs.

"The Queen, the Amir and Prince Philip," Duncan said, walking up to him.

Touzin asked, "Mrs Amir isn't coming?"

Duncan shook his finger. "They never do."

Two young women stepped in front of Touzin — "Excuse me" — laying a hand-painted silk cloth onto the top table.

Absolutely spectacular, in gold and shades of gold, it ran the entire 64-foot length and had a 30-inch drop at the sides. The motif was decidedly Arabic.

When they had it right, smooth and even, one of the women took more paint and, just where the Queen and the Amir would sit, coloured a large freehand scroll.

The Amir would probably never realize that these women spent two weeks making and painting this tablecloth. Nor would he ever know that he'd paid £4000 for it. At the end of the evening, it would be rolled up, put into a large box and stored somewhere in the Embassy, more than likely never to be used again.

An outside firm of florists had arrived at the Hotel with 360 boxes of flowers and greenery. It took them all night just to unload their vans. It took them all morning to unpack everything. Now, there were flowers everywhere — on tables and on the floor, and there were empty boxes on the floor too. There were peonies, lilies, snapdragons, delphiniums, sweet peas, and several thousand roses of at least a dozen different varieties. There was every colour imaginable.

The Amir's flower bill would come to £30,000.

Domingues sat down at the desk in the Banqueting maître d's minuscule office — off to the side of the Mirror Room, next to the waiter's service room — with an air of great confidence. He'd been through this before, having orchestrated hundreds of banquets — maybe even a thousand by now, he didn't know — because running the service at banquets was what he did for a living. Nor did it especially matter to him that it was the Queen who was going to dine here. He'd served her before, too. As far as he was concerned, a banquet was a banquet was a banquet.

"Glasses?" he asked Jarman. "Are they in?"

"Yes. There are 550 smaller glasses for water and 180 larger ones for juice."

"That's tight."

Jarman agreed. "That's very tight. Don't break any."

"We don't have any spare ones to break." Domingues handed him several sheets of paper, making up the evening's assignments.

Jarman studied it. "There are no Kuwaiti waiters."

He seemed surprised. "Since when?"

"Ah . . . that was the message from the Embassy. They called."

"Nice of someone to tell me." He took the seating plan back and corrected it. "You're sure?"

"I'm sure."

At 5:30, eight officers from the Royal Protection Group arrived to supplement the plain clothes Special Branch officers who were already on duty. There were seven large men and one rather slight woman.

Dressed in formal evening wear, they carried small portable radios in their pockets — no wires were hanging out of their ears — a heavy metal baton on their belts, just inside the fold of their dinner jackets, and a large pistol tucked into a shoulder holster under their arms.

There were now 18 armed plain clothes officers inside the Hotel, with six others covering the front and rear entrances, backed up by 80 uniformed police on the street to handle traffic and crowd control.

There were also four Kuwaiti Secret Service men, armed and deliberately visible, to reassure the Amir and the members of his government that they were safe, too.

Baxter greeted the eight and gave them a tour of the function rooms. He explained how the evening would go and described the little coloured stick-on dots that he'd issued to everyone from the Hotel. He took them downstairs and into the kitchen. He introduced them to the Chef, the sous-chefs and the cooks — the police nodded politely at everyone without making any comments — so that they could familiarize themselves with the faces they would be seeing throughout the evening.

The Chef, the sous-chefs and the cooks couldn't have cared less.

They'd been in the Hotel since 8 that morning and, even if this was just another banquet, the only thing that concerned them now was producing a meal for 172 people.

Lesnik had already briefed everybody and given them their assignments. He would have 15 people working with him at the banqueting finishing area, including William and Henry. Christian would stay in the restaurant kitchen because that had to function too.

The Back of House Manager temporarily threw everyone into a mild panic when he confessed that he couldn't find the Amir's yogurt pot. But it eventually turned up — under a pile of other silver in his office — and, when Lesnik took the little plastic container of super-market Greek no-fat yogurt, it slipped perfectly inside.

To test the fish, the Chef had seared it in a pan, then baked it in the oven. He'd carefully watched the time it took. While he'd been doing that, Derek had been making all the fruit juices. He'd delivered one glass of each to the Chef. Lesnik had found the kiwi juice too heavy, and the strawberry juice too sweet, so he'd added crushed ice to both to thin them out. It had left Derek barely enough time to make all the Danish pastries and all the croissants that Room Service would need in the morning.

That's when a French chef from Lyons showed up to pay his respects.

Chefs did that. They came to town and dropped in on their colleagues. No matter what else was going on, it was custom among the brotherhood to sit down with them for a glass of champagne. Part of it was camaraderie. Part of it was that a chef never knew when he was going to need a job. But some of it also had to do with being macho — see, in the middle of all this panic I've got things so well under control that I can take the time to drink champagne with you.

The chef from Lyons said he too collected antique cooking utensils, and admired the ones decorating Lesnik's office. He drooled over the 1925 nutmeg grater, as Lesnik poured the champagne. They drank a glassful, then Lesnik escorted him into the kitchen where he showed off the sauce to go with the fish.

When the visiting chef left, Lesnik called for his sous-chefs and took them upstairs to check out the Ballroom.

The Ambassador's wife was there, putting bowls of rose water and myrrh on the top table.

Suddenly, the room smelled of Kuwait.

~ 18 ~

FTER DICTATING A BUNCH OF letters to his secretary and taking a couple of phone calls, Touzin saw that it was 6 o'clock, and he told himself, if I don't get out of here now, I never will.

He left his office to walk the course.

Starting at the Ballroom entrance, moving slowly through the Rotunda and into the Reception Room — making certain that everything was perfect, ready for the evening — he stopped to take a good look at the falcon sitting in its cage.

A policeman wanted to know who he was.

Baxter rushed over to explain that he was the boss.

That amused him, especially when the policeman gave him one of those, I'm only doing my job, looks.

Now in the Ballroom, he put himself in the centre of the tent so that he could see if anything was obviously out of place. Instead, he found himself standing in the way of the florists, the themers, the electricians and the waiters. The only safe spot appeared to be behind the top table, so he went there, studied the room, then checked that all the other chairs along the top table were in a straight line. He moved the Queen's throne imperceptibly, the nervous gesture of a natural perfectionist.

"The cushion," he suddenly said out loud to no one in particular. "Where is the cushion?"

Everyone must have thought he was speaking to someone else.

"*Le coussin?*" He changed to French. Still no one answered.

He spotted Domingues. "The cushion for the gentleman whose back is no good . . ."

Someone from the other side of the room called out, "It's already on that chair. Over there. Towards the end."

"Oh." He looked again and saw that it was. "I think you need to put more salt in all of the salt cellars," he said to Domingues. "Some are only half filled."

Domingues grabbed a passing waiter and relayed the instruction.

Touzin now examined the fruit and the flower petals that lined the front of the top table, just high enough to block any view from the rest of the room of the Queen's plate.

He walked all the way to one end, then came back to the other, rearranging a few pieces of fruit that were almost falling out of their basket. He stopped at the chair with the cushion to centre it, before pondering the table one last time.

Content with that, he walked into the Mirror Room.

A baby grand was sitting just there.

"What's this?"

From the side of the room Rory Purcell answered, "A piano."

He spotted Domingues again. "This can't stay here. Why is it here?"

Domingues didn't know.

With waiters going past them in every direction, he enlisted Domingues and Purcell to help him push the piano to the far corner of the room, if for no other reason than to get it out of the way. But once it was there, Touzin decided it looked wrong. It was the only piece of furniture in an otherwise empty room. "Can't we get it out of here?"

Purcell said, "We have no place to put it."

He tried to think of what to do with it. "Can we put flowers on it?"

Domingues found a small bouquet and plonked it down on top of the piano. However, to Touzin's eyes, that made it even worse. "No. It looks as if we couldn't figure out what else to do with it. Take them off."

With loads of other things on his mind, Domingues removed the flowers. "They are only going to walk through this room on their way into the French Salon. No one will notice."

But Touzin noticed. He stared at the piano for several seconds, before conceding perhaps they didn't have much choice. "What about the room temperature."

"We've got the air-conditioning working full blast," Purcell told him.

"It's warm in here."

"It will be warmer when everyone sits down."

He continued into the French Salon. Everything there seemed to be ready, so he headed towards the Drawing Room. And at the far door, he nearly tripped over some wires.

"No." He exclaimed loudly. "Rory? These either come up or go under the carpet."

"What are they?" Purcell followed the wires into the Drawing Room, disappeared for a moment behind the door, then poked his head out to say, "It's the themer's sound system. We can't tuck them under the carpet here because the carpet doesn't come up. And if we tape the wires across the doorway, it will look horrible."

"Well, they can't stay like this. We can't have the Queen and the Amir flying head first into the Drawing Room."

Purcell suggested, "Why don't we just shut the door? Let them use the other one?"

Touzin thought about that, stepped back, and concluded that there was enough room for everyone to go through the nearer door.

"All right. Close it. Just make sure the wires are well hidden under the door."

While Purcell did that, Touzin returned to the Mirror Room, then walked into French Salon and through the door to the Drawing Room that the Queen and the Amir would use. "This is fine," he said. "It will work. When is Joe's meeting?"

That began promptly at 6:30.

Three large presentation boards sat on easels in the middle of the Drawing Room. The waiters — 62 men, most of them young, all of them dressed in evening clothes — filed into the room, then elbowed their way up to those easels to see what their specific assignments would be.

Jarman moved everyone back away from the easels and demanded attention, and, just like at school when the gym teacher blew his whistle, everyone stopped talking and waited for something to happen.

From his place in front of the easels, Domingues took the register. Oliveria. Hassan. Lopes. Cazals. Prosperi. And when each waiter heard his name, he responded, "Here" or "Present" or every now and then, "Si."

There were a few names Domingues had to call twice before the person attached to it responded. There were eight names he called three times. When no one answered, he scratched those off his list.

That done, he reminded them, "This is a very special occasion. It is important that you follow your instructions precisely. If you have any questions, you will ask me or Mr Jarman. No one else."

He described the pre-dinner drinks service. "During the reception and after dinner there will be fruit juices, soft drinks and mineral water only. No alcohol will be served at all. The drinks are strawberry juice, mango juice, lemon juice, orange juice, kiwi juice, apple juice and mineral water. At dinner, there will be only sparkling or still mineral water." He outlined the menu. Then he explained that waiters would work in teams, designated Waiter 1 and Waiter

2 — they could find their designation on the alphabetical list of names on the easels — and that each had very specific assignments.

"Soup course. Waiter 1 brings the bread, two baskets per table. Waiter 2 brings the butter. Both waiters leave. Waiter 1 brings the soup liner. Waiter 2 places the saucer on the liner and then remains by his table while Waiter 1 brings the soup into the room and holds the tray. Waiter 2 then places the soup cup onto the saucer. Then both waiters leave."

Domingues went through the entire meal, step by step. Clearing the soup. Bringing the fish. Clearing the fish. Bringing the lamb. Clearing the lamb. Bringing the dessert.

"There will be two waiters for the Queen and two waiters for the Amir," he went on. "The top table is butler service. The round tables are silver service with ladies being served first. You will start with the most senior, or highest-titled lady, complete all the ladies and then start with the most senior or highest-titled gentleman. Silver service is done on the left-hand side of the guest. Butler service is done on the left-hand side of the guest. All plated service is done on the right-hand side. All clearing is done on the right-hand side. All drinks are served from the right-hand side. Remember our rules. Be polite. Smile. Say, thank you. Say, excuse me please. But do not say anything more than that. If you need any help, signal for a head waiter."

Pausing to make certain that everyone understood, he tried to see over the heads of the men in the front row but he wasn't tall enough.

"There is to be a glass of orange juice on the table before sitting down. There is one yogurt for the Amir in a special container. And one Greek salad for the Amir for the main course. Any questions?"

There were none. So Domingues said, "Follow me," and led his troops into the Ballroom.

Jarman reminded them, "The service will be tight because there isn't a lot of room between the tables."

Domingues placed each team of waiters at their assigned table, reminded them they would have to be careful because the room was cramped, then went over the entire plan of service again.

Touzin was still bothered by the piano.

He stood in the Mirror Room, which was filled with flowers, staring at it for several minutes before an idea came to him. "I know what's wrong," he said out loud, motioning for Jarman, who was busy listening to Domingues. "Put a piano stool there."

Jarman didn't understand. "What do you want?"

"A piano stool."

"There won't be any music," he tried to explain.

"I know. Please find a piano stool."

Jarman didn't mention that the stool Touzin was looking for was already in place behind the Queen's throne at the top table. Instead, he thought fast, remembered where there was another one and asked someone to fetch it. When it appeared, Touzin took it and Jarman returned to his meeting with the waiters.

Touzin placed the piano stool in front of the keyboard. Then he stepped back and nodded affirmatively, "Now it looks like it belongs."

Leaving Domingues and Jarman with the waiters, he wandered downstairs to the kitchen, greeted everyone, then asked Lesnik — in an all too obvious way — "What does the fish taste like?"

"It's got a meaty taste," the Chef said, taking Touzin over to one of the stoves where a piece had been cooked. Touzin tasted it without the sauce — "Yes," he kept nodding — and then ate another piece, this time with the sauce.

The Lebanese caterer and one of the Kuwaitis noticed him and stood right there until Lesnik introduced them. They both handed Touzin their cards, as if to say, if you ever need a Lebanese caterer and a Kuwaiti cook, think of us.

Putting the cards in his pocket, he followed Lesnik to another stove to taste the soup — "It's got more of a pumpkin taste than before" — and the lamb with the sauce. "Delicious."

The caterer wanted Touzin to know, "The lamb here is the highest quality. I often order lamb in the UK and fly it out to Kuwait." Touzin nodded politely. The caterer invited him to taste the *machboos* and the *jerish*. Mohammed was there. The Chef gave him a warmer introduction and handed Touzin a fork.

"Normally when we make *machboos*," the caterer said while Touzin tasted the rice, "we leave the lamb on the bone. Tonight I have ordered it to be taken off the bone to make the service easier."

Lesnik let the remark pass.

Touzin told Mohammed he liked it.

Mohammed now offered him some *jerish*.

After tasting that, Touzin diplomatically assured Mohammed, "Very interesting."

Leaving the Kuwaitis there, Touzin and Lesnik went to the banqueting service area. On the way, they passed the Back of House Manager.

"Do we wash the Embassy's plates?" Touzin asked.

"We do."

Touzin nodded. "Just wanted to know."

They met Jarman rushing down the stairs. "There are two cancellations. We're trying to figure out where they're sitting to take their place off the tables. And the Lebanese bread," he said. "They've just decided that only the Amir will get Lebanese bread."

"What?" Lesnik couldn't believe it. "I have ordered enough for 200 people."

"That's what the Ambassador wants."

Lesnik looked at Touzin and shook his head.

"Also," Jarman went on, "I'm concerned with the timing of the dinner."

"I'm not," the Chef barked, but then must have realized just how tense Jarman was. "Andrew, everything is under control."

"We can't have people sitting around waiting for the next course."

Lesnik didn't need to be reminded of that, but Jarman wasn't Krenzer. "Andrew, trust me. It will be all right. I will have every course ready just in the nick of time. It will not be too soon so that it will get cold. It will not be too late so that they will have to wait." He took a small alarm clock out of his pocket and showed it to Jarman. "You tell me when to serve the soup. I will time everything else from that."

Touzin left them there. He had to change into his evening clothes. But first, he wanted to take another look at the Ballroom.

The tables were set. Two dozen candlesticks were out — two on each table — with nine nine-stem candelabras running the length of the head table. The candles were lit and the room lights were turned down.

The tent was shimmering with flowers.

The police were lined up on the Hotel side of the street.

Across the street, down the block and behind some barricades, about 30 protesters had assembled. A few of them were holding up a big sign in Arabic. It had something to do with Islam and how the Western media were always distorting the truth.

Two uniformed officers were standing with them, chatting quietly.

Now dressed for the evening, Touzin went into the Reception Room. The Ambassador was already there, wearing black robes and a headdress. His wife was next to him, wearing a long, flowery, dark-coloured dress. Touzin greeted them, chatted with them for a while — the Ambassador's young children were there and they were introduced to Touzin — then he discreetly checked his watch and, realizing it was time, excused himself to take up his position outside.

For a long time, everyone waited.

One guest arrived — self-consciously remarking that someone always had to be first — and then there were two more. And two more after that. Now cars were depositing guests at the Ballroom entrance, one after the other, while two of the Hotel's doormen helped ladies step out and tipped their hats to acknowledge the gentlemen.

Western men were in white tie. Arab men were in robes. Western women were in long dresses. There were very few Arab women.

Touzin greeted every guest — "Welcome to the Hotel" — and indicated that they were expected in the Reception Room.

There were many guests he did not know. But there were many he did. Two couples in particular he knew well enough that, when they arrived, he mentioned quietly to each of them that some of the other guests were assembling in the lounge. More people arrived. He introduced himself to all of them.

At one point, with no sign of care showing, he stopped briefly at Reception to ask, "Has Mr Halpern arrived yet?"

The clerk said, "No, not yet, sir."

"Be careful with him."

"We know, sir."

Then he returned to the Ballroom entrance, to continue greeting the Amir's guests. "Welcome to the Hotel."

When the Amir himself arrived — a huge Rolls-Royce with the Kuwait standard flying pulled up to the kerb, accompanied by two Rovers with police escorts inside — television lights came on. Two Arabs in Western dress, with camcorders on their shoulders, tried to get closer. The police held them back. But their lights were a signal to the bunch across the street to start shouting.

Security men surrounded the car.

The rear door opened and an old man in flowing black robes and headdress stepped out.

The protesters made a noise.

Except for the police, they were the only people in the street.

Touzin, now standing at the Ambassador's side, greeted the Amir and walked with him slowly along the carpet into the Reception Room.

More television lights came on.

And now every Arab in the room came up to him to pay homage — the Ambassador's wife and her children and other men in robes and headdresses — watched by the Hotel staff in their evening clothes, and armed security guards in theirs.

The Amir glanced briefly at the falcon — every now and then the bird fluttered its wings but most of the time it just sat on its perch, slightly bemused — and then the Ambassador showed the Amir where he was to stand to receive his guests.

Touzin went back to the street.

The Ambassador moved a few paces behind the Amir. The TV lights stayed on as five journalists, corralled into the corner, edged slightly forward and had to be told to step back, which they reluctantly did.

Then everything stopped.

The Amir stood with his hands folded across the front of his robes, looking as if he didn't know who to expect. He didn't smile. He didn't speak to anyone. He just stood there, where he'd been told to stand, and waited, as did everyone else.

That's when the Ambassador's wife remembered that the carpet leading in from the entrance to the Ballroom had not been sprinkled with perfume, so she summoned two young Kuwaitis in white uniforms who hurriedly did that.

Slowly but surely, more guests arrived. Westerners shook the Amir's hand and moved past him. Arabs embraced the Amir and moved past him.

Most of the guests were escorted away to the French Salon and the Drawing Room. The top-table guests formed a ragged half-circle at the back of the Reception Room, and stood there, talking quietly and sipping fruit juice, while they also waited.

The Amir did not drink anything.

It was a full honours evening, so the British wore their medals. The Foreign Secretary and his wife arrived. Then the Home Secretary and his wife arrived. Then the Secretary of State for Trade and Industry arrived with his wife. Prince and Princess Michael came next, followed by Princess Alexandra and her husband.

Then Prince Charles appeared.

He stepped into the room, alone, impeccably dressed with his medals and a sash across his chest and went straight to the Amir. With the Ambassador translating, Charles spoke to him for several minutes. He only moved away when other guests arrived. Gazing for a moment at the falcon, he proceeded to shake hands with the top-table guests, working the half-circle until he got to Princess Michael and Princess Alexandra. He kissed them both on the cheek, shook hands with their husbands and stood with them, to wait for his mother and father.

The schedule had the Queen arriving at 8:25.

But her car — deliberately, the exact same model Rolls-Royce that the Amir was using — with her standard flying on the roof, pulled up to the Ballroom entrance at 8:34.

Television lights again lit up the pavement.

The rear door was opened, the little step folded down and the Queen got out.

Touzin bowed, "Welcome to the Hotel."

The crowd across the street started making a noise again — the Queen gave them a quick look — and, with her husband at her side, walked into the Hotel.

As soon as she came into the Reception Room, flashbulbs went off.

It was 8:36.

Jarman quietly noted to a few of the others on the Hotel staff, "Her Majesty is never late. It's the schedule that's wrong."

Just as the Queen stepped into the Hotel, her chauffeur drove around the block to the rear of the Hotel — into the alley, blocked off by the police — where he parked in front of the Timekeeper's entrance, alongside the Amir's car and other official cars.

Downstairs in the kitchen, the soup was poured.

One floor above, in the Reading Room, Derek and five cooks started putting the desserts together.

For the guests waiting in the French Salon and in the Drawing Room, dinner was called. They were moved through the Mirror Room to their tables, where they were asked to remain standing. Once they were in, Domingues shut the doors and summoned his waiters, who'd been hiding behind the door of the service area.

They nearly filled the Mirror Room.

Waiters 1 had two baskets of bread each. Waiters 2 had the butter.

Domingues put them in three columns, one for each door — top table, middle of the room, bottom of the room — lining them up like a marching band about to start a parade.

The Queen wore a long gown, a lot of jewels and a tiara, and in her left hand she carried a tiny evening bag. One side of Prince Philip's chest was covered in medals, and he too had a sash.

As their son had before them, they chatted for a polite few moments with the Amir, and Philip moved past the Queen and spoke with the Ambassador. Then the Queen joined her husband, and together they walked over to the cage to look at the falcon.

The Amir waited with the Ambassador.

Philip pointed to the bird's claws and the Queen said something in a very quiet voice that made him smile. She left him there, to greet the line of top-table guests. Heels clicked. Men bowed. Women curtsied. Philip soon caught up with her. She smiled at everyone but spoke to some people longer than others. And when she got to her son — he was last in line — she leaned forward so that he could kiss the side of her face. "Mother."

He also kissed his father. "Papa."

Suddenly, for some unknown reason, the lights in the Reception Room dimmed for a second.

"Oh my." The Queen looked up and made a face, as if she wanted to say, the Hotel really should pay its electricity bill.

Her aide now appeared, whispering to the top-table guests, organizing them into a line, then inviting them to proceed into the Ballroom.

The Queen and the Amir were the final pair.

They entered together — all eyes were on them — but two steps into the room, she stopped. She looked around — at the tent bathed in candlelight and filled with an inconceivable amount of flowers.

For a woman whose life had been surrounded with so much opulence, even she was impressed.

Jarman raced down to the banqueting kitchen to tell the Chef it was time.

Lesnik calmly pulled the small alarm clock out of his pocket. The way he'd calculated it, from this point until the dessert was served, it would be 96 minutes. Everything he did from now on depended on that little clock. So he set the alarm.

Waiters served the bread.

Jarman was right, there wasn't a lot of space between the tables and only just enough behind the top table. But they managed it, and before long none of them took much notice. They simply got on with what they had to do.

Then the soup course was on its way.

Lesnik called out to the waiters, "Put tureens down and take trays away."

As the soup left the kitchen, he immediately started decorating trays of fish. "Who's doing prawns?"

Henry said, "Me, Chef."

"William?"

He answered, "Sauce, Chef."

Lesnik said, "All right, let me have the tray for the Queen and the Amir." One of the cooks handed it to him. "Fish like this . . ." He put four slices on the silver platter, "and prawns like this . . . facing inward."

Both William and Henry watched.

"Follow this pattern," Lesnik said.

The others began decorating the fish trays while Lesnik continued to rearrange the one for the Queen and the Amir. Suddenly, something about it didn't look right to him.

Henry called out, "Fish," and cooks brought more out of the oven. William called out, "Sauce," and cooks brought him sauce as he continued decorating the dish.

For a place where 15 people were busy, it was remarkably quiet. There was no idle talking at the service table — in fact, there was no talking at all, except for the Chef and the sous-chefs — because that's the way Lesnik wanted it. Not even the waiters were permitted to talk. Anyway, they were too professional to challenge him. They arrived in strict single file, silently filled their trays and left.

Touzin appeared, to watch the meal being rolled out. He stood near the Chef — but well out of the way — sipping half a cup of soup.

Lesnik continued toying with the platter for the Amir and the Queen. He kept rearranging the fish, until he finally decided that the problem was the platter. It was too big for only four slices. "I need some extra prawns here." A cook brought them to him and he filled out the platter with them.

Touzin noticed. "Now everyone will want extra prawns."

"But not everyone can have extra prawns," Lesnik smiled.

"Did you save any for me?"

"I've done eight extra portions. In case a plate falls or someone drops a service. Hope they don't. If they do, that's your dinner they dropped."

The waiters came for the fish and, by that time, the Chef was working on the lamb.

He prowled the banqueting station, confidently, in full charge. The real battle — getting the menu to work and getting the timings in his head — had been played out days ago. In his mind, this was just a re-enactment.

The doorman at the main entrance to the Hotel spotted Mr Halpern walking in the front door, carrying his own suitcase. He rushed over to take it from him. "Good evening, sir. Welcome back to the Hotel."

"What the hell is going on?" Halpern demanded. "And why the hell did the driver have to let me off at the corner? Why all the cops?"

"I'm very sorry about that, sir. We're having a Royal State Banquet in the main Ballroom. That's what all this security is about." He escorted Halpern to the Reception desk. "We've got the royal family here tonight, sir."

Halpern asked, "Which ones?"

"The Queen, sir. Prince Philip. And Prince Charles."

"I had to carry my own bag because the Queen of England came for dinner?" A smile crossed his face. "No kidding."

Domingues guarded the door to the service area, watching the waiters bringing up their trays.

One grabbed the wrong plate. He was supposed to have the *jerish* but took the *machboos*. The one who was supposed to have *machboos* started to argue about it. Domingues stopped them short. "Just take it," he ordered. They did.

He guarded the entrance to the Ballroom, too, watching the waiters making ready to enter the room.

Someone still had a cover on his tray. Domingues lifted it off. Someone else had a tie that wasn't straight. Domingues straightened it.

For each course he put them in line — "Waiter 1 here. Waiter 2 here. Come on. Let's go. Please. Let's go." — and when the doors were flung open, he sent them parading into the room, whispering "Good" and "In you go."

Touzin walked into the Ballroom to watch the service, to make certain everything was going exactly as they'd planned. Duncan was in the room too. And wherever they weren't, Jarman was.

Eight close protection officers dined at a table that had been set up for them in the Painted Room, just off the Reception Room. They had the same meal that the Queen and the Amir did. Except that they didn't all sit down at the same time. Some ate, while the others stood in the Mirror Room or looked into the French Salon or lingered for a few moments in the Drawing Room.

Then, suddenly, the gentleman at the top table who'd requested the cushion on the chair for his back stood up and hurried out of the Ballroom. He told one of the security men in the Reception Room that he was in terrible pain. Word went out over the portable radios that there was a potential problem. One of the officers escorted him to the Gentlemen's Cloakroom, where he helped the man lie down. Other officers joined them there, worried that it could be his heart. Word went to the command post to get the Hotel's nurse.

Within two minutes, Irene was there. Her first thought, too, was heart. She knelt next to the man.

But he told her, "It's my back."

One of the policemen said to her, "If it's his heart, we can get an ambulance here right away."

He kept saying, "It's my back," and, after looking more closely at him, she agreed that it wasn't his heart.

Another officer asked, "Sir, do you want me to tell your wife?"

"It's all right," he insisted.

"If you want to go home . . ." Irene started to say.

"No, I just want to lie here for a few minutes. Please. I'll be all right. Just tell my wife that I'm all right. It's my back . . ."

One of the officers went into the room to whisper into her ear that her husband was having back pains. "The nurse is with him."

She said, "Thank you," and kept on eating.

Someone had lined the Reading Room floor with blue plastic, obviously to protect it from spilled desserts and, as the cooks rushed around the room decorating plates, the blue plastic made a terrible noise.

On the other side of the screens, in the Foyer, the string ensemble was playing Sigmund Romberg.

As soon as the lamb was out of the kitchen, Lesnik, William, Henry and a few others beat a path to the Reading Room, leaving the junior cooks to clean up the banqueting service area. But Derek pretty much had everything under control. Glazed pears were already on all the plates.

Domingues continued to watch the Ballroom. A few candles had burned down, so he very discreetly made his way to the tables and changed them. Then, back in the Mirror Room, he told Jarman, "We'll clear in ten minutes."

Jarman passed that along to the Chef. "The lamb course will clear in ten minutes."

That was Lesnik's cue for the ice cream.

It took a couple of minutes to get the ice cream upstairs so, with eight minutes to go, cooks began dropping one scoop per plate into a little woven pastry basket.

Lesnik, Derek, William and Henry followed on their heels, up and down the seven tables, covering the ice cream with the basket top. Mint leaves — dipped in a gold sugar coating — were placed on top of that.

Touzin stayed out of everyone's way.

And then the waiters were there. Domingues was there too, directing them to carry the desserts carefully out of the Reading Room, along the corridor, and into the Mirror Room, where he lined them up, then opened the Ballroom doors.

Just as the final tray was taken away, the little alarm clock sounded in Lesnik's pocket.

It was exactly 96 minutes later.

The guests ate their ice cream politely — the way they'd eaten everything — and, when they were finished, they sat waiting until the Queen was done with hers.

She said something to the Amir and started to stand up. A footman pulled her chair away. The Amir began to stand up at the same time. A footman pulled his chair away. They rose together. Then everyone in the room stood up.

The doors to the Mirror Room opened.

The Queen moved along the back of the top table and stepped out of the Ballroom. Seeing that she was alone, she turned around and waited for Philip to join her.

Everyone else stayed in the Ballroom.

The two of them strolled through the Mirror Room, directed by Touzin towards the French Salon, but they stopped to admire a huge bouquet. Philip pointed to it and told his wife, "They must have emptied out the entire Chelsea Flower Show."

As soon as they were in the French Salon, everyone else left the Ballroom to join them there.

Waiters served coffee and *petits fours.*

Jarman reminded the Queen's aide that chairs were waiting for her and the Amir in the Drawing Room, but he answered that she would only go there if she wanted to. For the time being, he said, it seemed as if she was happy in the French Salon.

And that's where she stayed.

She stood for a while with the Amir, in the middle of the room, sipping her coffee and eating a tiny pastry. Then she circulated. So did Philip. So did Charles.

World-class minglers, they spoke of shoes and ships and sealing wax, of cabbages, and oil.

When the time came, the Queen gave her ADC the secret signal. It wasn't anything as obvious as a sharp tug on her right ear lobe, or standing for several seconds balanced on one foot, but whatever it was — probably nothing more than a glance in his direction — the ADC noticed.

Immediately, he passed the signal on to her close protection officer and word was just as quickly relayed to the chauffeur out back.

He drove the car up to the Ballroom entrance, parked too far from the kerb the first time and had to try again. The second time he wasn't happy with where the little step fell out of the rear door, so he wove back and forth until he got it just right. The police, both inside and outside the Hotel, were notified that the Queen was leaving.

The ADC brought the Amir and the Queen together.

Along with Prince Philip, the Ambassador, his wife, their body-guards and the translator, the Queen and the Amir walked down the corridor to the Ballroom entrance.

The chauffeur was holding open the rear door. The two Rovers that carried her police escort were also waiting. The protesters across the street started yelling. She thanked the Amir for the evening and the Amir bid her goodnight. The Queen and her husband climbed into their car and the close protection officers climbed into theirs.

Once she was gone, everyone else could leave.

Prince Charles said goodnight, and after he was gone the other royals made their exit too, in descending order. Then the Kuwaitis left. Then the rest of the guests left.

On his way out, the former Prime Minister Edward Heath asked someone, "Where is the bar?"

He was escorted into Touzin's office because the lounge was empty and a waiter was summoned. That's when Touzin promptly appeared — he has a knack for knowing where to be — and the two sat chatting amiably for twenty mintues. Then Heath stood up, said, "Don't bother, stay right there, I'll find my way out, thank you, goodnight," joined up with his bodyguard and left.

By that time, everyone else was gone.

Azoulai was growing increasingly concerned about a couple dining at a table on the far left side of the restaurant. A well-dressed man in his late 50s with a well-dressed woman easily 30 years his junior, they'd run up a sizeable bill, ordering everything à la carte. Normally that would not pose a problem. But they'd been drinking heavily for two and a half hours and were starting to get a bit noisy. They'd gone through a substantial amount of wine and were now onto vintage port. He was just about to wander over to their table, hoping to quieten them down, when the gentleman signalled for his bill.

Relieved that they were on their way out, he prepared it — dinner for two came to £355.50 — and delivered it to the table. "I hope everything was satisfactory."

"Fine, fine . . ." He was quite intoxicated. "Yes, fine." From inside his jacket pocket he produced a chequebook.

The care and handling of drunks was one of those skills a restaurant manager learns only by experience. In theory, the trick is to stay quiet, never to confront them, always to agree with them, and then to get them out of the place as fast as possible, without disturbing the other guests. But theory all too often gets chucked out the window and the moment Azoulai spotted the chequebook he knew he had a real problem.

Taking a very gentle tone, he explained, "I'm terribly sorry, sir, but it is Hotel policy not to accept cheques. However, we will happily take any major credit card . . ."

That was not what the guest wanted to hear. "Of course you accept cheques. What are you talking about? You've always taken my cheque . . ."

Azoulai knew he needed to be very careful. "Sir, it's the Hotel's policy . . ."

"Policy?" He pointed to the name of the bank written across it. "See this? Do you realize how much money you need to have an account at this place?" He was starting to get loud. "I happen to be a very good client here . . ."

The thing about very good clients was that Azoulai knew them all, and he'd never seen this fellow before. "If you would give me just a moment, sir, to see what I can do." He was in a bind and he needed to find a way out fast. "If you would be kind enough to fill out the cheque, please."

The man started scribbling. When he was finished, he handed over the cheque and a bank card. "You always take my cheques," he contended. "Don't give me that policy crap."

"While you're waiting, may I offer you something?" Azoulai motioned to the wine steward and said, in front of the clients, "Please give the lady and gentleman another glass of port, with my compliments." Then he excused himself.

Finding Salter in the Front Hall, he explained the situation.

"His name is Lowry and he claims to be a regular client of the Hotel. I've never seen him before."

So Salter and Azoulai went to the computer in the Reservations office to look for the man's guest history. There was none. Salter then checked to see if the man was on the NTBT ledger, or if any of the other hotels had put out a warning on him. There was nothing.

"May I see his cheque?" Salter studied it, then mumbled, "Let me try something." He picked up the phone and dialled a number. Some swanky banks, like this one, boasted that they never bounced a client's cheque. What many of those clients probably didn't know was that merchants — like the Hotel — had a special number they could ring, to clear certain cheques at any hour of the day or night.

After giving the operator who answered all the pertinent information, Salter and Azoulai had to wait only a few seconds before the operator confirmed that the cheque was good.

Returning to Lowry, Azoulai said, "Thank you very much, sir. I'm terribly sorry to have inconvenienced you. But I hope you will appreciate that it is Hotel policy . . ."

Lowry and his lady friend were far too pumped up with vintage port bravado to care about Hotel policy. "I'll have you know that the Manager here is a very good personal friend of mine. The General Manager. A personal friend. Mr . . . ah, Mr . . ."

Azoulai assured him, "Yes, sir."

"I'm a very good client here . . ."

He escorted the couple out of the restaurant and wished them a good evening.

"A personal friend of the Manager . . ." Lowry kept mumbling . . . "How dare you embarrass me by not accepting my cheque . . ."

Before Azoulai went home, he wrote up the incident for his logbook.

Salter put it into his log as well.

Jarman and ten of the people who'd worked the banquet with him set up a table in the Mirror Room to have dinner and celebrate.

The chef offered his staff a glass of champagne.

The movers came in to take away the rented furniture and the florists came in to take away the flowers. The handler took his falcon home and someone else took the cage. The tables were cleared. The themers arrived to strike the tent. The chairs were taken out of the room. Someone came to collect the glassware and cutlery.

Nearly 40 people worked through the night.

Around 2 am, a gentleman identifying himself as a Harley Street psychiatrist rang the Hotel and asked the switchboard if one of his patients, a certain Mrs Mancieri, was a guest. Without revealing anything, the operator automatically passed the call along to Salter.

"I want to know," the doctor explained, "if a patient of mine, Mrs Roberta Mancieri, is staying at the Hotel."

"I'm sorry," Salter said immediately, "but that is not the sort of information I can divulge."

"I assure you," the doctor went on, "that this is a very serious matter. I must know if she is staying at the Hotel."

"I'd like to help you, sir, but I'm afraid I cannot give you any information over the phone about our guests."

"Tell you what," the doctor said. "Have you got a house physician on call?"

"Yes, sir."

"Then ring him and have him ring me." The psychiatrist gave Salter his name and phone number.

Sensing that this might not be a prank call, Salter woke the house physician and explained the situation. The doctor said he knew the psychiatrist and that he would ring him straight away. A few minutes later, the doctor phoned to tell Salter, "I've spoken to him and he is concerned about his patient. Is there a Mrs Roberta Mancieri staying at the Hotel?"

Salter had already checked the computer. "Yes, sir, she's in a single. Room 440."

"What her doctor wants is that she not be permitted to leave the Hotel."

"I can't do that," Salter replied. "I can't restrain a guest. It's impossible."

"Has she had any Room Service?"

He looked again at the computer. "Apparently she's ordered some Diet Coke."

"All right then, no alcohol. If she rings Room Service and asks for a drink, can you refuse to serve her?"

"Yes. I'm sure we can. I'll inform the floor waiter right now."

"Has she been causing any trouble?"

"Not at all."

"Fine," the house physician said. "Just remember, no alcohol."

Salter repeated, "No alcohol," and when he hung up he passed that message along to Abel.

But Mrs Mancieri didn't ask for any alcohol, or anything else for that matter. Nor did she try to leave. Salter spent the night wondering what he would do if she came downstairs and wanted to go outside. In the end, he knew, he dare not stop her, especially if she was some sort of mad woman. But it never came to that. When he went to work the following night, he saw that she'd checked out earlier that day. He never heard again from the Harley Street psychiatrist. And Mrs Mancieri never came back to the Hotel.

When he arrived for work the next morning, Lesnik phoned the bakery that had supplied the Lebanese bread and persuaded them to take back half the order. The Hotel would have to keep the other half. But Lesnik figured he could sell some of it in the restaurant and find a use for whatever remained.

The dishes, cutlery and glasses that had been used the night before were washed and ready to be collected by the Embassy.

The uniforms were waiting to be returned to the hire shop.

The Ballroom was empty.

For 96 minutes and about £170,000, it had been a room of polite smiles and temperate conversation. A room filled with people wearing mildly uncomfortable clothes, who stood around making small talk as if their shoes were too tight. A room filled with people who waited until someone said they could leave, and then they left.

～ 19 ～

*T*OUZIN READ FROM THE LOGBOOKS. "Dr Brinker in 508 complained that his room gets too hot." He asked Purcell, "Why?"

"Just one of his strange ideas."

"Mrs Pollinger in 340 complained about noise in the next room." He looked at Buckolt, "Please tell her we're sorry for the problem and put a note in her guest history. Then let's get someone up there to take a look at the communicating doors and see what we can do to make things quieter on both sides."

"All right."

"Mrs Clancy phoned to say that her storage would be collected. Anyone know why?"

No one did.

"I'd like someone to find out and tell me what she says. If there's some reason she's leaving us, I'd like to know and maybe we can do something about it."

Buckolt said he would do that.

"There was a problem last night in the restaurant." Touzin turned to Salter. "A Mr Lowry?"

"Yes, sir." Salter explained, "Mr Lowry came in from outside with a date. There was a lot of drinking and when he was presented with the bill he produced a cheque. Mr Azoulai explained that the Hotel doesn't accept cheques. But the client didn't want to know and caused a scene."

That bothered Touzin. "Did he disturb any other guests?"

"Apparently he did."

"Didn't he have any credit cards?"

"I'm afraid that Mr Azoulai didn't have much choice. The man insisted on paying by cheque. It was drawn on a private bank so, before the client left, I got on the phone to clear it."

"Were you able to?"

"As a matter of fact, yes." Salter said, "Apparently the type of account the gentleman has requires a £3000 minimum balance."

Touzin's eyes opened wide. "Three thousand pounds minimum balance?" He looked around the room. "Who here has a private bank?"

Everyone chuckled.

Salter went on, "Mr Lowry kept insisting that he was a regular client of the Hotel. But there is no guest history and Mr Azoulai didn't know him."

Touzin asked, "Does anyone know him?" When no one seemed to, he wondered, "How was the reservation made?"

Salter answered, "I checked on that, sir. It was his office."

"I would like to have Mr Lowry's phone number." Touzin nodded to Krenzer. "Can you ask Monsieur Azoulai for a copy of the reservation. I will ring him myself and say that I am very sorry if there was a problem. Since he says he's such a regular client, perhaps we can turn him into one."

Salter added, "He kept telling Mr Azoulai that he was a very good personal friend of the General Manager. But he couldn't seem to remember your name."

"Hah." Touzin laughed.

Krenzer said, "I will get you his phone number."

"If he was drunk," Touzin said, "perhaps I shouldn't ring him too early." He paused for a moment — "Three thousand pounds minimum balance?" — raised his eyebrows and pushed the logbooks aside. Then he said to no one in particular, "It seems there was also a small problem with guests arriving to find that Brook Street was blocked off last night. A few of them had to carry their own luggage from the corner. We should have thought about that and put another doorman on. We'll know for next time."

"It wasn't as much of a problem as you think it was," Salter said. "When the reason for the inconvenience was explained to the guests, they understood."

"I noticed there was also a problem last night with photographers," Touzin said. "We had stanchions up, but no ropes and they got a little unruly. Again, we'll have to remember that for the next time."

Now he went around the room, "Anyone?" But everyone who'd worked the State Banquet seemed too tired to want to stretch this meeting any further.

Only a woman who'd come down from Personnel had anything to say. "We're trying to recruit a Reservations clerk, and although we've had a lot of applicants we can't get the kind of quality person we're looking for. The market is getting tougher because a lot of other quality hotels are looking for qualified people and there just aren't that many around."

Touzin understood. "It's an area where we are in difficulty. Why don't you get your requirements to me and we'll look at staffing levels. Don't wait until it reaches a crisis point." From there he somehow jumped to, "I want us to do more for children. Many people come here with their children and I think we should have certain amenities for them. Small bathrobes, that sort of thing." He turned to Krenzer. "I also want to put together a children's menu both for the restaurant and for Room Service."

Krenzer said, "Okay."

"Fruit and flowers in the rooms," Touzin mentioned. "They should be checked more regularly and replaced when they need to be."

Ronald promised, "I'll speak to the florists."

"The health club. Yesterday I cancelled our membership. There were several reasons. First of all, the club was men only, which was a problem for us when any female clients asked about going there. Then, guests complained about having to pay fees there. Instead, I have made arrangements to allow our clients full use of the facilities at our sister hotels, which includes the swimming pool. Even when our own health club is ready, they'll still be able to swim there if they want. And those facilities will be free of charge to our clients. It saves them money and saves us £25,000 a year, too." He said, "Robert, I'd like you to pull out a list of all our regular guests who used the racket club and fax them, I'll sign it, that we now have these new facilities. Stress the positive points."

Buckolt asked, "Does Head Office Sales know? It's a selling point for them too."

"Good idea."

Purcell cut in, "What happens if our clients decide instead to book into one of those other hotels?"

Touzin replied, "I've thought about that. So you'd better get our health club finished fast."

Purcell joked, "Can I put the £25,000 you just saved into my budget?"

Touzin answered, "I've already spent it in mine."

When no one had anything else, Buckolt went through the arrivals. "Mr Dimitri is in 120 . . ."

"I saw 120," Touzin cut in. "There are some tiles broken in the bathroom."

Buckolt corrected him, "That's 220."

Touzin said, "Oh."

Ronald added, "And we've already taken care of it."
Touzin said, "Oh," a second time.

The meeting ended.

Struggling with the arrivals log and several sheets of computer print-outs, Robert Buckolt stepped through the door that led back into his own office. He sat at his desk, looked at his computer screen and suddenly realized he had a problem. Five rooms were due to come on line early that morning, and none of them had. He'd booked Mr and Mrs Glover into 520 — they were regular guests and would be arriving soon — except 520 wouldn't be ready.

On a hunch, he checked the Glovers' guest history and found that last time they'd been in 120. Apparently, they'd liked that room. But Mr Dimitri was in 120. He tried 220. The problem there was that he'd already booked Mr Mathers into that room. But Mr Mathers wouldn't be arriving until mid-morning. He'd never stayed at the Hotel before, so he didn't yet have a room preference.

Buckolt kept punching keys.

He took Mr Mathers out of 220 and put Mr and Mrs Glover there. Then he tried to figure out what to do with Mr Mathers. He thought about 320, the same sort of room, but that wasn't available. However, 440 was still open, except Dr and Mrs Robert Nagler were booked into it from tomorrow. So he moved Mr Mathers into 440 and, after checking to see that there wasn't anything in their guest history to say they preferred 440, he put the Naglers in 430.

That's when a call came in from the reservations manager of another five-star hotel. He had a Japanese gentleman, Mr Fujimura, who'd just arrived, claiming to have a reservation. But they didn't have anything for him. What's more, they couldn't accommodate him. "Can you bail us out? Do you have a large double?"

Buckolt ran through his list of available rooms. "How many nights?"

"Six."

"Ah . . ." This sort of thing wasn't supposed to happen, but everyone in the hotel business knew it did, all too often. A businessman thought his secretary had confirmed a room and she hadn't. Someone thought their fax had got through announcing an arrival, and it hadn't. Someone made a booking for two nights then got to the hotel and said they wanted to stay for a week.

He wondered about the Naglers. If he put them in 330, he could give Mr Fujimura 430. Then all he had to do was hope that the people now in 330 wouldn't suddenly decide to stay an extra day. "Yes, I can take him."

The fellow said, "We'll send him right over."

After typing the reservation into the computer, Buckolt walked out of his office to the Reception desk. He explained the situation to Alastair and Michael.

Ten minutes later a Japanese gentleman came bashfully up to the desk. Both Reservations clerks stood up and Michael said, "Good morning Mr Fujimura."

"But I have never been here before." The man stopped in his tracks. "I am very flattered. But how do you know my name?"

The two Reception clerks grinned. "Welcome to the Hotel."

One lucky guess had clearly made Mr Fujimura's day.

The meeting ended.

Carole Ronald hurried upstairs to start hers.

Rory Purcell heard his bleeper sound and, when he dialled his office, someone told him there was a leak in the maids' service area on the fourth floor.

Andrew Pierron went back to Michael Duncan's office. They were trying to come up with a way that the computer could measure the daily financial position of the Hotel, with the specifics for everyone's "business." The idea was that the staff should start to think about each department as a business — the Food and Beverage business, the Concierge business, the Reservations business — and have a gauge printed out for them every day.

Philippe Krenzer went back to his office which, for the first time since he'd come to the Hotel, was empty. Andrew Jarman and the others had the day off.

Adam Salter went downstairs, got out of his dinner jacket, climbed into his car and headed home to sleep.

♚

The meeting ended.

François Touzin left his office to stroll along the Ballroom corridor, through the Reception Room and into the Ballroom. The tent was gone. The flowers were gone. The last of the furniture was on the way out.

From there he wandered downstairs and into the kitchen. He thanked everyone for last night.

Back upstairs, the restaurant seemed too quiet and he made a mental note to remind Krenzer again that they needed to do something about increasing their breakfast business.

Moving through the empty Foyer, he was happy to find the Front Hall very busy.

As inconspicuously as he could, he made his way up the grand staircase, along the mezzanine and then up the smaller staircase to the first floor. From the far corner of that floor, he had a perfect view of the Front Hall.

He often stood there, unnoticed, watching people coming into the Hotel, watching people leaving the Hotel, watching the Front Hall porters.

This time he waited there for ten minutes.

The Concierge never once stood with his back to the door.

And a smiling François Touzin assured himself, we're making progress.

Epilogue

A FEW MONTHS LATER, Mario Lesnik left the Hotel.

After a dozen years of fighting the stoves, when another Executive Chef job came along, kind of out of the blue, he figured it was time to move on. It was time, he decided, for new challenges. Touzin threw him a going-away party and even Philippe Krenzer came to have a drink and wish him luck. A British chef replaced him. Ironically, shortly after he left, the à la carte menus in the restaurant went back to being written in English and French.

The Balsamic vinegar was returned to the supplier and the truffle supply was run down. They still stock truffles in that locked freezer, except now they don't hold much more than £5000 worth. The difference was not put in the bank to earn interest.

When Touzin learned that there was no French flag in that cupboard in the corner of the upholstery shop, he bought one. Because it amuses him, it now flies alongside the Union Jack, the Stars and Stripes and the European Flag above the Hotel's entrance.

Michael Duncan left. His wife and children were in France and after a while he decided that was really where he wanted to be. Andrew Jarman left. He was invited to become Assistant Manager of the Royal Household at Buckingham Palace. Roy Barron retired.

PAR claimed his briefcase. The sixth-floor refurbishment was completed on time. Mrs Widdicombe passed away.

The incident of the missing gun continued to play on Touzin's mind. It was so troubling to him, that he ordered a full review of the Hotel's security procedures. And the system was promptly changed, at great expense, to make absolutely certain that no one could ever again get into the wrong room.

And the potato crisis ended in its sixth week.

Spuds had gone through more than two dozen varieties before a supplier sent in a French potato. He took some, peeled them and prepared the crisps the same way he always did. As soon as he cooked them, he knew. Triumphantly, he called the Chef.

As soon as Lesnik saw them, he knew.

Later, François Touzin was on his way to the restaurant kitchen, walking through the little alcove at the rear of the Foyer, behind the screen that hid the kitchen doors. He spotted a bowl of crisps waiting there to be served. Automatically, he popped one into his mouth.

And as soon as he tasted it, he knew too.

647.9442
R   Robinson, Jeffrey

The hotel

DUE DATE
